Another Bloody Love Letter

Also by Anthony Loyd

My War Gone By, I Miss It So

ANOTHER BLOODY LOVE LETTER

ANTHONY LOYD

headline
review

Copyright © 2007 Anthony Loyd

The right of Anthony Loyd to be identified as the Author
of the Work has been asserted by him in accordance with the
Copyright, Designs and Patents Act 1988.

First published in 2007
by HEADLINE REVIEW
An imprint of Headline Publishing Group

1

Cataloguing in Publication Data is available from the British Library

Hardback 978 0 7553 1479 9
Trade paperback 978 0 7553 1483 6

Typeset in Palatino by Avon DataSet Ltd,
Bidford-on-Avon, Warwickshire

Printed and bound in Great Britain by
Mackays of Chatham plc, Chatham, Kent

Headline's policy is to use papers that are natural, renewable and
recyclable products and made from wood grown in sustainable forests.
The logging and manufacturing processes are expected to conform
to the environmental regulations of the country of origin.

HEADLINE PUBLISHING GROUP
A division of Hachette Livre UK Ltd
338 Euston Road
London NW1 3BH

www.reviewbooks.co.uk
www.hodderheadline.com

For my mother, The Brother, and Delilah.
None ever met.
They do so here.

GLOSSARY

APC: armoured personnel carrier.

DB: Državna Bezbednost, Serbia's state security service.

haram: forbidden to Muslims.

KLA: Kosovo Liberation Army, the insurgent force of Albanians opposed to Serb rule of Kosovo.

Kosovar: an Albanian living in Kosovo.

Kosovo: the southern province of Serbia whose two million population are predominantly Albanian.

madrassa: Islamic religious school.

mujahedin: plural of mujahed, translates literally as 'strugglers', or in context as 'holy warriors'. Used by Islamic fighters throughout the world, in Afghanistan the term generally applied to fighters serving the Northern Alliance.

Northern Alliance: the union of various mujahedin groups, representing several Afghan ethnicities, who joined together in northern Afghanistan to fight the Taliban.

panga: square-tipped machete.

peshmerga: Kurdish guerrilla. The word translates as 'those who face death'.

PKK: Kurdistan Workers Party, the militant separatist organisation of Kurds aspiring to independence. Also known as KADEK.

RPG: rocket propelled grenade.

RUF: Revolutionary United Front.

schwerpunkt: the deciding moment of thrust in a battle.

shalwar-kameez: the knee-length unbloused shirt and loose baggy trousers worn by most Afghan males.

shura: a meeting, usually conducted among Afghan elders or commanders, to discuss important matters.

SLA: Sierra Leonean Army.

Talib: translates as 'seeker'. Singular of 'Taliban', the predominantly Pashtun fundamentalist force in Afghanistan.

Yugoslavia: now defunct, during the Kosovo war the term referred to the federation of Serbia and Montenegro.

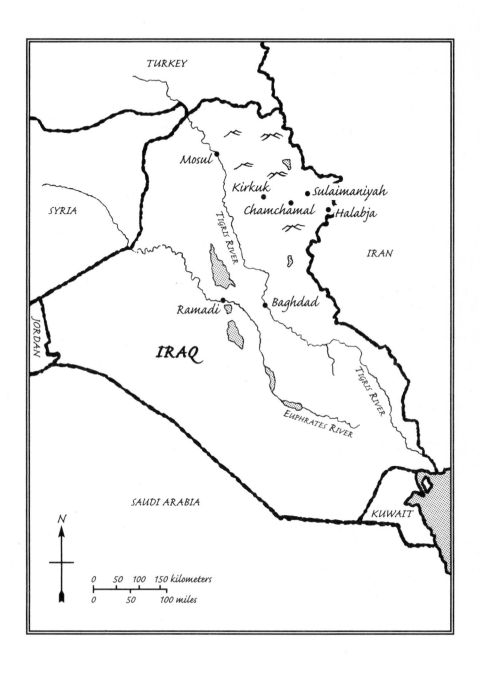

TURKEY

Mosul

SYRIA

Kirkuk

Sulaimaniyah

Chamchamal

Halabja

Tigris River

IRAN

Ramadi

Baghdad

Tigris River

IRAQ

Euphrates River

JORDAN

SAUDI ARABIA

KUWAIT

N

0   50   100   150 kilometers

0   50   100 miles

SERBIA

MONTENEGRO

Prekaz

Lauša • • Srbica

Čičavica
Mountains

Likošane

Priština

Drenica
River

Istinić

Berisha
Mountain

Dečane

Glođane

Senik

KOSOVO

Tropoja

Račak

Lepenac River

Bajram Curri

ALBANIA

Skopje

MACEDONIA

N

0   10   20   30   40 kilometers

0   10   20   30 miles

Tirana

GUINEA

Kontah

Makeni

Rogberi
Junction

Kamrabai

Lunsar

Magburaka

Freetown

SIERRA LEONE

NORTH ATLANTIC OCEAN

N

LIBERIA

0   20   40   60   80 kilometers

0   20   40   60 miles

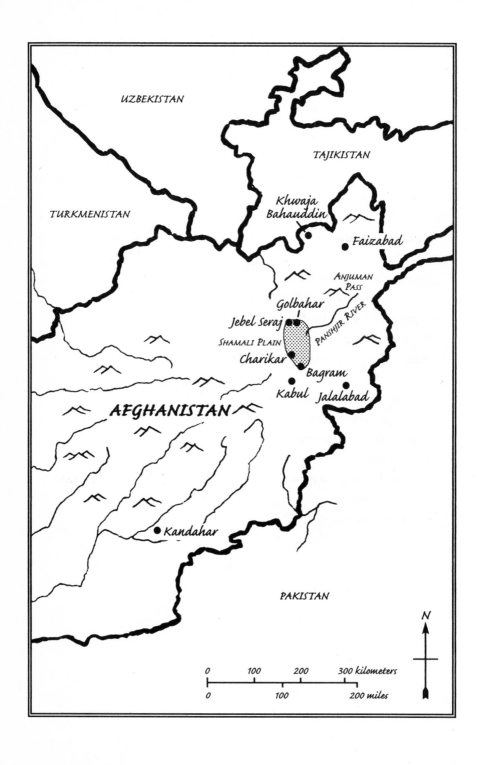

UZBEKISTAN

TAJIKISTAN

TURKMENISTAN

Khwaja
Bahauddin

● Faizabad

ANJUMAN
PASS

Golbahar

Jebel Seraj

SHAMALI PLAIN

Charikar

PANSHJIR RIVER

Bagram

Kabul   Jalalabad

AFGHANISTAN

● Kandahar

PAKISTAN

N

0   100   200   300 kilometers

0   100   200 miles

Everyone Sang

Everyone suddenly burst out singing;
And I was filled with such delight
As prisoned birds must find in freedom,
Winging wildly across the white
Orchards and dark-green fields; on-on-and out of sight.

Everyone's voice was suddenly lifted;
And beauty came like the setting sun:
My heart was shaken with tears: and horror
Drifted away . . . O, but Everyone
Was a bird; and the song was wordless; the singing will never be done.

Siegfried Sassoon (1886–1967)

PROLOGUE

Iraq, Winter 2004

The day was nearly done, the fire fight over and the mission all but complete when the question arrived, slipping from a soldier's mouth in an unbroken slice of sound, so quick that it seemed almost like a single word. A senior NCO with an Airborne flash on one shoulder, older than most of the others, he was a compact, muscular man, his cheek bulging with a wad of chewing tobacco. Behind him, across the river, a dead young American was soaring up into the sky on the floor of a helicopter fuselage, bloody and dirty inside a bag: first wrap for the start of the long journey home, where he would arrive so clean, so cold, but so neatly presented, casked beneath the Stars and Stripes. Beside us, Carlisle was still hyped and trembling, jaw muscles bunching and twitching on the adrenalin rush, his rifle barrel uncooled. All along the banks of the river fire teams were checking their ammunition, regaining their breath and shaking out to move forward once again, more in ritual than hope by that stage, for they knew their quarry was long gone.

The NCO might have looked angry – for soldiers often display bitterness towards a journalist the moment they lose one of their number – but there was no trace of malice in his voice or eyes. Instead he seemed just curious, as if merely wanting to know whether the death of the young American was worthy of a story, somehow justifying my presence there. The question was punch enough though, unwittingly as intrusive and complex as anything I had ever asked as a reporter. One way or another, it had haunted me across the years, an unanswerable stalker at the close of every day in every war, hungrier by the hour.

1

'Hey,' he said, 'you get what you were looking for?'

I paused for a second, still unsure of precisely what to say, even though I knew that I had some sort of reply by then. It had come to me a few months earlier, on my first day in Baghdad, the loneliest in my life, as I stared from a hotel balcony across the city, already capital to a thousand and one tombstone tales of dead dreams and broken hope. But it would have taken too long to use that answer on that afternoon in Al Anbar. So I said something about people not having to die for me to be there, sounding defensive without intending to, abandoning my belief in the brush-off's credibility even as I tried to shore it up in my own mind, and left it at that. The soldier shrugged and walked away. He was probably asking himself the same question. It hovers over most men in war, second stepping their every move like an unborn twin.

It had been an altogether haunted day. Right from the moment when Bravo Company had dismounted from their vehicles on the northern bank of the Euphrates, formed up and crossed the mission start line beneath the bright blue of the winter dawn they had been pursued, the eyes of the unseen insurgents watching their every move. Chasing them too was the ghost of Charlie Cong. Charlie, with his ethereal Chinese Kalashnikov and spectral satchel charge; Charlie, chattering through the rotorblade throb of two overhead Hueys; whispering among the tall rush beds that divided the paddy fields and irrigation ditches; lurking in his black pyjamas under the palm trees; eating his bag of rice in the shadows thrown by a fat, cold sun. Watching. Waiting.

Adjusting their equipment and glancing around them, the soldiers knew Charlie was near. For soldiers know that there is no place more haunted than a war zone; that ghosts chase you across years, generations and continents; that Vietnam was too close; that haunting can be personal and malicious and goddamn you'd better believe it. But none of them mentioned it, at least not directly. It would have been bad karma. And no one wanted to mention the V-word lest it actually incite matters.

Except for Carlisle. He came right out with it. If I was near the end of my trip, the point at which I could no longer listen to a war song without knowing that I had heard it many times before, but sat there anyway waiting for something new, too long term an investor in the venture to sell my shares, Carlisle was at the beginning of his. We had barely exchanged a word on the route to the drop-off point. Together with Bravo Company's commander, a quietly spoken, authoritative young captain, we had travelled by Humvee in the reflective silence that characterises a sleep-broken ride to the start of a ground operation, staring ahead as the grey, undulating desert around us gave way to the vegetated alluvial plane that borders the Euphrates, wondering if everyone was still going to be around to remount their vehicles at the mission's end.

Stepping from the Humvee and surveying the scene, the reeds and flat fields, the lean-to farmers' shacks walled with bamboo and roofed with palm leaves, the peasant women grinding flour in stone pots around small fires watched by children with inscrutable dark eyes, and the slick, brown, slow-moving expanse of the river, Carlisle tilted back the brim of his helmet and spat on the ground. He was a tall, rangy man with an aquiline nose, pale Celtic eyes and a straight mouth that hinted of something mean.

'My father was in the special forces in Vietnam,' he began, speaking towards the river as if challenging the landscape. 'He did four tours there between '69 and '73. He was shot in the Mekong Delta but survived, hiding beneath the body of one of his buddies after his platoon took ninety per cent casualties and the VC went through them, finishing off the survivors.

'He was a great soldier,' he added as an afterthought, spitting again, 'but a lousy husband and an even worse father. He died when he was forty-eight. He lived life hard.' He said nothing more, just continued to gaze out at the river.

I smiled inwardly. It was as if he had learned the story by rote, in the same way as most young men explain their presence in war until the heat loosens up the wax on their wings and they take a dive, and have to come up with some other logic. Yet, if the Americans had their ghosts in attendance that day, I had my own, too. A whole patrol of them. They always grouped in close on a mission: the fat Serb waiter; the Albanian mafia chief; Allieu in his tatty shoes, sweaty under a West African sun. People I knew personally; others I recognised only as bodies; places;

sounds; goodbyes, said and unsaid. I liked to think of them as 'friendlies', but knew that I could not count on every one. Dave would at best want to cut me some sort of deal for his loyalty; Halil always demanded a down payment in advance. Would they disappear into a black fog if something went wrong, I sometimes wondered, or would my first awareness of the end of it all be the moment when a Land-Rover pulled up, the door opened, and Kurt leaned out to ask if I wanted a ride?

The sappers and infantry began moving forward in extended lines across the paddy fields, a few bearing mine detectors; each laden with assault rifle, grenades, pistol and ammunition. The mission involved a lengthy sweep to search for the weapons caches of an otherwise invisible enemy. Across the Euphrates the city of Ramadi, capital of Al Anbar Province, sat brooding on the south bank behind a treeline of palms and thick foliage.

Al Anbar already occupied the unrivalled number-one position of threat to the Americans in Iraq. Stretching eastwards into the country from the border with Syria, it was a vast swath of Sunni territory uniquely hostile to the coalition presence. Foreign fighters, former Ba'athists, local Islamicists, tribal warriors and a new wave of indigenous insurgents competed there in disarray with little more strategic aim than to take American lives. Known generically by the Americans as the 'Hajis', the insurgents were not so much a single force as a spangle-cracked gang movement, linked at best by shifting ad hoc alliances, anger and opportunism, but their anarchic approach to warfare carried a weighty strike, and the highest proportion of American soldiers sent home from Iraq with the zip-snap epitaph of a closing body-bag had breathed their last in Al Anbar.

'Am I doing something wrong?' the brigade's Catholic chaplain, vexed at his inability to save his men's life through prayer, told me he often asked himself.

'No,' I should have said. 'It's just a war. It doesn't care who it kills or why. Don't take it personally.' But I said nothing. It was his first operational tour. He would have to work it out for himself; something he could do only by staying around long enough. Meantime, struggling to make his reckoning with God, he still held on to the forlorn hope that the negotiations may result in an amnesty. He verged close to tears when he described giving the last rites to dying soldiers, and admitted that the experience was so draining that at times he walked away weeping. It was an intimate confession. Once, I may have privately sneered at his predicament, for the crushing of another's hope can be cruel sport to behold from the pedestal of nihilist certainty. But that time was gone. Suffering and loss can be livid catalysts to enlightenment; and they can make war, a place of so many lost farewells, an obvious starting point for a man to begin searching for his peace. Not that it offers a guaranteed path to the grail. Only a few days previously another of the unit's chaplains, overwhelmed by the challenges to his faith, resigned his commission and left Iraq to reconsider his position. He said that he could no longer accept working without a gun.

The sun ascended and the cool of the morning surrendered to a sullen heat. There was no sign of any combat-age Iraqi males. Instead, as the American search lines converged on the few dismal farmsteads they found only goats, chickens, women and children. One kid, unsmiling, snot-nosed and under-dressed, offered an orange to a soldier. The man accepted it, grinned, and turned away.

'Better not suck it in case it explodes,' he confided, only half joking.

Four small reconnaissance craft, crewed by marines and engineers, joined the operation. Bristling with mounted machine-guns, the boats careered across the Euphrates from bank to bank, their heavy wash slapping at the reed beds.

'Just like *Apocalypse Now*, 'cept without the grass and acid,' a marine noted with rueful enthusiasm, nostalgic for a time he had never known. Sure. Just like *Apocalypse Now*. So like it in fact, that it seemed only a few frames away until Mister Clean got wasted in an ambush. I could almost feel it coming.

Some barely out of college and experiencing their first foreign country, many of the younger American soldiers in Iraq were living in their own war films, life and art enmeshing in a freakish coupling to a contemporary soundtrack of thrash metal and gangsta rap, unaware that war seldom has a clear end, and never a final credit. War stories are the same, at best an incomplete fragment of momentous pattern, words in a day of a perpetual cycle. History diminishes wars, boiling each down to a singular happening defined between two dates. The reality is always more nebulous, the current beginning far earlier than the moment which is subsequently recognised, the overspill lasting long afterwards, and for each individual involved the experience has a deeply personal definition, usually remembered in a fashion totally disconnected from time and event. It was only sometimes, much later, that I could ever look back and define a particular phase. Iraq marked the end of one of them.

Things were never going to be the same again. That certainty was not borne from merely being older. Nor was it related to the country's fading wish-list, the lack of faith in the war, or the fact that it was being lost, resistance reseeded and multiplied by the success in every clash of a coalition force whose concept of victory had been diminished to little more than whatever lay down a gun-sight. Instead, a personal era had died between the NCO's question, its answer, and the lessons of death that lay between.

Soon the crew in one craft discovered a large weapons cache of mortar rounds and artillery shells concealed on the bankside. Soldiers planted a charge among the ordnance and blew it up. The blast reverberated up the river, sending a flock of white egrets into the sky.

'We usually sink all the Iraqi boats along the banks when we find a cache,' a marine implored the sapper colonel, call sign Brokenheart Six, pointing at a handful of empty fishing vessels bobbing temptingly in the reeds.

'Well, you're not sinking all the boats today,' the colonel overruled, as cool, wise and resolute as his call sign suggested, too many lines on his face to allow him to indulge in overkill.

By late afternoon the winter sun had grown fatter and sunk deeper, and a brooding tiredness settled on the soldiers. No longer were the search lines straight and true. They began to break, waver and lag. Up the dykes and across the ditches they continued, though, under the palms, through the overgrown orchards, past the abandoned farms and the women without men, the soldiers' energy waning as the shadows lengthened.

'Too long. We've been in the same area too long,' a lieutenant warned quietly, fixing his fingers into claws and drawing his hands slowly together.

I grew tired, and my thoughts started to drift, back to when the itch began, the first time I had been in Iraq, quite unbloodied. A soldier seeking quick answers, much like Carlisle was now . . .

It had been winter then as now, that time of my first war, and on the eve of invasion the omens were propitious and death a stranger. In the previous weeks of waiting the desert skies had often remained closed and brooding, the light opaque and tinged with the orange of sandstorms. By night a thin black rain had fallen upon us from dark clouds as we huddled in our shell scrapes, spattering our battle dress with the grey residue of burning oil fields, while plunging temperatures had turned our water bottles into maracas alive with the chinking of ice. But as we received our final orders at the edge of the Iraqi border, as if in blessing the night skies cleared to reveal a shining cosmos above us so perfect in detail that peering up from beneath the brims of our helmets we could chart the passage of the satellites cruising the battlefield from the heavens; and note the silver starlight reflecting from the wings of the distant attack jets flying their lonesome missions.

We had been the tiny playing cards in the momentous hand crafted by our most senior commanders, and were at the fulcrum of our destiny. Or so it had seemed. Months of planning had gone into the pattern of our assembly; millions of man hours of intelligence, experience, training and intuition shaping then reshaping our army's composition and deployment in readiness for the moment when we would be cast on to the table into battle. Our form, wholesome and varnished with such precision, would change in an instant in reaction to the arch-dynamic of war: chaos.

For whatever the odds and whatever the preparation, once the final arrow is etched on to a general's map and the last lance-corporal finishes briefing his fire team, an army marches into the dark valley of the unknown and unforeseen. The definition of the script dissolves with the first acid drop spatter of bullets, scattering presumption to the skies in a hail of torn confetti fragments that cascade with their own momentum, shifting shape and direction as the fighting spreads, the fate of individuals remaining either unseen and unnoticed in the disguise of the moving mass, or shimmering to the ground alone, remarkable perhaps for some solitary act of courage, cowardice or dying.

Oblivious to these finer details in the cocksure vanity of youth, as the artillery barrages thumped across the horizon and the desert ran alive with the sudden movement of thousands of armoured vehicles, I was war's blind novice. Small surprise that laden with the drama of the moment suggesting imminent ordeal and epiphany, I would augur so wrong. I always got it wrong with Iraq.

A single piper had played as our battalion left its departure point to cross through the enemy's breached front line. It was a romantic gesture in keeping with the unit's Scottish origins, but as we sat hunched together in our vehicles, a clanking mélange of flesh, cloth, anti-tank rockets, grenades, ammunition and rifles, the throb of engines and roar of an escorting American tank squadron stole the skirl's every note. Perhaps I should have read more significance into the desert's theft of 'Scotland the Brave', but once inside Iraq a strange storm accompanied our passage, bestowing our self-perception with the mantle of might and rightful vengeance. Bolts of lightning threw themselves from waterless clouds and angled on to the flat wastes of the desert; a sudden and unnatural crosswind collected the lustreless sand into drifting thigh-high waves so that middle-distance infantrymen appeared as ethereal, truncated figures floating legless through the war zone's lunar landscapes.

I did not have to be there: my own regiment was thousands of miles away. I was a volunteer, tacked on to a new unit a few weeks previously. Nor was I in Iraq to serve some noble ideal. I cared little as to whether the coalition's war to eject Saddam from Kuwait was legitimate or justified. Twenty-four years old, a soldier for five years, totally ignorant of war's random handouts of tragedy and reward, I was there simply to fulfil my dreams of glory, reach through the darkness of danger and adversity and seize the burning laurels that were the birthright of my ancestors.

War, as I saw it, was a natural and necessary rite of passage. It afforded the chance to discover if I was brave in action; and provided the opportunity to be seen to be brave in action. Bravery was challenging death. Bravery was being cool under fire. Bravery was shooting someone who was trying to shoot you. Bravery was ostensibly a male preserve and was proved, exclusively, in war. Bravery made you a man. It was the very point of joining the infantry in the first place, and as I jolted into southern Iraq, knowing my new comrades little better than strangers sharing a compartment on a long train journey, I felt sure my moment was upon me. Perhaps I would even see Baghdad, I mused happily. The seizure of the city would carry a far greater sense of fulfilment than some mere perambulation around a referenceless desert. Though the overthrow of Saddam had not been part of our stated aims, who could tell what secret plans lay in the minds of our distant commanders, or what effect our advance would have on the Ba'athist regime?

However, it turned out to be a very short war, just five days long. And in those hundred hours, between the deceptive manifestations of nature, the occasional vista of burning Iraqi armour and the rumble of artillery, action remained an elusive fugitive, conducted far from my eager curiosity in an abstract theatre of growing disappointment.

We encountered one Iraqi unit whose position had been hit and bypassed by advance armoured coalition forces. As our company crawled towards it, the prospect that there may have lurked, among the underfed, ill-led, demoralised and clearly defeated troops before us, a group of diehards intent on further fight, brought an excitement that negated any trace of fear. My only concern was that my rifle would jam once the shooting started and deny me a rightful kill. Irritatingly, though, the windborne sand kept running into my eyes through the sides of my frayed goggles and as I slithered forward on my belly the motion of my shoulders pushed the heavy radio set on my back against my helmet, bashing its brim repeatedly on to the bridge of my nose. 'Christ,' I mumbled, eyes streaming, pushing the brim back for the umpteenth time, angry that this trivial irritation was interfering on the threshold of so profound a moment. 'Shit. Fuck.'

Then the first Iraqi troops began to clamber from their bunkers, dirty white flags and hands raised, and with their appearance my dreams of glory melted miserably into the dust. In the ritual choreography of the battlefield as they walked towards us in supplication we broke position, first to a kneel, then to a crouch, standing finally once it was obvious no fight would be given. After that it was a fairly nonchalant exercise akin to herding intelligent and acquiescent cattle into a central group to be searched and taken away.

Trucks rolled up to remove the prisoners and I took a walk through the deserted position with another soldier, noticing the abandoned weaponry, dirty matting, scattered piles of shit, and grime-crusted cooking utensils that were the legacy of the Iraqis' defeat. The wind still whipped sand around our legs, but save for the eerie rustle of these millions of moving granules there was silence.

The ceasefire halted our advance after another forty-eight hours. The top round in my magazine, a tracer, was the same one I had placed there five days earlier. It shone at me accusingly. Far, far away from Baghdad, we looped east from Iraq, into Kuwait, then south back to Saudi Arabia. The desert no longer represented an archway to initiation and had instead become a meaningless vacuum echoing with some sort of incomprehensible joke. Cheated and confused, I felt tricked by fate and could not wait to leave it.

Six weeks later the battalion flew back to its barracks in Britain. It was the end of my service in the army and I had no wish to re-enlist. Having handed in my kit and signed a few forms, suddenly baseless after so long in uniform, I boarded a train to a station near my mother's rural home and took a taxi for the final leg of the journey.

'Been away?' the driver asked, peering at my sunburned face through his rear-view mirror as the cab started its twisting descent through a country lane.

'Holiday,' I replied curtly, slumping lower in the seat in an attempt to deflect the conversation.

'Somewhere nice?'

'Not really.'

A bright strip of bunting fluttered in the driveway of my mother's cottage, the welcome to a son come home from war. It seemed so taunting and undeserved at that moment that I told the driver to pass the house, and had him drop me off in a deserted stretch of the lane where I could collect my emotions before walking back alone and knocking on the front door. My sulky introspection did not survive contact with my mother's unconditional delight at seeing me again, the leaping terrier or the general buzz unique to the English countryside in April. For a few days the spring greenery alone, erupting around the cottage from the surrounding woods and fields, was itself an elixir to my mood after so many weeks of drab sand.

Soon, though, the seeming deceit of the war's non-event began to gnaw at me once more. Looking at pictures of the family's men, seeing their uniforms and the medal ribbons gleaned in both world wars, I wondered if their wars, real wars, had provided them with an answer; if medals were enough, or whether *behind the hinted smiles and steadfast stares they had felt as vexed and empty-handed as I did.*

Thirteen years later, in Baghdad, on a day when it seemed I had no more company than war itself, the memories of that earlier homecoming, so narcissistic and innocent, had found a final resonance; each detail somehow echoed in belated answer. Epiphany? It is an arrogant word of claim, suggesting more completion than the human state is capable of. What I had found, though lumpy and tarnished as an uncut gem, was much more real than epiphany. As Bravo Company continued its weary trudge along the Euphrates, I turned it over in my mind once more, trying to digest it. It was not the reply I thought I was looking for . . .

Contact! A burst of gunfire, then a second, then a third, and the nought-to-ninety-in-a-second rip and roar of the adrenalin rush that momentarily left my mind cartwheeling in its wake. Fire in front, then gunshots across one flank, crossed by more from another; soldiers piling into ditches; a Huey overhead, its machine-gun blazing away. Rolling down into a culvert the fear was immediate: the pressure of thousands of tons of water squeezing down on my chest. But as my thoughts scrabbled for traction, the old, familiar voice of gun battle override stepped in. Oxygenating, strong, it buoyed me up from the deep spin of shock with simple instructions. Breathe, it ordered. Think. Be calm. (And if you can't be calm – then try to look it.) The fear began to subside a little, and the pressure reduced. Others must have heard it too. For just a few seconds every man there had been an individual lost in his own world of instinct, fright and confusion, until that voice poured oil upon their fragmentation, congealing the disparate moments into shaking cohesion.

Concealed insurgents lying on both river banks had ambushed one of the reconnaissance craft and turned their fire on to Bravo Company. In the boat a sapper was hit in the neck, dropping dead to the deck as another soldier fell wounded beside him. The boats fired back and in the Humvee cupolas gunners on the .50 cals joined the fray. Beside his commander's vehicle, Carlisle dropped to the ground and raised his

M-16. He saw two men in the undergrowth ahead of him and began shooting.

'I got one!' he yelled, juddering with the excitement at having so quickly found what he thought he was looking for, as an Iraqi interpreter muttered, 'Cool it, cool it.'

Then it all subsided as quickly as it had begun, the chattering heave of noise suddenly exhaling into no more than a crackle or two, then silence, save for the shouts of the commanders regrouping their men, and the blood singing in my ears. Even time regained its usual pace, stepping back from the yawning void of action that dazes every participant so that they can no more tell with any precision how long a fight has lasted than estimate the duration of a fantasy.

'I didn't even have to think about it!' Carlisle shivered on in the aftermath, still aboard the adrenalin carousel, seeking quick confirmation for his kill. 'I don't just think I got him. I *know* it! Man, was that exciting!'

Yet there was no trace of the insurgents, neither dead nor alive. I clambered up from the ground, patted invisible sand from my clothes for the sake of something to do, and saw the NCO walking towards me, the question already forming on his lips as the medevac chopper came in to dust-off the American casualties, the clatter of its blades cutting over the rippling murmur of the river. More than any reply I could have come up with that day of one more war, one more war story, the noise, so naked in hope and the desire to save, already seemed some kind of an answer in its own right: sound-ink signature to another bloody love letter.

CHAPTER 1

Kosovo, February 1999

I always hated the Kosovo crows. During winter in Priština the edge between day and night was unfailingly marked by a Gothic passage, as they swarmed in their thousands through the fading light like an ill wind to roost in the city's warm underbelly: unremitting, relentless harbingers of the carrion ahead, vulgar guardians to secrets past. In some of the more remote mountain villages elderly Serbs would tell you that they were the spirits of slain Serb fighters, killed in the Battle of Kosovo Polje when an invading Ottoman army trounced Prince Lazar's forces on the 'Field of the Black Birds' just outside Priština in 1389, an occasion which marked the ascendance of the Turks' domination of the Balkans, and sowed the seeds for so much of what followed. There is a ticking clock and haunted hill in every Serb heart, entities they utilise for both their self-definition and justification. Sooner or later, even their most casual conversations click back six centuries for a starting point, a quick wheeze of concertina closure before the lengthy outward breath that spans the ages later; the centuries-long trail of tensions, manipulations, betrayals and bloodshed that mounts towards another war, rocking the cradle for the next generation with whispers of past injustice and future vengeance.

So when the sudden beat of wings rustled just above me I instinctively hunched and grimaced.

'Huh! You see that crow come out of nowhere and swoop you?' Kurt laughed.

'Think I'm blind or something?'

'It looked like the angel of death to me,' he continued, in amused appeal to my superstition.

'Right. Thanks man.' I grinned back, but was unsettled and spooked. I had lied: that time I had not seen the bird.

Shrugging away the moment, I looked back at the body in front of us, trying to piece together the man's killing in my mind. By battlefield standards it had been a casual affair. The victim was in his twenties. Dressed in a blue woollen jersey and jeans, probably an insurgent, no ID, he lay sprawled at the edge of a Kosovar village, shot twice in the chest, palms open and fingers outstretched, his wristwatch, cheap enough to avoid being looted, still marking time. It attracted my attention. Tick-tick-tick on a dead man's wrist: movement and noise from the inanimate; stillness and silence from what had been alive. In two days the man would be black and swollen; another two weeks, open and crawling; two months more, just scattered bones. And the watch might still be ticking.

His posture and the little details around him indicated that he had not been killed in action. Two empty pistol bullet casings lay at his feet, as well as a fresh Yugoslav cigarette butt. His executioner had been a Serb soldier who smoked. The corpse had a little facial bruising but bore no sign of torture. Likely he had been a Kosovo Liberation Army scout sent to the area to see what was going on, had been caught, questioned, slapped around and shot. Or maybe he was just a civilian who did not make good his escape in time. The Serbs would scarcely have bothered to differentiate, and it did not take much for an Albanian male of fighting age, stopped by security forces in a rural area during operations, to get a bullet.

Perched like an eyrie in the mountains many miles south of Priština, the cluster of houses behind the dead man, nearly a mile above sea level, smouldered dismally in the midday sun. Serb tanks and mortars had pulverised them a day earlier, before the infantry moved in and torched what remained. The centre of the village was little more than rubble, any surviving houses gutted by flame. The mosque had been raked with shellfire and vandalised. The village's registration office, home to the birth certificates and identity papers needed by Albanians to exist as Yugoslav citizens, had also been ransacked: Yugoslav and Albanian flags lying trampled in ironic partnership in the dust outside. Other than the occasional crash of falling masonry and plaintive keening of a pair of circling falcons, the village was totally silent.

After so many years of practice, the Serbs had 'ethnic cleansing' down to a fine art. Insurgents need a civilian population in which to survive and recruit just as lice need hair. Western armies try to isolate them from their host communities by a parallel political strategy – a diplomatic olive branch beside the military fist. Not so the Serbs. In Kosovo they shaved the entire scalp, purging guerrilla and civilian alike from their homes, interpreting the scorched earth that remained behind as 'pacified'. They were taking a gamble, though, assuming that they could either get away with the strategy of fire, ash and occasional nonchalant massacre which was pitching thousands of people from their land, or else endure a few consequent, token NATO air strikes. It was typical of their arrogance, but at that moment did not appear such an ill-conceived assessment: no one was in a great hurry to go to war with Yugoslavia over a province that was smaller than Wales.

There was no trace of the other villagers apart for one very old man who rambled, dazed and alone, through the ruins. He had fled his home when the Serb attack began, but had become separated from his family in the confusion, and without enough strength to escape across the mountains unaided, he had returned to the village, where Serb soldiers had pummelled him with their rifle butts, leaving his face bruised and puffy.

It was a tired scene. Almost boring. The deaths of strangers had expunged my naivety long before. In Bosnia, that old, dead friend of a war, I had seen their bodies tossed and chopped like salad by shellfire, riddled with bullets; burned, splintered, cracked; bone-bleached, green-rotten, peach-fresh; single, group, multiple; soldier, civilian; man, woman, child. Dull neighbours, war dead had become so familiar by that stage of my life that I could no longer even class the dreams they haunted as nightmares. Life was cheap, I thought; it was an easy conclusion to reach when greeted by the remains of people I had never known. From time to time an especially remarkable corpse or massacre still evoked some flickering sense of poignancy and loss, but most provided only more evidence of my own inurement. It was a bad relationship to have with the dead. For, just as a soldier who is prepared to kill but not to die becomes little more than a common murderer, a reporter standing beneath the umbrella of cynicism in a conflict is little more than a parasite and a fool, half blind at that.

Other than the corpse's watch, the most salient aspect of the situation that day seemed to be the vista, a beautiful green tumble of plateau, slopes and oak trees framed by the spring-washed blue sky.

'Beautiful, huh?'

'Yeah. Amazing.'

'Mmmm. Wow.'

We clambered into our car and pulled away, leaving the old man to stumble through the ruins of his village with just the ticking corpse for company. A single stray dog, a handsome creature with trusting eyes and thick tan coat pursued us frantically across the mountain tracks, seemingly desperate not to be left behind, beckoning to our consciences until we picked up speed and it became no more than a shrinking brown flurry in the distance.

Two hours later we were back at Beba's. He was a charming man and we were friends. A Serb gangland daddy who had graduated from loan sharking and debt enforcement into hookers and casinos, he had risen quickly through the power echelons in Priština's underworld to become a mid-ranking godfather, nineties Balkan style: shell suit, shades, pistol and baseball cap. Only the transmissions of power and violence invoked memories of Brando's Don Vito, but the reality was the same. In his early forties, well over six feet tall, he was a bear of a man with the kind of face that could be either ugly or good-looking, depending on the light and his mood. Married to a Muslim woman, Vera, predictably he kept some heavy company, and numbered both the paramilitary warlord Zeljko Raznatovic, better known to the world as 'Arkan', and founder members of the KLA among his erstwhile comrades. The mob, always the last institution to fall apart in a war, was a very integrated scene in Kosovo at the time.

A foreigner needs a good base in a conflict, somewhere secure, preferably with running water and electricity, to which they can withdraw at night, wash, eat and sleep. Additionally, due to the endemic violent crime that accompanies most wars, a host is required with rather different qualities to the normal social requirements. Savvy and solid, with a finger on every strand of the city's web, Beba was thus an ideal patriarch. Better still, his hotel in Priština, positioned bordering a tawdry strip of trees and litter-strewn wasteland, was a converted bordello. With some fifteen rooms arranged in squares over two floors, each surrounding an open furnished atrium where once clients had drunk and smoked prior to and after their rendezvous with the girls, the horizontal bedside mirrors, thick carpets and padded doors all remained, so that whatever the newer transformations of kitsch decor there was no disguising the building's original prupose. The sexual ambience was still so strong that, sleeping there alone, you were more conscious of your loneliness as the night descended than was the case in other beds, other rooms, other places.

For the whores were long gone and did not return, despite occasional entreaties to Beba. Instead, the building took its cash from a different type of punter: men and women versed in the currencies of violence from wars the world over but the Balkans in particular; dramatic and self-dramatising; concerned and callous; mostly white and middle class and angry and childless; selfish through circumstance but often kind by inclination; sometimes brave; invariably great pretenders. Us. War correspondents, to use the professional term.

I ordered an espresso from the bar, went up to my room, lit a cigarette and rang the boss, wondering what the market in the newspaper's London office was that day for a corpse, a burned village and a beaten old man. If the appetite was right then the machine would hoover up even a single death story. Distracted by some other event in the world, it had to be a multiple killing to gain their attention. It seemed that they were interested, so I flicked through my notes, sketched the story in long hand, and began to tap away at my laptop. An hour or so later I had finished, so I poured myself a glass of wine and wandered outside in search of company, wondering what else the day would bring.

Kosovo's was a very strange war, such as it was a war, in those few months leading up to NATO air strikes, its trajectory erratic and unpredictable. My intimacy with it lay not in an immersion with fighting, but more in the languid dividing periods that segmented the conflict in an on–off series of spasms. Until its final eventual rush, watching the conflict progress was the same as looking at a cheap firework. The touchpaper was alight but hissed only reluctantly. Occasionally a sudden spark and flare of energy suggested speedy acceleration and imminent explosion, causing held breath and tightened stomach, only to dwindle again to a sullen sputter. Then the pattern would repeat, the only difference being the shortening length of time between creep and crackle.

And never once during the whole conflict could I shake the impression that my engagement with the place was really to find an ending to a war that was already lost and finished. As if I was having an affair with the younger sister of a dead lover, I went through the motions in the hope of seeing some similar expression or gesture, of discovering even a trace of the passion I had once known in Bosnia. In this regard at least, from beginning to end, Kosovo left me quite bereft. Goodbyes are hard to chase. But there were other rewards.

So much as any war has a clear beginning, Kosovo's had a specific moment of violence from which the greater conflict emerged. Most of those involved were either already dead or had disappeared in one way or another by the time, much later, that Kurt and I found three survivors who told us what had happened, how it had all started. Their story involved a mutant tree, four men in a car, some policemen and that first trigger pull. It set the pattern for the evolution of the whole war: the skirmishes and massacres that accelerated across Kosovo into a wave of bloodletting and pogrom; the hundreds of thousands of people burned out of their homes and purged from their own country; a monolithic and criminal state organisation running amok through the province; and the fateful moment when NATO dragged itself into the conflict with the reluctant enthusiasm of a racehorse-owner entering a prized stallion in a donkey derby, and began to bomb Yugoslavia.

On the eastern side of the small Kosovar village of Likošane, deep in the Drenica Valley, caught between green fields and the junction of an earthen track, grows a legendary oak. According to the village elders, three hundred years earlier the shoots from six acorns had entwined together at the spot. Intrigued by the deformed sapling, generations of Albanian villagers protected the tree from livestock, watching it develop over time into six equal trunks spreading from one root. A local landmark, it became known as the 'Six Brothers', and after the Second World War the communists claimed that its unique growth symbolised Yugoslavia's six-republic federation.

Every insurgency has its heartland, and the Drenica Valley was Kosovo's, akin to Northern Ireland's South Armagh, Lebanon's Bekaa Valley, Chechnya's Vedeno Gorge, Iraq's Al Anbar. A gentle roll of fertile farmland criss-crossed by untarmacked roadways and encroached by deciduous woodland, the valley curls northwards into the centre of the province from beneath the Crnoljeva Mountains. Quaint stone-walled villages and gurgling streams gave Drenica a benign guise, yet the hearts of the Albanian communities living there were singularly forged by antipathy towards Serb rule and the desire for independence. A bastion of Albanian resistance throughout the centuries, by the mid-1990s Drenica had become an unwritten no-go zone for the Belgrade authorities, a parallel society within Yugoslavia where police ventured at their peril.

On 28 February 1998 the shadows thrown westwards from the deformed oak by the rising sun fell on the frozen soil of a land at peace. By the time the shadows had turned eastwards at the close of the short winter day that peace was at an end, and blood and bullet casings speckled the tree's snow-scabbed roots.

Early that morning, a car had approached the tree. The skies were wind-blown and clear, the ground patched with snow and muddied by a hesitant spring thaw. Inside the vehicle were four armed fighters from Ushtria Clirimtare e Kosoves, better known as the Kosovo Liberation Army. At that time, the KLA was viewed largely as a myth, its existence and activities confined to rumour and speculation, at least to the eyes of the outside world. With the exception of those in Drenica and the Serb security forces, even most Kosovars regarded it as little more than a piece of contemporary rural folklore.

Yet these fighters were real enough and, as they drove past the oak, a Serb special police unit hiding in a nearby farmhouse sprang an ambush. One of the KLA men was hit by a bullet in the arm. Together with the others, he rolled from the car and ran to take up position by the tree, destroying a police Lada Niva that appeared on the scene with a rocket-propelled grenade. One of his companions then shot up another police vehicle with a machine-gun. Two policemen were killed, several more wounded.

Both sides called for back-up on their radios. Five KLA cars from neighbouring Drenica villages raced to the scene, among their occupants a selection of men who were to become famous in the coming war, including Adem Yashari, a tough Drenica gunslinger who would gain posthumous notoriety only a few days later.

A silver Audi was first to arrive at the tree. By this time the Serbs had a helicopter gunship in action, while armoured personnel carriers and regular troops advanced from the east. The Audi crew collected the fighter who had been wounded in the initial exchange, only to become casualties themselves, injured as shrapnel from an exploding rocket tore into their car. Bleeding profusely, the driver succeeded in reaching the nearby hamlet of Prelloc, where he crashed the vehicle into the wall of a house. Rescued by local Kosovars, the entire group escaped. The rusted Audi remains beside the wall to this day, an unlikely memorial to day one of the conflict.

In retributive mood, and harried on their flanks by fresh KLA gunmen, the Serb security forces advanced into Likošane. What happened next, as angry, confused soldiers encountered bemused civilians, was herald to all that ensued.

Having killed two Albanian farmers in a house near the oak, the Serb forces moved upon the compound of the Ahmetaj family. Engineers and intellectuals, the Ahmetajs were not KLA members, but their innocence was no deterrent to the Serbs' wrath. The police rammed down the compound's iron gates with an armoured vehicle and rushed inside. Amid the screaming of women and children, the Serbs dragged ten men from the house and began beating them. The beating continued for twelve hours. All ten were ultimately killed, not one by a bullet. When the police and army finally withdrew they took the bodies with them and left the ground littered with hair, flesh, teeth and bits of broken bone.

A total of twenty-five people were killed by the Serbs in Likošane that day. By the end of the week, when Adem Yashari and his family had been slain en masse too, gunned down by Serb police in their family compound in Prekaz having refused to surrender, the body count had risen to eighty-two, including twenty-five women and children.

So it began.

Oblivious to all this, it was not until four days after the oak tree ambush that I awoke to events. I was drinking coffee in a London street when the realisation came. The café was full, so I was sitting outside, hunched and disconsolate in the cold morning, vacant with sleeplessness, smoking, disconnected thoughts drifting through my mind, trying to collect myself in readiness for the day ahead. In the early stages of a drug rehabilitation programme, my mind was about as far as it was possible to be from Kosovo.

Then, flicking open a folded newspaper, the front-page photograph burned through the mists. It showed thousands of crouching Kosovars, praying before a line of coffins in a bare field outside Likošane. At their forefront stood a small boy, proud and insolent in his grief, holding up an Albanian flag, the black double-headed eagle superimposed over a scarlet ground. The report below the picture was brief, for details of what had happened at Likošane were scant at that stage, but the photo said enough to me. A small breeze shimmered into the morning's listless sails.

Already familiar with the Balkans, I knew enough of Kosovo's recent history to realise that the Likošane killings would have a seismic effect. Once an autonomous province within the Yugoslav federation, the Albanians there, who comprised over 90 per cent of Kosovo's two million population, had lost their power nine years earlier when the Serb supremo Slobodan Milošević, stacking the nationalist tinder beneath his vision of a Greater Serbia, changed the constitution and handed

Kosovo's rule directly to Belgrade. Thousands of Albanians had their jobs taken by Serbs, and the moment marked the start of a decade of oppression which in turn spawned the first cells of KLA fighters. A full-scale war in Kosovo, regarded by some Serbs as the very cradle of their civilisation, thus became only a matter of time as the Belgrade authorities in the province grew ever more oppressive in their efforts to subjugate the increasingly restless Albanians.

So, as news of the Likošane massacre spread, villagers throughout Kosovo, both Serb and Albanian, dusted off the weapons most Balkan households have stored beneath the eaves and floorboards and readied themselves for what they knew must come. For a time during the spring the conflict stalled as quickly as it had begun. The KLA stepped out of the shadows to control rural Albanian communities, but fighting was minimal, and the Serbs hesitated over further strikes or encroachment. It was an eerie period of phoney insurgency.

At the very start of summer, the engine suddenly sprang into life once more as along the province's southern border with Albania the Serbs began to raid Kosovar communities loyal to the KLA. Black smoke from burning houses gathered above bucolic green valleys and small bands of refugees began to flee into the mountains. It was a serious enough development for my boss to call me, reignite the freelance contract I held with the paper, and ask me to proceed to Priština.

No sooner had the phone call ended than I felt the delicious thumping farewell refrain begin, flaying me from the chaffing skin of my London world of rehab, relapse, routine normality and unutterable boredom with the scalpel precision of a renowned plastic surgeon. I threw some clothes into a bag, collected my sat-phone, cash, a flak-jacket and a plane ticket from the office a day or two later, and turned away from the clustering barnacle growths of life's trivia and problems, bidding goodbye to my peacetime alter ego without a backward glance, jumping through the breach on another great escape.

Travelling first through northern Albania, then on to Macedonia, I took a cab across the border and arrived in Kosovo one morning in early July. The war was still a nascent, low-intensity insurgency, and apart from the groups of sour-tempered, blue-uniformed Serb police huddled behind sandbagged checkpoints on the roads, its presence was all but invisible to the casual observer. The cab completed the final stretch of road and as we dropped over the last gentle ridge-line, Priština appeared suddenly before us. An inglorious mélange of communist architecture spiked with the occasional mosque, Kosovo's capital, its flat sprawl rising in a slight climb on hills to the east, was crowned by a brown summer smog produced by the nearby power plants – the romantically named Kosovo A and B, located there years before by Tito, in a brotherhood and unity middle-finger salute to Serb nationalism, on the very site of the ancient Kosovo Polje battlefield.

If not the most foreboding entry into a conflict, the day would yet see some drama. And it was Kurt who started it.

A colleague once described Kurt as the most famous war correspondent you have never heard of, a double honour because, contrary to popular belief, public recognition is an eroding canker on a reporter's integrity, eating away at the humility so essential for the work with the sharp incisors of vanity and ego.

We had first met in Sarajevo five years earlier. Bureau chief of a top news agency, he had already been there for a year when I turned up, and was the brave leader of Bosnia's reporters, as daring, sharp and resolute as a Wolfpack commander. A stammering wannabe correspondent, I knocked timorously on the door of his office at the suggestion of someone I had asked for professional advice. I was living with a Bosnian Serb family in a bad quarter of the city blown through by fighting, knew little about journalism, had no contacts and nothing to offer, and bore the painful aura of a fool about to die in rash endeavour.

Intense, even burning, yet with a mouth that sat on the edge of perpetual amusement, Kurt listened to my story of half-arsed aspiration and ill-defined plans from behind his desk with a series of punctuating 'uh-huh's and 'hmmm's, as if my hitch-hiking around Bosnia in the hope of getting a break was an entirely rational and laudable exercise. Perhaps my gamble in being there had appealed to his private motivations, for behind him lay his own long march. The son of a US marine who had seen action in the Pacific in the Second World War, exempted from service in Vietnam due to his appalling eyesight, Kurt was a former Rhodes scholar who had abandoned a safe and well-paid job running the New York transport system more than a decade earlier to gamble his chances as a freelance journalist based in Singapore. Already in his forties at the time, this new-found vocation had quickly taken him to wars in Sri Lanka and Afghanistan, then on to northern Iraq, where he had lived among the Kurds during their brief victory, long retreat and civil war in the wake of the first Gulf conflict. It was a strange choice to have made at that stage in his life, one which launched him on a course of solitude, danger and hardship that would have tested men half his age. But in the vernacular of the field, Kurt was one tough motherfucker.

Or maybe he just liked my irresponsibility. Whatever the case, in Bosnia we had become friends, travelling together whenever the chance arose, long before the Balkan fires had blown east to Kosovo. Hooking up with him in Priština on that first day, I found that my arrival coincided with a minor but newsworthy event. An observer group of foreign diplomats was touring Kosovo on a fact-finding mission. Though potentially tedious fare, in shadowing their cortège in a Land-Rover with Kurt, I knew I would receive an excellent brief on the situation, as well as see the lie of the land at first hand.

However, from the very moment it left the city, the diplomats' convoy of vehicles lost its cohesion as it was joined by vehicles belonging to local Serb and Kosovar journalists, as well as those of foreign reporters. Then, as it neared the destroyed village of Prekaz, one of the first tour stops and the site where Adem Yashari and his family had been killed, a red saloon broke from the rear of the cortège and sped to the front, taking an intimidatory swerve at a cameraman standing by the verge as it did so, missing him by inches.

'Who the fuck are those guys?' Kurt murmured, his attention suddenly fixed on the saloon, irritated by this apparently motiveless display of aggression. With only small encouragement from me, and using skills learned on a racing track, he gunned his Land-Rover forward, cut up the saloon and wheelspan a few stones its way as we turned down an unsurfaced track. Minutes later the entire convoy drew to a halt in Prekaz and Kurt stormed up to the saloon. Inside, ominously, sat three large men who looked more like bouncers than journalists. 'I don't know who you are or who you work for but you just about ran down that cameraman,' Kurt remonstrated. 'What's the rush?'

The men said nothing, and instead stared woodenly ahead through the windscreen. With no other option and puzzled by the silence, we walked away through the growing gaggle of other journalists. Seconds later, in a coordinated move, two of the men pushed past on either side of Kurt while the third squared up to him and gave him a mighty punch, snapping his head back and sending his glasses flying off into the stratosphere. There were quite a number of other reporters present by that stage, perhaps as many as forty. Yet when that single blow landed a space the size of a small coliseum appeared around Kurt and me as our media colleagues fled the scene in a clatter of abandoned pens, television tripods and dictaphones.

As Kurt staggered I was faced with an awful quandary. His attacker was huge. Wearing baggy trousers and a sweatshirt, he had blond cropped hair, a slab-like, brick-red face and a physique that suggested the labour of many months spent in a gym. Should I hit him and hope for the best or avoid confrontation and be shamed?

I slugged him smack in the face, a real barnstormer that came up from waist level, straightened on the curve, gathering some shoulder behind it to plant itself square on the left side of his jaw with a deep and delightful 'thwack'. It was a fantastic moment. In a squandered life of many shames that punch still ranks highly for its sense of overall achievement and honourable statement.

Retribution, however, was not long in coming. Unfamiliar with the art of physical violence, save for a few cartoon-starred recollections of boxing at Sandhurst, I stood back to admire my craftsmanship, optimistic that the fight was at an end. Unmoved and unflinching, the man stared down at me with an expression of slight puzzlement in his blue cop-soul eyes, rubbing his jaw thoughtfully. It seemed some time had passed since anybody had last punched him in the mouth. Finally, he paused from this motion, grunted a one-word Serbian curse, then unleashed a fast and furious barrage of karate kicks into my ribs that sent me pirouetting over the ground like a spinning top. The pain was immediate, sharp and continuous, and the breath left my body in a spasmodic series of expulsions in time to his kicks. But just as my vision began to granulate and standing up no longer seemed an option, Kurt stepped back into the fray.

'OK, you want to do it?' he addressed my assailant, eyes blazing, hurling his notebook gauntlet-style to the ground and raising his fists. 'Then let's do it!'

Our protagonist appeared taken aback by this new broadside threat. Together with his two henchmen, similarly attired bruisers who still loitered on the flanks, he could have pulped Kurt and me across the Prekaz fields, but looking at the fearless outrage of the new challenger it was clear they would have to do just that in order to extricate themselves from the situation: Kurt's fury was obviously not going to be cowed by a simple beating. And by this time the diplomats' security detail were moving in on the scene, as the accusing murmur of 'DB' grew among the Kosovar journalists. For these were no renegade bodyguards or happenstance thugs. The troika were Državna Bezbednost, Serb secret police, infiltrating the cortège to gather intelligence. But in true Serb style they had now blown their cover, unable to resist the chance for some bullying and intimidation.

Growling threats over their shoulders, they backed down, pushed past us and left, one ostentatiously adjusting a pistol concealed in his waistband just so we got the future message. I count the conclusions to bad situations from which I emerge still standing as victories, so this was a major triumph. I had fought the law and the law had not won, if only by default.

'You OK?' Kurt asked me, groping blindly in the grass for his missing specs. 'That was quite a punch you gave him. The guy was so big I didn't know whether to hit him or you.'

'Without your glasses I'm surprised you could see who to hit at all,' I quipped back, a little louder than perhaps was necessary, and with enough enforced bravado to give any of our returning swift-heeled colleagues the impression that I punched it out with the DB on a regular basis.

Little could have been further from the truth. When it came to fighting with large, professional roughnecks I knew the taste of humble pie and was as well-practised at climb-down as the next man. The experience of living with a drug habit in London had led me to rationalise and justify capitulation so many times in so many ways that surrender was an option I could take unblinking. I would not have belted the cop on my own behalf, nor on that of any other man but Kurt. But then Kurt was a man unlike any other I have met, or ever expect to, a rare and inspirational comet who one way or another affected the lives of almost everybody who met him, and many who did not. He was a pure force in a tainted world, a beacon of integrity: brilliant. And such essence needs protection for the world crushes the good fast. It crushes the bad too, but it just takes more time.

Difficult and uncompromising, as a war correspondent he was a one-man Zeitgeist to the small band of Balkan war reporters, the standard bearer to our values. His work was succinct, sincere and consistently credible, its power singly lifting the level of reportage throughout the Bosnian and Kosovo conflicts. Innumerable journalists can crank out professional reports, observe and criticise. Kurt was different because of his vision and profound, Solomon-like sense of justice. Fuelled by an angry compassion, contained by common sense, this foresight and talent to discern righteousness beyond simple truth set him apart; and in allowing him to reveal a moral context within his stories it took him far beyond what most reporters are capable of doing. This ability also earned him many opponents, and was at odds with the upper echelons of a profession more concerned with fiscal success than ethics and morality.

As an enemy he was a moody, intolerant, dominating, headstrong son-of-a-bitch, a man to be feared. If he thought you were a hypocrite you would know about it immediately. If you tried to turn him over, however subliminally, he would pick up on it and say 'fuck you' to your face then and there. His extreme IQ and zero bullshit tolerance made him the terror of military and civilian spokesmen, propagandists whose job is necessarily to lie, twist and confuse, and even the best of them displayed no more agility in fending off his line of questioning than a seal pup attempting to escape the blows of a clubber in the Baring Straits.

His involvement with war was the inevitable product of his being, for he was a man physically and mentally at his best in conflict, and he glowed in that environment. War both completed and complemented him. It soothed his frustration, jousted his impatient will, and he found no better soil to nurture his acute sense of right and wrong than that which lay beneath the shadow of the gun. Under his ascetic, cerebral exterior swam delight, fury and compulsion. The friction made him a brave, focused man with a hunger for the testing ground of action.

I cannot say that he did not love war. I can say that sometimes he hated it. Either way, he knew he was damn good in it. It was a knowledge that had its limits, for ultimately the mystery of the man lay in his innocence: the inspirational energy within him was mirrored by a perplexed humility, ensuring that he never really knew how important he was. He was my friend, my mentor. I was not looking for another father to replace my own, dead four years by then but absent much longer. Nevertheless, Kurt embodied goodness and wisdom to a degree I could never have imagined should I have had a thousand fathers. Whatever the darkness of addiction or life's other pitfalls, I could fall back on the certainty that Kurt was somewhere out there, and that his continued existence meant everything would work out fine in the end. He had a shine about him, the glow of assurance and invincibility that encouraged me to stick close and believe in hope. And, in my mind, he was never going to die.

The likelihood of my own death in a war zone seemed a far more rational concept to entertain, tedious even, by comparison to thoughts of Kurt getting killed. He was the Yang to war's Yin; near namesake to *The Heart of Darkness*'s central figure – Conrad's Inner Station agent, Coppola's Colonel. Yet pushing way up the river, peering into the abyss, he had not fallen into the same trap: his genius never slid into madness. Instead, he defied the depths and shadows with an aura of light about him so unique, so essentially good, that it suggested the canopy would never, should never, close in and the creep of night fall.

Among the small, edgy central group of war photographers and correspondents, whose membership was the result of mysterious code and hidden trial known only to themselves, he was known as Brother Number One.

Taking a kicking from the DB on his behalf was the least I would have endured for him. He was a great man, and it was my fortune to be his friend. Small wonder then that my abiding recollection of the short, squalid war in Kosovo is that it was the backdrop to our friendship. Not a bad way, perhaps, to remember a war.

CHAPTER 2

Drawing its first breaths, the young insurgency was initially of such low intensity as to be vapid, characterised more by abduction, kidnap and sectarian murder than 'real' fighting. Occasionally, when the Serbs had the mood upon them, a column would push towards a KLA stronghold and the guerrillas and their families would flee before it, usually without fight, leaving their houses to be torched and plundered. For the most part, however, the Serbs seemed dazzled by the rapid advent of the KLA, and though there were some heated exchanges along the Albanian–Kosovar border as regular Serb troops sought to close down insurgent infiltration routes, the interior was patrolled merely by police. Without the backing of the army, they appeared unable to do much more than protect urban zones and establish checkpoints along the province's main roads, leaving the hinterland to the KLA.

As a result, the insurgency was a very rural affair, and Priština itself was left curiously undisturbed by the tensions. The city's cafés and bars remained full; the shops were open; the Serb and Albanian youth, barely distinguishable from each other until they spoke in different tongues, came out in force during the sultry evenings to promenade along boulevards alive with the tedious thump of techno; thoughts of war seemed a world away.

Following the Prekaz punch-up we passed these summer weeks of stand-off in leisurely enough fashion. Most mornings we would rise early and leave the city behind us, driving out into the countryside, either following up on a sniff of trouble gleaned from the previous day or trawling the interior in speculative venture, using the Gordian network of rural tracks that link Albanian villages to bypass the Serb checkpoints. There were few front lines as such, though an increasing number of villages, both Serb and Albanian, were protected by a light screen of armed locals.

The Serbs were predictable and their psychology was familiar to us from earlier Balkan wars. It was the KLA who were the unknown quantity in Kosovo, and in whose hands the future of the conflict lay, so we used the absence of major events during the summer to spend as much time as we could in their company. Inward looking, closed and secretive to a degree that made the Serbs seem transparent by comparison I only ever got to know one of the KLA guerrillas with any familiarity, however, and his unique forthrightness sprang from a mind too wired to be considered anything like normal.

Sami had first tried to kill a Serb policeman with a bow and arrow. One of five brothers, born in Lauša, a small Drenica town with a long history of nationalist sentiment and armed resistance, he was a tall, rangy thirty-year-old, bearded and with the shining eyes of a biblical prophet. If not exactly mad, then Sami was decidedly peculiar. Seven years before the oak tree ambush, he had met secretly with a group of friends, similarly minded young Kosovar hot-heads sickened by their community's passive resistance towards Belgrade rule. Together they elected to start a war themselves. Deciding that a surreptitious assassination tactic was the most appropriate opening gambit, they purchased high-grade archery equipment in Germany, returned home and spent a whole summer hiding in bushes twanging arrows at police patrols. Frustrated by their inability to get a bull's-eye, they upgraded their weaponry, buying an Albanian Kalashnikov smuggled in over the mountain border. The rearmament succeeded, a thirty-round clip of 7.62 mm blowing away the last of their Robin Hood aspirations as well as a cop, and Sami fled Kosovo on the run from the Yugoslav authorities to start a new life as a construction worker in Germany, wanted back home for murder.

But in November 1997, watching TV in his cramped *Gastarbeiter* quarters, he saw that his primary school teacher in Lauša had been killed in a Serb drive-by shooting. The man's funeral was attended by thousands of Kosovars. Present too was a small group of uniformed KLA, the first time the guerrillas had ever been seen in public. Dodging border controls, Sami returned to Lauša and hitched up with his old comrades. Things were different by then. Budding insurgents were no longer social outcasts, scurrying through the undergrowth on half-arsed clandestine missions. Kosovars were impatient for change and the sense-less killing of the teacher had a ripple effect throughout the province. An armed struggle, so long eschewed by the majority of Kosovars, started to become a feasible option in the minds of many people. There were more weapons, too: RPGs, hand grenades and explosives were coming through the forests on mule trains, purchased from mafia gangs in Albania who that year had inherited their country's entire arsenal after the army deserted its barracks en masse. During the oak tree ambush Sami was one of the principal protagonists, part of a KLA team sent in to extricate the initial casualties. As he described it, the day was a dream come true.

'I have been waited since 1991 for this moment,' he told me in his fractured English, eyes closed as if in rapture. 'This moment for when it is time to stand and fight, this moment of truth for the Kosovo.'

By the time I met him that summer he was brazenly walking around Lauša dressed in US Army surplus combat fatigues, his Kalashnikov a by now familiar extension of his hand. He and his brothers liked Kurt, and if there was nothing else happening we would drop by and hang out, drink some coffee and listen to Sami's latest madcap idea, made all the more surreal by his habit when excited of muddling German with English so that an imagined stalk of a Serb tank became: 'I have good plan for destroying one Serbish Panzer mit rockets.'

Lauša was nominally secured by a few KLA posts at its fringe, manned by a mixture of goofy teenagers and lined, middle-aged men, smiling and childishly self-important with their weapons. Barely a five-minute drive north of them, along a minor road flanked by deciduous woodland and low green hills, sat the Serb-controlled town Srbica, an urban wasteland of crop-headed men, depressed concrete streets and suspicious stares. That the Serbs did not at that moment attack from it and instantly overrun Lauša was more due to their ponderousness than the capability of the KLA. Whenever they changed their mind, there would be little to stop them.

Fervid and passionate, Sami may have been odd, but he was one of the best the KLA had at the time. Most of the other KLA fighters looked like prime candidates for a mass grave. Though commanded by men with noms-de-guerre like 'Snake' and 'Steel' and technically organised throughout the province among seven operational zones, the 'army' was in fact a factionalised guerrilla group, more an expression of a loose desire to shed the Belgrade shackle than a structured force with a manifesto. The bulk of its fighters were simple Kosovar villagers who had long hated the Serbs and in the sudden absence of police patrols had the chance to wear a uniform and tout an assault rifle. To these men add a sprinkle of idealists, freedom fighters, Marxist–Leninists, Albanian nationalists, mafiosi and former prisoners of conscience, and you had the KLA. It was always more of a spectrum than a unit. With the sudden realisation that a small core group of militants with a hard agenda were engaged in fire fights with the Serbs, one and all felt that their moment was upon them.

Yet, if in some ways the KLA looked like a joke, a paper tiger slow to hit and quick to run, enough of their commanders had made a strategic assessment based on the lessons learned from the war in Bosnia, just as the Serbs had done. Only unlike the Serbs they had got it right, and realised that their own vulnerability on the ground was at the same time their greatest asset. They knew that there was no magnanimity or mercy in the victorious Serb heart, and that once suitably enraged the Serb military machine would claw its way through village after village, kicking the embers of resistance across the province through the tight chain of Albanian group consciousness, igniting a cycle of reaction and counter-reaction until the Western powers, their patience with Milošević already at breaking point, intervened. No Balkan war has ever been won without the intervention of foreign power, and the KLA knew that all they had to do to achieve this in their favour was swing the pendulum, stay in existence and survive the Serb crackdown. And that crackdown was inevitable. The Serbs would rather burn in hell than compromise, and it was clear that it was only a matter of time before their dumbfounded sledgehammer would recollect its sense and plough down on the ripe insurgent fruit, just as the KLA desired.

As that slow summer ended, the Serb blow began to fall.

The change came as suddenly as an unseasonable storm, with the Serb army pulling its troops away from Kosovo's border with Albania in early August to push them into the province's hinterland on offensive operations. Whatever its speed, so little resistance was offered by the KLA that the Serb advance seemed more like a huge humanitarian abuse than an act of a war, a vandal raid intended simply to punish rural communities for their support of the insurgents. At first, like droplets of mercury regrouping, the pattern of Serb attack merged from a series of disconnected incidents – an infantry assault on a KLA village here, a route cleared there, shelling elsewhere – into wider action.

Days after its start, Serb troops found the charred remains of human bodies at a kiln in a remote Kosovar village south of Priština. The victims were allegedly Serbs executed by the KLA. Revenge was immediate. Within hours of the discovery the Serbs began to bombard a group of several thousand Kosovar refugees hiding in the forest outside Senik, a village a few miles beyond the kiln. The firing went on throughout the night and into the next morning, leaving seventeen dead and more than fifty wounded. A United Nations vehicle chanced upon the aftermath the following day. Inside was a man I had known since the Bosnian war, a witness already familiar with Balkan savagery. Yet he was still shaking with rage when I saw him later that afternoon in Priština, where he gave me and Kurt directions to the massacre site. He said he had been alerted to the scene when thousands of refugees had poured from the undergrowth begging for help. Walking into the forest, he had found the ground littered with ripped bodies, abandoned clothes, shoes, passports and wrecked domestic items. The trees were torn with shrapnel and a few tractors, used to transport the refugees' supplies, were aflame. Among the dead were several women and old people, a four-year-old boy with his head blown off, and a newborn baby. He saw no evidence of the KLA.

By the time we reached Senik the bodies had been buried, but there were still brains and babies' boots lying on the forest floor; a woman's scalp, locks of hair and gore hanging from the trees. Aside from the human remains pasted up and down the slopes, the moments of terrified pandemonium that had followed the first incoming Serb shells were still clearly visible in the charred panoply of strewn clothing and shoes, shredded sacks of flour and burned tractors, their metal molten by the heat of phosphorous grenades used by the Serb infantry who had walked down to follow up the bombardment by destroying whatever was left. Every single vehicle and cart, packed with household belongings and supplies to ensure the survival of the refugees, had been destroyed. Judging by the hair and brain matter coating a treaded lump of rubber, one victim appeared to have had part of a tractor tyre blown through their head. Among the wounded was a mother whose hands had been blown off when shrapnel scythed the child she was cradling from her arms.

After that the situation seemed to change overnight. Sami and his KLA colleagues simply disappeared, either escaping to the hills or abandoning their uniforms and joining the fearful refugee columns who fled one way or another across central and southern Kosovo. Suddenly our mornings at Beba's were given a new sense of urgency: the war was moving again and we with it. Some days we would seem to lock effortlessly on to that specific zone where the action and the story lay, electrified and malignant. I would see the fear, the sadness, the anger of those on the run; hear the shellfire and watch the flames and my dead emotions would reignite, hard-edged, real and immediate; the clanking tread of the war machine a high-voltage blast of oxygenating meaning and reintegration that had me shuddering back to life like Frankenstein's monster awakening courtesy of the thunderbolt. My whole world shrank to a space defined by the dawn and dusk of each day. Beyond it nothing existed and my life at home could have been that of another man. Even my addiction became no more relevant than a rumour of a haunted house in another country's capital.

Less than a week after the killings at Senik, after yet another circuitous cross-country ride dodging checkpoints, Kurt and I drove straight into an advancing Serb column. Halting our Land-Rover in an empty meadow we saw dense, black smoke pouring into the sky, belching from flaming villages in valleys around each point of the compass face. Dozens of Serb tanks, personnel carriers and truck-mounted anti-aircraft guns swept suddenly from a group of shattered ruins towards us in a roar of engines and grinding tracks; the crews coal-eyed and dust-covered from the sleepless work of the past few days; infantrymen clinging to the vehicle sides like bunches of camouflaged grapes, swinging with each lurch of their armoured host.

Behind these troops no single Kosovar remained, living or dead. Man, woman and child: the populations of every village in an expansive south-western triangle of the province were on the run ahead of the Serb push in panicking refugee columns which clambered through the woods and hills as if escaping a barbarian scourge. The corpses of abandoned dogs and livestock littered the fields, killed by the Serbs in lieu of the vanishing KLA; smashed cars and tractors lay ground and overturned by tanks in the verges of roads; bandana-clad militiamen stepped forward in the column's wake to loot and burn whatever the shelling and shooting had missed. Little, if any, resistance had been shown, and the exodus seemed to have pre-empted the advance, so the Serbs moved through a depopulated zone, destroying as they wished.

The army caught up with the refugees at Istinić two days later. In that small town forty thousand Kosovars, a fraction of those escaping the purges elsewhere, were corralled by closing cordons of Serb troops, having fled their homes on foot or by cart over the previous fortnight and then wandered aimlessly through the woods and hills with little plan other than to survive. Hungry, frightened, thirsty, they crowded away from the surrounding Serbs towards the centre of the town, clustered so thickly together in the narrow streets and fields that it was difficult to move. Their sweat, their smell, their heat, their fear combined to produce an atmosphere of claustrophobic dread, which was accentuated by the coils of smoke spiralling upwards from their homes in the burning villages beyond. The aged and infirm, newborn babies, small children and adults alike, they awaited their fate with sweat-sheened faces and eyes dulled through exhaustion. Many were sick, and without medical attention the state of the ill and wounded was worsening.

As we pushed through them, trying to concentrate on individuals' accounts above the clamour of voices vying to be heard, a man yelled out to me. He was lying on an improvised wooden litter and green pus was already seeping through the clumsy bandages on his shrapnel-shattered arm.

'Where is Europe? Where is America?' he shouted.

I stared back at him in silence.

The Serbs toyed with them for a few days, filtering off some men for 'questioning'. Then, in the absence of any better plan, they drove the remainder into the interior again, pushing them back towards their wrecked homes with stinging switches and robotic threats blasted from Tannoys mounted on the APCs. 'Move, move, move,' the loudspeakers bade repeatedly, as police whipped at the legs and backsides of the refugees. 'If you do not comply, force shall be used.'

The scene resembled South Africa under apartheid: obsolete, unsustainable, obscene. Where indeed were Europe and America? Unfortunately, the nascent war had the wrong kind of suck. The world in general and America in particular were obsessed at the time with the emerging details of the Clinton–Lewinsky blowjob, and Kosovo could not compete with Monica's mouth. The scale of suffering, however intense, was not enough to draw the West's attention away from sexual trivia and towards moral conscience, in spite of the prophetic shadow of Bosnia's Srebrenica massacre, barely three years old at that point. As a reporter in Kosovo that autumn, getting the message out was like shouting into a bucket of wet sand.

By November, over a quarter of a million rural Kosovar civilians were living among the ruined shells of their burned villages, or in improvised bow tents in the woods, their harvest uncollected and rotten, facing a winter without aid. The KLA had dispersed. Behind them, lying between the furrows of Serb tank tracks, a terrible and implacable hatred had been sown. The KLA plan was working well.

*

Inevitably, the conflict had a flipside, one we came across while driving in the wake of the offensive in early September. It was a day of curdling humidity, the sun invisible behind a gloomy sky of heavy cloud with no hint of return. Kurt was at the wheel, and the Land-Rover lurched and bumped its way through a marshland near Glođane, a bleak wilderness of grey scrubland, mud and dwarfed, dying trees: a good place to kill, a lonely one to die. To our flank smouldered Rznić, an abandoned Kosovar village hit by the Serbs a day or two previously, its mosque felled skittle-like by a tank shell.

In the way of close friendship, between easy silences our conversation covered an eclectic mix stitching past and present in interrupting leaps that, while entirely comprehensible to us, would have appeared almost unintelligible to an outsider.

'Is this a war?' I asked, as the landscape smeared past us. 'Doesn't feel like it. More like looking at some sort of punishment by fire and enforced vagrancy.'

'Hmmm. I know what you mean. Like watching one great crime.'

'Did your father talk much about the war in the Pacific?'

'No. Not a lot. He told me one time there was a beach assault on some Jap-held island and he was in the second wave of assault craft.'

'Look at those stunted trees. Dead man's gulch. Did we take a wrong turn? I keep expecting to see a vulture. Second wave? Must have had a pretty bad time.'

'Serb police in the woods on our left. See them?'

'There's more up ahead. Huh. What's wrong here? Summer and the grass is grey. What a place to die. Don't leave your bones here, Kurt.'

'I don't plan to. If it ever happens though, just remember to tell people I died trying to save a child.'

'Sure. I'll say you were hit while running away. That I tried to stop you but you just kept running and squealing.'

'Thanks. I knew I could count on you. So he hit the beach, but there was nothing left for him to do.'

'What do you mean "nothing left to do"? He was a marine medic.'

'He said there was nothing left to do because the first wave were already dead on the beach. There was no one left alive to treat.'

'Jesus.'

'Yeah. Hey – you smell that?'

The pungent scent of decaying flesh wafted into the vehicle as on our left a narrow river, the Bistrica, swung into view, funnelled into a fast flow through an open concrete culvert that ejected the water over a fall into a deep pool. Floating face down in the pool, spinning grotesquely in the current's eddies, were two men and a woman, their skin whitened, stretching out the fabric of their clothes in a button-popping bloat. Another five corpses lay at the edge of the culvert wall, twisted in the usual undignified contortions of violent death, a desiccated mess of bone and oozing flesh. Above them the impact of bullets had chipped a line at chest level along the concrete. The occasional bone and item of muddied clothing emerging from the bankside's red silt suggested older victims lay buried there, too.

It was a KLA execution site, and the slain were more likely to be Serb civilians, murdered to settle a local score or merely on account of their ethnicity, than captured reservists or soldiers. Whatever their status, a Serb falling into the hands of the KLA was unlikely to see much future beyond the scraped soil of a shallow grave, and scores of them had disappeared that summer. Serb police were already at the scene, staring hatefully into the waters of the Bistrica.

Disgust constricted my throat as I looked at the gaping dead. The decomposition of the bodies was at varying stages, so they must have been killed at different times, frogmarched out as individuals or small groups over the course of the summer by grinning hick local heroes to that bleak, ugly place, stood at the river's edge over the rotting bodies of other Serbs, and shot in the back. There is nothing like the scene of a war crime in the empty après-killing silence in which to feel the reverberation of evil, as if the act itself causes a rip in the ether, allowing space for it to echo on devolved from the march of time.

The killing of Serbs such as these was central to the KLA's strategy of provocation, and the torture and murder of innocents came easily enough to both sides. Unlike Bosnia, where a multi-ethnic Slav ideal had often existed between the wars, in Kosovo, with the exception of Priština and a few other urban centres, the Serb and Albanian communities were already partitioned into their own respective zones throughout the province by de facto ethnic divides. Beyond living within the same geographical border, neither group had ever 'coexisted' in any meaningful sense. Intermarriage was rare. Socialising between the two ethnicities was confined to the urban elites. Neither side liked the other, nor ever had done. Atrocity occurred quickly in the Balkans, even between similar ethnic groups. In Kosovo, as in any war between different races, it found an especially fluid passage.

But – and it was a big but – the dead we saw that day, whose killers deserved their own corner of hell, did not level culpability in Kosovo. The Kosovars' desire for independence, the central energy in the conflict, was borne from legitimate grievances resulting from their repression at the hands of the Serb authorities. However repulsive the KLA's criminality, in comparison to the Serbs, who used purge and massacre as a state policy, they were small-time offenders, at least until victory further empowered them. The details might have been entirely semantic to the war's victims, and the cause of greater good was never more than weak in an essentially nationalistic equation, but they were crucial tools in our unwholesome effort to search through war's moral miasma to identify the lesser evil.

It was more than a little monstrous to be able to leave the relative luxuries of Priština each morning, drive a few miles down the road and encounter large groups of people experiencing abject terror and hardship, then return to a warm room to write accounts of the day before dining and drinking well, and ultimately falling asleep while musing on the job's pleasures. Yet that corruption was unavoidable. War makes monsters of most humans at some point or other and whenever my brain jammed trying to work out the morality of my emotions as a reporter in war the clarion echo of old soldiers' philosophy rallied my senses, at least enough to block out the questions: 'We're 'ere because we're 'ere because we're 'ere.' It was a vital job and someone had to do it. Whatever the reasons, rights and wrongs, reporting was the vocation of my choice, and I understood that shame was sometimes an inevitable part of the life it gave me. Admitting to it was uncomfortable, but less cretinoid than claiming, as a few reporters did, that they were solely honoured witnesses.

And if slightly troubled on the September evening of my thirty-second birthday, it was not morality that gnawed at my thoughts. Beba and Kurt had organised an evening feast in celebration. Seated at the head of a long table beneath the crow-shit-crusted boughs of Beba's garden, flanked by my comrades, I stared across a candlelit sentinel line of whisky and wine bottles, glowing red and amber over plates heaped with pork and lamb, and savoured the moment as best I could.

Dan and Mickey were the waiters at the event, Beba's very own Tweedledee and -dum. Mickey, a slight and broken man in his forties, had lost double his entire life's savings in one of Beba's casinos, and now worked for him in a type of grateful servitude as an alternative to repaying the impossible debt. Dan was both revolting and delightful. Twenty-eight years old, he was so fat as to be nearly spherical, and as the hotel barman would swear obscenely at guests while taking their orders in a fraudulent display of Tourette's syndrome. Claiming to have fallen in love with Elly, a key figure of our circle, at times he resorted to serenading her while twirling a pink umbrella over his shoulder in parody of Gene Kelly, flicking his tongue with flagrant sexual suggestion through the gap where his two front teeth had rotted away when he could not remember the words. Beba had already sacked him twice for stealing from the till but he had been reinstated each time after tearfully explaining, full of a remorse that may even have been genuine, that he was a kleptomaniac who could not help himself.

Kurt gave a quick speech and raised me a toast as a precursor to the usual drunken abandonment in which the gang familiarly indulged. There were two exceptions to this ritual. Sitting to my right, Kurt himself, as controlled as ever, drank only a single glass of wine, and I doubt he finished that. Aside from an annual evening's blow-out he scarcely ever drank, stating simply that there was too much to do in too little time even without a hangover. He knew well enough that I was a heroin addict but it was the one thing we scarcely ever discussed. Just once or twice he had remarked, apropos of nothing in particular, that he understood repetitive compulsion and said that in his case he felt driven to seek confrontation. I was grateful for his further silence. It was a subject of shame that I did not wish to discuss with someone I respected so highly. Moreover, I knew that talking about it seldom helped. It was a lonely fight that I would win or lose alone. Mutual friends had told me that he wished me to talk about it more, but was waiting until I felt the time was right. By the time it was right, it was too late.

Miguel was not drinking either. The long, tall Spaniard, beak-nosed and gaunt like a young Jean Reno, preferred coffee and cigarettes. By then he was a renowned cameraman. We had met many years earlier in Bosnia and shared a special link in that we were the only two, so far as we knew, who had travelled to the Balkans on a whim to try our luck in the war and had succeeded in sticking the course. He had created an unforgettable impression even at our very first meeting. It was night and I was sitting outside the porch of a Croat home in central Bosnia, drinking whisky with a scar-faced British officer when Miguel rolled in out of the blackness on a motorbike, with a pen-torch clamped between his teeth providing the only illumination for the road ahead. I had tracked the distant growl of the machine, tried and failed to twin it with the approach of that tiny white beam through the dark ink of the war's night, and was wordless and amazed by the time he pulled in beside us and dismounted.

'Good evening,' he began in heavily accented English, serious and sincere as a late summer breeze. 'I am looking for a girl.'

What an entrance. It left us no option but to laugh and see this latter-day high plains drifter right, give him something to eat, hear his story and find him a place to sleep. He also thought he loved Elly. What was it about her? Every other nut and Don Quixote across the Balkans was in love with the brunette former shoe-shop assistant from Hounslow, causing her own travels to be hallmarked by a trademark smile of sweet dismissal. Miguel was off again at dawn, a lonely figure on his bike, chasing his paramour through the war's empty roads.

The encounter had been the start of a strong friendship. A lawyer by trade, the eldest son of an old and aristocratic family from Barcelona, Miguel was a member of Opus Dei, a devout believer tortured by the demands of his exacting faith, whose only vices were tobacco and caffeine. Yet we bridged our differences effortlessly and became close. He was a unique individual, as driven by moral imperatives as was Kurt.

As a group, most of us present that evening in Priština were part of the media's feral echelon, as far removed from news-desk journalists as drovers are from auctioneers. Kosovo's conflict was not yet a mass-media event and, at that stage, was covered by no more than a small cadre of reporters. The majority of those at the table were veterans of previous Balkan wars, restless souls known to me long before I had arrived in Kosovo; and most were in some way outsiders outside of war, a status that at once dissociated them from their lives at home and helped them to operate effectively when abroad. Each of us was fragmented in some way, and we had all been drawn to this place for deeper reasons than the simple execution of our professional duties. We found that war gave us a sort of completion, plugging our holed spirits. Without it, we were in danger of drowning in the listless drift of the seas of peace and the mundane. But if we found personal tourniquets in war, even in part, then the issue of what else we were searching for grew ever more clouded and distant. For whatever war's rewards, its debts were greater and accrued with interest. So we kept looking forward through neccessity, narrowing the question concerning what we were looking for to the next story, the next war, in order to ignore how deep the plunge beneath us grew.

Bosnia sat at the table with us as an invisible guest. It was there that I had first fallen in with this tribe of correspondents. Having left the British Army, I had hitched to Sarajevo at the start of 1993, dissatisfied by the experiences of Northern Ireland and the first Gulf War, which had offered none of the challenges I had sought. Twenty-six years old and confounded by the trivia and seeming meaninglessness of life, I wanted to explore the edge of a frontier in a shrinking world, touch the extreme and find fulfilment by testing and proving myself in war. It was not such an abnormal desire. Young men the world over have traditionally sought a similar path of initiation. But in the increasingly saccharine and narrow globalised environment the rituals of manhood had become twisted and confusing, to me at least.

Raised by talkative women, my childhood perception of what it took to be a man had long before attached itself to the wartime experiences of my family's silent males, notably those on my mother's side. Her father, a quiet biomathematician who had volunteered to join the RAF at the start of the Second World War, was awarded the Distinguished Flying Cross after a mission in the skies over Europe. During my childhood, his silence over the war was absolute. The medal was concealed in a secret location and was not discovered until after his death. This reluctance to discuss his heroism intrigued me. Did he find what he was looking for?

Many years later, and after wars of my own, I read the letters he had sent to his wife between bombing missions. They chart a journey into total war that is at once terrible and fascinating. At first they are the words of a homesick and sensitive man, a volunteer much older than most of his peers, whose individualism and intelligence bridle against the clumsy coarseness of basic training. They change tack as he describes the appalling realisation of the killing and destruction he is being trained to perform, a task so at odds with his pre-war scientific trips to the Galapagos and Peru. Then his missions begin, flying in a Wellington bomber: the first deaths of friends, most of whom would be killed as members of the service which suffered the highest casualties in the war, leave him totally bereft. But next a delight emerges. Is this brutalisation or an overfamiliarity with death and killing? Both?

After a night raid on a German naval base: 'have been back at the old game again and enjoying it immensely . . . got a rare kick out of the flak and the cones of searchlights . . . a new zest for life has glowed up in me'. Then, after a series of raids:

Got in my Paris raid – no longer the fun that it was – the factories are very heavily defended now – guns and searchlights in hundreds and an extensive balloon barrage . . . made a low level attack going straight through . . . hails of flak, being hit again and again, and pranged the bloody factory . . . circled over Paris at 1000 foot, could see every street and building as clear as day – at the lowest part of our dive we could see the Eiffel Tower well above us . . . eventually landed at Maidenhead – a horrible bumpy business as our hydraulics had been shot away, tyres were holed, and all sorts of things had been shot up. Old U for Uncle [his plane's call sign] is still there – too much of a casualty to be moved as yet. They came down and picked us up . . . for a 1000 aircraft business on the next night . . . we then heard that of the 4 crews especially selected for the attack we were the only ones to have made it there and back . . . I wish I had seen Cologne. I believe one could see the great cathedral as plain as day amongst a great sea of flames. Went to Essen two days later . . . it was burning quite nicely both that night and the next when we went again.

He completed two full operational tours, nearly sixty bombing runs – a tally that he had a one in five chance of surviving. The letters ceased the moment the war ended. No conclusion. No answer.

By contrast, my mother's grandfather – a one-eyed, one-armed beau sabreur multiply wounded in a series of conflicts – had loved war from the very start. Awarded the Victoria Cross for his actions leading an attack on the second day of the Battle of the Somme, he fought in almost every campaign between the Boer War and the end of the Second World War. Dying peacefully in Ireland in his eighties, I found his written reminiscences, tellingly entitled 'Happy Odyssey', much less inform- ative as to the real nature of war than my grandfather's letters.

He encapsulated the entire Somme experience of his battalion's advance across no man's land to the bitter hand-to-hand fighting beyond in ten short paragraphs, all but devoid of detail, and predictably with no mention of either the medal or the actions for which it was awarded: 'desperate moment of chaos . . . advanced regardless . . . appalling casualties . . . captured La Boisselle . . . had no idea how comfortably the Hun lived in his deep dug-outs . . . tired and thirsty and waiting with our tongues hanging out for the water'. Without the occasional reference to the dead and a few French place names, he could have been describing a tough away match with a rival public school.

It was only when I went to war myself that I realised, despite very real examples of personal courage displayed by soldiers, much of war's glory and greatness is myth, a necessary projection concocted to allow the perpetuation of mass killing, and that veterans are silent afterwards sometimes through modesty, sometimes through an unwillingness to revisit the horror, but as often because they simply cannot explain their part in orchestrated slaughter, particularly if they enjoyed it. In the ignorance of my youth, though, aware only that I knew little of life and nothing of death, I had regarded war as the natural and necessary right of passage to rectify my situation, and grew keen to follow the precedent of bravery set for me by these men.

If I had wanted to see war's real face close and raving, then in Bosnia I found more than I ever could have bargained for. Stumbling through a combination of intent and coincidence into journalism, among the country's blood-rich hills and fields I saw action aplenty, though never gleaned much satisfaction from my quest for courage, discovering my own bravery to be an irritating quarry, hard to hold captive, capricious and requiring perpetual rechallenge, fickle to circumstance and vague rules of its own. It was not that I did not possess courage, just that proving it did not appear to solve anything, and the fewer answers it gave me the more questions I asked of it. Some men are *always* brave, often because the limits of their imagination exempt them from fear, so the exact extent of their bravery is hard to judge. Others give themselves easily to cowardice – a quality which lurks as a potential vice in most men's hearts – cutting and running at the first hint of danger. The middle echelon among whom I found myself, thankful not to be among the latter group, irritated not to be one of the former, experience courage as an increasingly unreliable guest, offering diminishing returns according to how much it is expended. It is hard to be old and bold as a war reporter, and you grow old quickly: a few near-death fire fights, the weight of a corpse in your arms and your sense of mortality advances exponentially. After that bravery is like an old man's libido: you can still get it up on a good day, but the shame of any failure is biting.

In Bosnia, amid the fluctuating hypocrisy of the United Nations, the bigotry of the British government's policy, the triumph of hate and the savage murder of a multi-ethnic dream, what I found as a certitude instead was a sense of internal definition and passionate involvement. Between 1992 and the end of 1995 just over two hours' flying time away from Heathrow more than 200,000 people, the majority of them Muslims, were slaughtered. Set free by Europe's stunning moral failure and refusal to intervene, the forces of nationalism and religious intolerance, emanating principally from Bosnia's Serbs and Croats, were allowed to crush the more tolerant aspirations of the state's Muslim community then re-form them in their own mould. Rather than confuse the immature self-awareness I had possessed at twenty-six, by the time I returned home at thirty the Bosnian war had catalysed opinions and emotions that hallmarked my life: the dry sponge had come back sodden. The level of killing, suffering and misery so fanned in Bosnia by international lassitude shaped me and my colleagues to a degree unlikely to be surpassed by any other experience in our lives. To some extent, once it was over we were never more than stepchildren to our peacetime lives. We had crawled through the dark underworld of Europe's belly, enmeshed in the cataclysmic breakdown of a terrible, pointless and preventable war, and emerged at its conclusion to return to our respective homes, smashed-teeth romantics in a street-party where no one cared. The B-side of the curse was the sheer high-octane thrill I had got out of the war. It had taken me to peaks of excitement, life affirmation and sensory enhancement. If at times it had been whimsically perverse, it was no more so than peace. And for all its cruelty, in its bosom I had found a rich inheritance: voice, meaning, clarity, definition, a very powerful cocktail; the ultimate means of escape from the reptilian slither of uncertainty lying at the bottom of personal ravines.

But stepping from Srebrenica's silent, bone-twigged forests at the war's end, I had gained no real sense of fulfilment from the Bosnian experience. The question of what I was looking for or had hoped to find had whispered around me throughout but remained as unresolved as ever, in spite of everything that I had seen by then. If anything, Bosnia's legacy was a sense of yearning for repetition: an echo rather than a reply. And whatever passions that conflict had evoked in me, I remained haunted by the suspicion that I had little more understanding of war than as the participant of an adventure into other people's deaths, a voyage from which I had emerged both naive and cynical: a strange double negative that preserved a state of ignorant limbo.

It was not the only discord on my mind that night of my birthday. Even as I sank back into the warm fug of camaraderie and drink among the serenade of chinking glass, friends' voices and women's laughter, there was the awareness of further unease. Somewhere out there, I could hear the soft tread of a hidden pursuer. It was my other life, and it was closing in fast. In only a few more days I would have to leave Kosovo and return home. My visa had to be renewed in London; besides which, it was time for another stint in rehab. I did not know what would befall me there, only that I could not escape it.

Very late that night and very drunk, I fell asleep on a sofa in the hallway of the hotel's upper floor. Awaking at dawn, I stumbled to my room. The face in the bathroom mirror was grotesque, a horror-film patchwork of fake scars etched on my skin with a burned cork. Hours later, over breakfast, Dan laughed uproariously between curses and described how he had crept up to my sleeping form and marked me with the cutlass slashes. I laughed a little but it seemed a very strange and slightly perverse act.

Not long afterwards I saw Dan's face similarly carved, staring up at me with dead eyes from a police photograph in a file of John Does. Someone had butchered him with an adze. For, in just a few short months, much would change in Kosovo, and the the real killing had yet to begin.

CHAPTER 3

London, September 1998

Coming home from Kosovo and the itch was upon me even before I had collected my bags from the arrivals carousel at Heathrow and cleared customs. I knew that soon, probably within a few hours, the feeling would change into a full-blown craving. The aftermath of any war assignment, no matter how intense, bland, long or short the experience, always left me spinning in the homecoming splashdown, rattling in searing heat like a spent sputnik re-entering the earth's atmosphere. I never missed heroin while abroad. Its thrall ceased the moment I was on an outbound aircraft. Returning with the mission complete, though, I bubbled uselessly in the seas of a strange planet, bad company, ill tempered, restless, desiring immediately to drink, take smack or screw as some sort of concluding freeze off: alternatives that only ever speeded the revving engines of the perpetual longing. By the time I was in the taxi to my flat the sensation had transformed into a growing, vice-like tension, both physical and mental, which reduced my thoughts to a numbed, deadlocked yearning and stretched me on the rack between one voice which called for resistance and another demanding release.

I sought no company that evening. My tempestuous girlfriend had given the door to our relationship, already badly splintered, a final slam a few months before and elected to pursue her life without the encumbrance of a drug-addicted boyfriend, leaving me to swing the chains alone, admiring their broken links with dim regret. Though I had other friends in the city, there were very few whom I felt comfortable with at that stage of my life. Once it had seemed that every night was an extended sweep of bars or clubs in their company. But those days were over. Most of my erstwhile drug-taking gang had since crossed over the sidelines one way or another, cleaning up or running down. The former did not want to see me due to the precarious threat posed by my own continuing on–off use; the latter I wished to avoid as they guaranteed further relapse at a time when I wished to clean up. The mid-ground of non-addicts were in turn divided between the more hedonistic, who felt my presence was too disquieting for an enjoyable evening – struggling addicts are heavy night-time companions – and those whose artless ability to satisfy themselves with just a drink or two caused me more envy than I could bear.

I unlocked the front door to my flat and hauled my bags upstairs, wrinkling my nose at the mouse-food stink that wafted up through the building, emanating from the Portuguese deli below. I was living alone, so there were no surprises waiting for me. The unopened pile of mail sat on my desk, untouched from where I had left it before going on assignment. Only the dust was a little thicker. I drummed my fingers on the back of the chair, lit a cigarette, sat down, stood up, paced around, decided to call my dealer, stopped myself, sat down, stood up, reached for the phone and halted, brain squirming in a wrestle with choice and the fight for time. All it ever took was a phone call. And the phone was right beside me. Inches away from my fingertips.

Relapse. There were a thousand ways to do it, between the cold-blooded set-ups whereby I allowed myself several days' warning of deliberate betrayal before calling my dealer, days in which I would concoct a deceptive smokescreen fight of stoic abstinence, and the ejaculatory decision of an instant that seemed to storm through the battlements of my conscious intent to stay clean from the inside, like a psychic fifth column. Sometimes the cravings were fleeting and passed of their own volition. On other occasions they could be easily fended off, and would return in weaker form. Then there were periods when they appeared to merge and mount, and several consecutive days and nights would pass in white-knuckle shriek until I gave in. Mapless in the fog of this struggle, I had no idea how each evening would end. The only certainty was that the more I used, the stronger were the cravings.

Addiction does not wait. It is not a neutral force. Like hell it sucks and the more you feed it the harder it pulls.

My state was no longer one of total isolation, though. Since the start of the year I had Core to fall back on. All I had to do, I reminded myself, was make it until morning without using and get myself back to Core.

Fourteen cigarettes, two hours and thirty-two paced laps of the flat later, the whispering was undiminished so I left the building and walked the streets for a while in figures of eight. Anything just to keep moving and stay away from the phone. It began to rain, muffling the city's sounds, painting the pavements red and orange in Matisse-like strokes of reflected light. Held in the steady embrace of this smarting impact, I cared little whether I was wet or dry, and wondered instead at the apparent carefree ignorance of those I passed by, London's unbombed generation, for whom war was still an unimaginable and alien experience. Sometimes I begrudged them their palliative cloak. At others I recognised it as no more than the reward of too old a peace. Mostly, I cared neither way.

Eventually I passed the hour mark at which I knew my dealer closed for business and turned off his phone, so I headed back to my flat. My energy began to wane and the craving slowly diminished with it. Sleep crept upon me, tentative and unconvinced. I dreamed of rotting fish in a dry riverbed. It was an otherwise clean night. When I awoke the craving had gone. It returned in force as soon as I realised this. But by that stage I was already hurrying downstairs in search of sanctuary.

Built in the mid-nineteenth century to house railway workers constructing Marylebone Station, my destination was a two-storey, terraced, brown-brick cottage in Lisson Grove. By the early 1980s, it had become home to a group of heroin-addicted squatters who, as they sought to break free from the drug, had transformed it into a rough-and-ready non-residential rehab centre with funding from the local council. Named the Core Trust, its grey tile roof was overlooked by an encirclement of offices and flats. Invisible to the street, Core's connection to the outside world lay in a narrow arched alleyway that gave it an aura of secrecy, suggesting that it could be found only by those in real need.

Beyond the alley, a thin apron of patio fronted the cottage, bordered by a high wall that further added to the sense of sequestration.

As I walked through the arch I could see a group of people standing at one end of the patio, talking and smoking: my fellow addicts. I was happy to see them, and the gaggle opened slightly to allow me to join it, then closed ranks again. Their conversation picked up at the point it had left off with my arrival. To my relief, there was no particular interest in the fact that I had been away in a foreign war. They had battles of their own to deal with that were part of the most complex war of all, and were engaged in a desperate struggle with a cruel and unforgiving enemy: themselves.

Only nine months earlier, on my first day at the place, I had taken one glance at the same people, the coke-heads, boozers, pill-poppers, crackerjacks and smackers, the stuff and pukers, and thought my inclusion among them had been a terrible mistake. Most had the dazed, glazed eyes of boxers bouncing awkwardly off the ropes, uncertain how to survive the next punch, naked but for the diminishing hope of victory. By comparison, I had felt very sane, certain of finding salvation through *schadenfreude*, if nothing else.

Looking again now, much had changed. No longer an anonymous segregated spangle of hard-bitten habitués whose problems I could use to downplay the extent of my own habit, the close confines of Core's small community ensured that since that first day they had become illuminated as individuals. Dancer, psychic, actor, con: no common thread of class, education or profession existed among us. There were serial rehabilitators who could spin yarns on clean-up clinics like old lags reminiscing about prisons; addicts whose addiction had morphed with time from one substance to another, allowing them to muse on the days before alcoholism when they had been heroin addicts, the mid-ground in a drug history that had begun as clubbing speed freaks. Then there were those who had spun off the roundabout after only a few years' addiction to a single drug. Drug history counted for little, as experience did not equate to status. Young or old, we were all members of a dark club, unified by the awareness that none of us could leave by the door through which we had entered.

I cared for a few of them deeply, and felt a positive neutrality towards most of the others. There were just one or two who could have relapsed and died without causing me more than a second's fleeting interest. Some, like me, had made the wrong choices. Others had backgrounds in life that had offered little choice at all. A few had been crushed by such cruel hands of fate that I wondered how they had any alternative other than to exempt themselves from the pain of their lives with drug abuse. The unshakeable suspicion always lurked deep within me that these three categories marking the definition between option and necessity were the frontiers between sin and innocence. There was something of the choice of Eve in all of us but some were more guilty than others.

There were several staging posts in the descending road down which I had slithered to Core.

In the easy abandon of my teens I had first tested out heroin while travelling in Southeast Asia. It reappeared much later in my life in the company of a group of London friends with whom I lived after leaving the army. Hardcore libertines, we thought we were cool and beautiful and turned on. Maybe we were. But chasing the dragon as the rightful elixir of our excess was a bridge we did not realise we had crossed until it fell down behind us.

To some degree, that early use was an inevitable result of my curiosity. If it was Eden's apple, then heroin changed its appeal through the ages: from the green baize door at the end of the long corridor, forbidden to children by grown-ups until that first parental absence allowed tiptoed tread and the turn of the handle; through teenage rock 'n' roll reality; finally consolidating its image as an adulthood front line that demanded crossing. Into the arms of oblivion, into the dreams of love, surf the days and nights on a silver board far above the clouded cares of the world, weightless, wonderful, golden, glowing: heroin put me right where I wanted to be and I embarked on my relationship with it arms and eyes wide open. It gave me a feeling of completion I never knew I had lacked, but subsequently could never forget. And every time I had a hit it permeated and penetrated the depths of my being a little further. Without it, I felt normal. Crap.

Like the clanking carriages of a train as it pulls out of the station, bumping buffers as they jerk behind the engine in the moments between resistance and momentum, my habit had been pulled and pushed along behind me during the Bosnian war. For months at a time I had exchanged the abandonment of the drug for the fulfilment of the conflict, then come home for a break and swapped mistresses. War for work, heroin for holidays: the pattern had been part of the desire for extremes I had sought. But after three years the war in Bosnia had ended and I had come home for good. No bunting, flags or medals awaited, just a warm wasteland. And the dragon had turned. Now it chased me.

Two years later the vista lying before me had been an endgame void. The party was long over, the clique of drug friends either in rehab or manning their lone satellite outposts of solitary use. My sense of control was reduced to that of a shanked baitfish unable to swim beyond the limit of its line. Scoring and using were more familiar points in each day than eating and drinking. The highs were lower, the lows longer. Fractured will and a complete lack of self-trust stalked my waking hours and intruded into my dreams. Shame and fear burgeoned, and the lies were many.

Weeks passed at a time in which I had seemed to do little more than sprawl wasted in the bathroom of my London flat drifting in and out of stupor. Occasionally the newspaper would call up, activate the freelance contract I held, and send me on a short assignment to another war, provoking a new paroxysm of fear at the thought of the cold turkey it would involve. Coming down from heroin en route to rank venues such as Liberia and Chechnya left little desire for a repeat performance. Life was becoming unbearable, breaking up and falling apart.

Friends could take or leave it; girlfriends could stay or go. Though I felt little responsibility to anyone other than myself, the effect of my addiction upon my mother and sister was devastating. My parents' early and bitter divorce, combined with the speedy deaths of my mother's parents and only sister, had reduced our family unit to a tight-knit nuclear troika. Whatever the independence of our separate lives, the three of us were very close. Indeed, across the years and in spite of the time I had spent away – at boarding school, in the army, on smack, as a foreign correspondent – I counted my mother as my greatest friend. Our relationship was complex but tested and had traversed many difficulties. There were subjects that she, my sister and I held private, but we were honest and open in our dealings with one another, and despite the occasional blazing row our communication left no unexamined source of resentment.

They were proud of my work abroad, and had never once expressed a wish for me to choose a safer vocation. I knew that they privately dreaded the potential call from my boss informing them that I had been killed or wounded on assignment, so whenever I returned to London I always telephoned each to let them know I was back. But I also realised that the news released another fear in them. They had been aware of my addiction for some time, long pre-dating the moment I had sought professional help. It had been too obvious to conceal. Once no more than a tolerably wayward and ill-disciplined son and brother, after leaving the army I had become a disruptive and difficult presence during visits to my mother's home. As time passed, and especially after the war in Bosnia had ended, I spent more and more time incommunicado in London, and whenever I did turn up to see her I was wasted and sick, prone to frightening rages or catatonic depressions. Our few outings as a family were disasters: a birthday treat to the theatre ended up with my passing out in the stalls; I nearly killed the three of us when nodding out at the wheel driving to a film. After weeks of silence I would arrive at her house at five in the morning, off my head, barely coherent and not having slept for days, determined to say goodbye before catching a flight for an assignment.

Never one to duck an issue, she had confronted it full on, trying first to counsel and advise me, then seeking professional advice on how to cope with my problem. Accepting finally that she could not cure her own son, unable to deal with the pain of my presence, and hoping to define some sort of limit, she had asked me no longer to come to her home. It was a grim request. My family were of huge importance to me, and I felt as though I was tearing it apart. In fleeting periods of health I emerged from heroin to be crushed by the shame of causing so much pain to a person I so loved. Shame was never enough, though, and rather than become part of the solution it became part of the problem, snowballing into a massive sense of worthlessness and guilt that fired up the furnace even more. Worse than breakdown, I seemed to fall beneath a total moral collapse.

'One day soon, Ant, someone is going to call me and tell me you've been found dead on the floor,' my mother told me one day, shaking with the effort of holding back her tears. 'When you die it will break my heart. It will break my heart if you die in war, but at least I can tell myself you were killed doing something you loved. Have you any idea how that feels?'

My sister Natasha, younger than me by four years, a woman of flint-like resolve beneath a gentle exterior, was equally horrified by my decline. Though we both lived in London and were strong friends in our own right, for the two years before I first went to Core we hardly saw each other and barely even communicated by phone. She found me less absent and disturbing as a memory than as a presence.

It was not guilt that finally led me to Core, though. Nor was there some single, illuminating, rock-bottom moment.

In its essence addiction is an abstention in the pro-life vote. Unwilling or unable to accept the terms their existence has to offer, an addict takes a wander into the limbo of oblivion. Some find that space unacceptable too, and die quickly, by intent or accident. Others decide that they want to enter the light again, and have the strength of that wish prosecuted as they try clean-up. Those occupying the centre ground gamble their lives in spiritual absentia, as the platform beneath their feet gets smaller and smaller. You have to be a real Houdini to sustain addiction indefinitely. The skill required for long-term survival is too much for almost everyone, the cards get fewer with every deal, and the misery mounts. Having rolled with it for several years, I found the pain of life with heroin to be worse than that of life without it. In the face of this gradual dissolution into wretchedness I blinked first and tried to surrender, attempting to clean up unaided. I failed, once, twice, a dozen times, and with each defeat my sense of loathing became worse and the appetite to get wasted stronger. If only the drug had been a woman I had fallen in love with. Another soul in the bad affair might at least have catalysed a final repulsion and severance instead of the implacable and eternal grind of my deepening adoration that mere powder allowed.

At this point some users roll over in the face of their addiction and die without a murmur of further dissent. Some elect to accept their habit, maintaining it for as long as they can, stoically shouldering every new depredation and robbery it imposes upon them as the circles of damage spread wider and the grip of the web grows tighter. Others, like me, try to enlist assistance in calling it quits. The stakes of that decision are high, for any self-perceived failure to break addiction increases the magnetic appeal of the drug of choice even more. And the very moment when I acknowledged that I was incapable of healing myself unaided was the point at which addiction cracked its knuckles and decided on a brain-frying course of wanton malice. For it does not accept any surrender, no matter how unconditional. Once it had broken me, it picked me up, shook me, humiliated me, and found something else to smash. There is always more to lose as an addict, some previously unnoticed morsel of hope or pride to be exposed with the relish of a ghost-faced conjurer and then destroyed. The route out is a long desert march through the labyrinth of the soul, and stragglers disappear. I thought I would give it a go, though. I did not want to die on the bathroom floor.

Typical of many addicts queuing up on the quayside for the no-return voyage beneath a live-fast-die-young banner, as soon as I had actually seen the dark ship hove into view and the skull and crossbones fluttering from its mast, I started edging backwards against the press of those around me, murmuring, 'Wait a minute . . .', and had then promptly tried to cut another deal to get through the turnstile back to safety. I sought outside help with a fistful of caveats, still determined to control the terms of my recovery. I did not want to give up my job as a correspondent. Nor did I want to go through the total abstinence twelve-step regime of Narcotics Anonymous, handing myself in like a yellow-bellied rocker who trades his addiction for a salvation fixation and grows up to be just like his dad. This standpoint was not merely a creation of my addiction. A deeply ingrained sense of adventure was integral to my expectation of life, and I did not wish to sacrifice it to the tedious self-denial systems that seemed to have transformed so many reformed addicts' lives into controlled backyard perambulations.

The social worker assigned to me by my London borough's drug help unit – an imposing, fire-bellied woman in her forties – had been curiously understanding of this logic. Our first meeting had taken place in a dismal office beneath the Westway nearly a year earlier. It had involved a lengthy discussion on the killing of Blair Peach by the police in an anti-fascist riot she had attended, probably as a participant, in 1979, and the work of war photographer Don McCullin, one of her heroes. This encouraging introduction complete, I had been referred to Core.

Spruced up a little since its squat days of the eighties, Core still possessed a maverick reputation in the world of rehab, specialising in an alternative approach to drug rehabilitation involving acupuncture, holistic treatment and psychotherapy. At odds with most other rehabilitative ideologies, it did not believe that addiction was an incurable disease that at best could only be contained. Rather than reprogramme an addict through the behemoths of fear and denial so favoured by standard systems, it attempted instead to enlighten addicts concerning the nature of the choices they had made in their lives and those they could still make, giving them the space and strength to make drug use an option rather than a necessity: remind the lotus eaters of an alternative dish and teach them how to swim. After that, success or failure was down to each individual. It accepted me for a provisional year-long period, later extended to a second, and agreed to allow me to take assignments when required, presumably on the premise that addicts with jobs are better off than those without.

Core's client community was perhaps twenty strong, dependent on relapse rates, its members encouraged in their precarious recoveries by a small team of staff. Imbued with an atmosphere of benevolence and espousing a calming 'know thyself' philosophy, there seemed few rules, though violence led to immediate dismissal and rudeness was discouraged. Relapse was, of course, frowned upon, but it did not necessarily result in banishment, as long as the client showed some inclination to learn from the experience, a point I noted early. To its critics, Core was too loose and libertarian an environment to gain enough grip with addicts, and the attrition rate was certainly high: clients frequently disappeared, never to return. Yet Core's supporters pointed out that those who survived the programme tended to have a better chance of staying clean back in the outside world, and were capable of living a life without the tag of 'addict' shadowing their every dawn.

In the early months of my time there, prior to going to Kosovo, I had been too miserable and perturbed to make a conscious choice to try to outwit the system, but somewhere inside me the low cunning of the heroin hook made me see it as an environment that could be worked and outmanoeuvred. Furthermore, Core's non-residential status meant that at the end of each day I returned home to my flat, where my habit murmured longing entreaties, like the voices in a schizophrenic's head. A short time into the programme I used heroin again, the start of a new pattern: displaying just enough commitment to stay at Core, but relapsing frequently enough to maintain my drug sharehold. There was the width of the razor's edge between my wanting to clean up and my desire to remain an addict, and its cutting award varied, one side or the other gaining ascendancy from day to day.

However, though I limped along with no noticeable progress, my attendance at the programme did at least prevent me from returning to daily drug use during those early months. Fixated by time, speed and event, I found it hard to understand the source of this holding influence upon me, for the routine of days at Core seemed quite unmarked by specific happening. On occasions I even seemed to share with my fellow-clients an active delight in recollecting of our downfalls. The patio outside the building, where we gathered to smoke in breaks between sessions, became the scene of blissful escape. Incredible drug legends were swapped as we stood there hunched together, cawing rooks on a good perch. Among the standard addict stories of excessive promiscuity, gambling, financial ruin, crime and self-harm, the second-degree proclivities familiar to most of us, there were occasional accounts of fantastical addictive behaviour.

'Did I tell you about the Curry Kid?' one of our number, a compact alcoholic coker in his forties, would chirp up. Everyone would pause between drags, waiting to hear yet another novel tale of addiction freakdom. The Curry Kid, as Mick told it, apparently from first-hand experience at having known him at a previous clinic, was a top city executive whose fix was adrenalin released by the hottest curries imaginable. Soon the man was bunking off work thrice daily to get Bangladeshi chefs in Brick Lane to cook him conflagrating specials. His stomach started to burn out. He got cancer of the bowel. He lost his job, his home, his wife. And still he could not stop gorging on curry, dying for that adrenal hit. Oh, how we laughed! Why could he not have overdosed on drugs, choked on his own vomit or drunk himself to death like a normal person?

But there was little chance of similar escape in the daily group meetings. Here the braggadocio of junk-life war stories failed, swept away by the tide of reality and lapping waves loaded with the fat blue fruit of sorrow. A mother might talk of losing the custody of her children due to her drug use, a father admit to robbing his family to pay for his habit, a woman recall doing time in Holloway as a crackhead and coming out a smack addict. A friend once spoke of waking from an opiate dream and calling home to discover that his mother had died three months earlier. On another occasion the same man described regaining consciousness beside the body of an accomplice, dead through overdose. He seized the cadaver's wallet and ran off to score. I wasn't shocked; I found his logic perfectly comprehensible.

Yet, confronted by such admissions, the room would go quiet and the stillness penetrate deep inside. Against the heavy yawn of silence a quiet inner voice would remind me that there was no plateau to addiction, no cavalry galloping forward with tootling bugle to save me from being overrun. My only resources in the fight were whatever I could gather in myself. Which did not seem to amount to much. Among the floor cushions of that unfurnished room, remarkable only for its drab walls and flopping pot plants, one face always stared at me with a fixed, unwavering gaze: potential defeat. The inherent faith of youth that I once had in my fortuitous ability always somehow to scrape clear of serious danger was drained empty. A struggle had finally arrived that I feared I might lose.

Core's once-weekly acupuncture sessions were more uplifting. Lying down half naked in the middle of the day and being stuck full of needles had an effect upon me of almost magical resonance, and for at least forty-eight hours after each pricking I experienced a rare sense of stillness, proper appetite, and the desire to sleep.

By contrast, therapy began as a naturally uncomfortable affair; though, if nothing else, it provided a great opportunity to sit in front of a stranger and vent my spleen over whatever took my fancy. On the first few occasions I rattled through my life's key dates in the expectation that the shrink, a large, dark-haired man with an enigmatic scar on one side of his face, would interject with sudden diagnosis. It never happened. Once I had explained my heroin CV, I entered a discomforting zone whereby I could either waste fifty minutes in annoyed silence, waiting for him to say something, or rummage around my brain for more imaginative takes on the situation. The only noticeable change was that with each session, his scar, at first so noticeable, seemed to fade. At least one of us was getting something out of it.

I always grappled for some logical reason for my addiction, some culpable past event to put in the dock and take my blame. But I could never find one. Even the rages that sprang forward so easily from memories of my father seemed too trite, too convenient, too clichéd, to weave into a noose from which to hang heroin. Instead I laboured under the unpleasant suspicion that my short concentration span and minuscule patience threshold had made war and smack inevitable pastimes. Lingering as another, and no more consoling, option was that my brain might be one of those flawed models that just happened not to like itself.

War was seldom a subject that arose with the therapist at Core, and with good reason. War had not produced my drug addiction, nor was I totally convinced by the platitudes of those who suggested it was an addiction in itself. I felt fairly grounded in my relationship with war. It was certainly an environment full of compulsion and attraction, and one that fired my imagination, but my inability to find tranquillity in peace was more the question at stake. It would have been too simple to regard heroin as some sort of self-medication to the horrors I had seen. Instead I felt victim to nothing but self-execution. Yet, as time went by, while it provided no immediate cure, therapy offered a kind of sound boarding for my conscience: the self-division required to go and score was becoming more difficult to achieve the more sessions I had.

Returning now to Core from Kosovo, I felt an immediate sense of reconnection with the place. If only because I had been away on assignment, I had, after all, been clean for several weeks. Shortly after my arrival home, the Serbs outdid themselves, massacring the inhabitants of a Kosovar village and provoking such a wave of international condemnation that a ceasefire ensued. The province returned to its state of uneasy, low-intensity tension for the rest of autumn and into winter, allowing me to concentrate on fighting smack. I managed a full clean week, then a second, then a third. The cravings diluted and diminished. Everything seemed to be going smoothly. The sense of well-being was suffocating and quite unmanageable.

It was an unremarkable afternoon when I next relapsed. The sun kept its heat through autumn clouds, so I chose to walk home from Core. I had nothing in particular to do and took my time with the journey. Heroin was close to my thoughts only in that I was indulging in a little euphoric self-congratulation over my short success in dodging it, and inflating my hopes of a future. By the time I reached my flat, I had extended this train of thought to the point where I decided I had broken the back of my addiction, so I chose to get wasted in celebration.

Cathy took my call. She and her husband Dave had been my dealers for a few years. We had a simple but effective system of designated rendezvous points identified by number codes. I would phone them, they would tell me to meet one or other of them at a certain number, and a fifteen-minute drive later we would hook up and do the deal. The arrangement meant that they never had to have addicts turning up at their home, attracting the attention of the police or neighbours, and I never had to worry about walking into a bust. There is more to addiction than just taking drugs.

Though I had not seen either of them since my return from Kosovo, beforehand I had usually dealt with Dave. He had been getting sicker over the last year or so, wasting away, waxen skin stretched across his face with increasing tautness, the rings around his eyes growing wider, darker and deeper until he began to resemble a medieval illustration of Death. A dirty needle had caused septicaemia to spread into one of his legs, and after years on heroin his body had few resources left to fight the infection. He was still chirpy enough whenever I saw him, though, greeting me with a collusive 'All right, Anthony?' as he hobbled up to trade off through my car window, smiling gamely through his few surviving teeth. Spare framed and once handsome, in a previous time he had been a hard man in the London underworld, but little remained to suggest his past form now, other than the occasional flash of raptorial gaze and the undercurrent of internal tension his presence produced, like the dim, rolling smear of a lighthouse seen from a fog-bound deck.

Cathy's voice sounded notably flat and expressionless on the phone that afternoon, but then neither they nor I ever gave much away in conversation. It was an established business relationship that did not require any illumination of the personal details of each other's lives. I liked them, though. They were discreet and reliable. But I was surprised when she told me simply to turn up at their home. It was a break from the usual protocol.

Already stoked with the anticipation of scoring, I left my flat and drove westwards across London, dog-legging through a series of bland residential streets, avoiding the traffic of the major roads, ticking off the minutes to the pick up.

Cathy met me in the forecourt of their estate as I parked, walking towards me with her arms folded across her chest. Bleach-blond hair, blue eyes and a face of tough, sharp, elfin features, she carried about her something of the gangster moll.

'Dave's dead,' she began, her voice soft and slightly husky. 'Died this morning.'

She was wasted, but I could see the grief peeping behind the glowing iciness of her retinas. I stepped forward, told her I was sorry, and took her in my arms. She emitted a couple of dry sobs.

There is little emotional quarter given by an addict on the edge of scoring, no time for the burden of prisoners, no secondary tasks in a mission that is simply to get the gear and get away to a place where they can use it as fast as possible. Not wishing this sudden surprise drama to interfere with the deal, my mind made a quick assessment. Dave was dead, a second-degree heroin death, and that might have upset Cathy, addict and wife, enough to discourage her from selling me, client and fellow addict, more heroin, the killer of her husband. On the other hand, she was already wasted and had allowed me to get this far.

I was not totally devoid of feeling, but any sentiment I had at that moment was more a thin by-product of cerebral activity than anything deeper. So as I held her, wondering how best to extract the drug from this challenging social situation, I reflected coolly that only a few hours after her husband's death Cathy was being clasped not by a family member or a friend but by a punter come to score: a grim epitaph for a dealer. But that's heroin for you.

We broke from our embrace. She gave me a quick stare and, saving me from momentary awkwardness, squeezed a cellophaned bundle of three heroin wraps into my hand as if my token display of sympathy had been enough. I slipped her the cash, told her I was sorry once more and turned back towards my car, thankful that the whole shenanigan had not taken too long.

'Hey, Anthony,' she called after me as I opened the door.

Oh no, I thought.

'Need any more, you just give me a call, right?'

Hotwheeling it back to get high alone at home, in Shepherd's Bush I ran into traffic. Unable to tolerate the delay, I cut around the Green and turned south into Hammersmith. I stopped the car in an empty street and pulled a spectacles case from beneath my seat. Inside was a sheet of foil, a lighter and a tube pipe. Grooving a narrow trench line down one side of the foil, I shuffled a generous mound of the gear into one end, cooked the heap into a brown pool and chased a run, taking the hit lying across the seats with my head in the footwell. A glorious numbness spread across my face and cascaded into the pit of my stomach, pumping a rush of blood into my groin. I smirked and spluttered over the smoke's bitter exhalation as my brain fired up with a pinball zing, and war, Core and smack went ring-a-ring-a-roseying across wondrous dance floors, the discord of the past minutes, hours, years orchestrating themselves into single mellifluous harmony.

I sat up and lolled back into my seat, awash with serotonin, mouth grinning slackly in a greedy smile, a strange, orgasmic hint of nausea in the back of my throat. Too bad about Dave, I thought, and wondered whether I should let someone else know from among his client base, before deciding quickly not to bother. Perfect peace at eighty quid a gram: it was bound to involve a little collateral damage. After a while, I turned the ignition and began a slow cruise back to my flat.

From the bottom of a deep cavern a small voice beckoned, reminding me that once again I was falling through the net, running back into the abyss, using, getting wasted: that tomorrow it would all be worse. But I barely heeded it. Not at that moment anyway; not with two further wraps of gear in my pocket to ward off the punch of remorse for another twenty-four hours. Just this one more time, I told myself though the slick fuzz of anaesthesia, just this one more time.

I made it back to Core a couple of days later. Sitting on the floor in a group meeting, pasty-faced and goggle-eyed, I stared fixedly out of the window, burgeoning post-heroin depression amplifying my sense of misery, and told myself that I hated the place and everyone there. A metal-on-metal screech shivered through my brain.

The cravings were more intense after that. A fortnight later I scored again, took another little deferral on life, and waited, hitch-hiking for redemption on an empty road. The pattern repeated itself: sometimes up, sometimes down, more clean than not, but always struggling. Autumn slowly turned to winter, time seeming to pass in the circles of a one-winged fly.

CHAPTER 4

Kosovo, February 1999

The sun was up and as we drove towards the forested Čičavica Mountains its cloudless morning light revealed the Drenica Valley behind us in perfect detail. Looking from the Land-Rover window I could see miles of pasture glittering below us with billions of crystals of the previous night's light frost; dozens of villages, semi-destroyed in the offensive of the previous summer and autumn, their red-brick walls smeared with smoke stains, light blue plastic sheeting stretched across the newly laid roof timbers; dull-woolled flocks of ant-like sheep; and the slow, patient tread of solitary shepherds, white fezzes on their heads, staves in their hands. There was no immediate suggestion in this landscape of tranquil rhythm that harm lay so close at hand.

Then as the woodland of fir and birch closed in around the Land-Rover to obscure the view, we heard the first sporadic thump, muffled and distant, of Serb artillery. On either side of the track, bunkers and shell scrapes lay dug into the forest floor. A day earlier they had been occupied by the KLA. Now they were empty, and as we drove forward their abandonment began to load within me an awareness of malice, heightened by the faraway sound of grinding tank treads.

There were five of us in the vehicle that day: me and Kurt; Mark, a South African cameraman and former soldier; Yanis, an impetuous and talented Greek photographer whose fast temper and humour had disgraced most of the world's war zones over the previous decade; and our interpreter, a young Kosovar woman who sat gawping in the back with an expression of shocked wonder that I guess lay somewhere between rapture and fright.

We were a sharp team, the total of our combined war experiences allowing us to cut our margins of error finer than most, generating as it did that most essential of survival tools: intuition. Some asset. Never more reliable than a double agent, the better honed intuition becomes, the more likely it is to screw you over, smother you with unnecessary fear, or suddenly switch off and allow false confidence to strip you bare, and send you walking into a place you should never go, thinking, 'Today's surely not the day,' reading 'left' when the word was 'right'.

Supernatural gift or just a fast subconscious computation, as a general guide, however, intuition takes over where logic leaves off in war; and when all else fails it can take the money and give you some silver back: your life. Kurt respected it, even rejoiced in it, but he knew its limitations and the only time I ever saw him doubt his own ability ultimately to win clear came in the aftermath of that morning's events.

For, in an instant of burning clarity, I realised we were about to drive into a minefield.

'Stop, stop, stop,' I called.

We stopped. Trying to shape what was more sensation than calculation into a digestible theory, I explained that I believed the KLA had mined the track ahead as they withdrew in order to hit the advancing Serb tanks. We turned back. There was no dissent from the others, but I still felt uneasy; for, though confident in my call, I was concerned that the group might think I had the fear upon me. The subsequent silence in the Land-Rover was a little heavy for my sensitivities.

However, seconds later vindication arrived and it was glorious. Leaping into the track before us a KLA commander, flanked by a pair of bodyguards, waved us down. He had a pair of binoculars around his neck and fingered them nervously, looking both relieved and slightly sheepish as he spoke. 'You stopped your vehicle ten metres before the first string of our anti-tank mines,' he said in a sprinted rush. 'We tried to shout and warn you as you passed but you couldn't hear.'

We laughed long and loud in the fashion of men who have just walked up and knocked on mortality's door, then stepped back from the threshold. It was a good sound, not so much a noise of life affirmation as a serenade to our skill, our unity, our collective wisdom. It was deserved.

Kurt, all white teeth and flashing eyes, turned to face our stunned interpreter. 'That's why we are still alive,' he told her, 'because in this car, between the four of us, you have about fifty years' and forty wars' experience . . . and we're damn good.'

Later in the day, though, back in Priština at Beba's, he had grown reflective, analysing what had happened, what it meant, and what he could learn from it in the way that he always did about anything significant. 'You know,' he said after a while, 'we survived today because of the intuition we have developed through our experience.' He sipped on a Coke and drummed his fingers. 'And the more wars we go to, the more our intuition develops and the more our confidence in it grows. But intuition isn't always twenty–twenty. So one day all our confidence and knowledge and experience will lead us around a corner to somewhere we shouldn't go . . .'

Looking at him, I waited for something else, a conclusion perhaps. But there was none and he said nothing more, just stared away into the distance. He was unnaturally quiet for the rest of the day.

My own interpretation of the event was different. I thought I had saved him, and could do so again.

I had arrived back in Kosovo a few weeks prior to the minefield incident. If not a picture of health, I could have looked a lot worse. Rather than tire of my lagging presence, before this latest departure to the Balkans the staff at Core had offered to extend my time with them by a second year, having apparently identified some latent hope in my situation. I felt rather flattered. Regarding the war as a rewarding break from the dazing, Sisyphean rehab cycle, I happily concurred and quickly left London for Kosovo, arriving in January, slightly disconcerted by the karmic connotations of funding my future rehabilitation through war work, but not overly so.

Whatever the slowness of the previous summer, by that stage it was obvious Kosovo was going to blow open, and the days rushed tumbling in one upon the other, so fast that it seemed I would wake one morning, travel the back roads and return to Beba's by dusk to find that a week had passed.

Forced upon the Serbs by the international community, the hole-riddled ceasefire deal which had ended the fighting the previous autumn was the last figleaf left covering Europe's basic lack of desire to go to war with Yugoslavia. Under its terms the Serbs were supposed to have pulled some of their troops out of Kosovo and kept the rest in barracks. The Serbs had gone along with the deal but only because they had already achieved much of what they wanted – scorching the KLA out of their home environment, and a quarter of a million civilians with them.

However, the flaw in the Serb strategy was that, far from crushing the KLA, in terrorising so much of the Kosovar population they had merely booted support for the guerrillas right across the province like spores from an upturned mushroom. In the early winter lull the guerrillas had come back as prevalent as ever; and, like any insurgent force in the wake of a long march, they had new arms, a more organised structure and a harder agenda.

In the new year the ceasefire had begun to fall apart throughout Kosovo as the chafing dynamo of provocation and reaction kick-started again, with the clashes more frequent than ever before. In mid-January, days before my return, Serb units had entered the village of Račak following up on a skirmish with the KLA. Over a period of several hours they killed forty-five Kosovar civilians. Some of the dead were shot while trying to escape. Most were executed at close range in a gully outside the village. Vanguard to the wave of diplomatic condemnation which ensued, American, British and French leaders pushed for a last-ditch diplomatic solution for the province, backed by the threat of force. Summoning Serb and Albanian leaders to a chateau in Rambouillet, just south-east of Paris, they hoped to squeeze them into signing an agreement for an interim solution in Kosovo which envisaged a NATO peacekeeping force deploying to the province, the demilitarisation of the

KLA, a reduction of Serb police and military units based there, and eventual elections for self-rule in a template that respected the province's place within Yugoslavia.

Ostensibly the plan should have worked, for the alternatives were bleak. The Serbs knew that if they refused to sign up at Rambouillet they could be bombed by NATO. Conversely, the Albanian delegation feared that if they baulked at the agreement they may be abandoned by the international community to the tender mercies of Belgrade. But this logic missed a key element: Milošević was not afraid of air strikes. Together with his inner sanctum of advisers, he never believed that NATO would be able to maintain the cohesion to see through such an operation. And besides, he saw any potential bombing campaign as a convenient umbrella under which to initiate a final solution to purge the majority of Kosovars from the province and leave the remainder so terrified as to be no threat at all. Linked to NATO's own phantom assumption – that air strikes would be fast and conclusive – the Serbs' double-or-quits gambit set up a chain reaction that once ignited would result in the deaths of thousands of people in just seventy-eight days.

Yet, as each side gambled towards disaster at Rambouillet and the hopes of peace diminished as the negotiations dragged, stumbled, stalled, broke, then reconvened, on the ground in Kosovo the language of the gun spoke unchecked, louder each day in clear and confident voice.

I was never afraid to say 'no' to a plan, and on several occasions during this period of escalating violence, I found myself in the unlikely role of chaperone calling a veto to one of Kurt's more impulsive suggestions. Driving towards a beleaguered KLA base at the edge of the Drenica Valley one afternoon, we saw a patrol of ten insurgents preparing to move on to an exposed ridgeline, barren of cover other than the odd dwarf oak. The air was sharp and cold, the skies clear, visibility excellent, and the occasional Serb tank and mortar round were already blasting against the slopes, sending flint and shrapnel skimming through the target zone. The KLA, unshaven, already fatigued and ill-tempered with the combat of the previous days, had little time for conversation. Yet, as they filed off in ascent, Kurt suggested we should accompany them. It seemed a bad idea. I had full respect for the skills of Serb artillery observers and did not wish to be caught up in a barrage on a coverless ridge with a group of jittery KLA fighters. With perfect manners but obvious disappointment, Kurt agreed. Minutes later, their eyes attracted by the movement on the slope, the Serbs sent a barrage of mortar fire across its length, obscuring the area in clouds of brown dust.

'Huh, good call man,' Kurt applauded me generously, 'they're getting quite a drubbing.'

Regardless of having my concerns so legitimised, I felt uncomfortable with the sudden diversity in our judgement of acceptable risk, which challenged my sense of courage. 'Enough' is never an easy call to make, for risk is an essential part of a war reporter's vocation. Without exposing themselves to danger, journalists can never understand fear, a principal element of war, and lose insight into the minds of those experiencing the fighting at first hand.

Besides, truth is no easy find in a fighting zone. It lies growling and expectant, and can be reached only by those compelled or foolhardy enough to attempt the journey to discover it for themselves. Allowed to escape unsought, truth travels a quantum leap into the world of the press conference, military statement, political interview, contact's phone call; and is filtered through tertiary reporting into very different guise, a stale and contorted package, moulded and abused to suit the ends of the deliverer's agenda. Which is why war correspondents exist: intrinsically flawed characters prepared to take a chance and push through the breach to deny the propagandists their prisoners. To some degree, too, sprinting across harm's way was a desirable cap on our profits from carnage, deflecting some of the guilt the job evoked. Gun-shy, hotel-bound war correspondents are contemptible for their unlimited corruption.

The prospect of dying was a shadow that haunted every assignment, a non-negotiable clause in our contract with war. The potential of a slamming bullet or searing lump of shrapnel received a tick in the box from each journalist getting on a plane to work in conflict. We could not deploy to an environment to witness people killing one another and expect to remain wholly untouched ourselves. War reporting was not an exercise in bungee jumping, and a return ticket was never guaranteed. This awareness posed a disturbing dilemma. We were not soldiers, serving the orders of authority. We were not civilians, trapped in war. Our choice to be there was entirely our own responsibility. It was our profession but it was also our delight. So was our presence in a war ever so important that it could outweigh the impact that our death would have on the families we had left at home? We had to believe so.

We all felt it to some degree, the fluttering of our lives as cat-stalked birds in the cages of thin grass we had placed around them. One evening, congratulating Miguel on his latest daring footage of a KLA raid, I saw his face screw into a mask of pain. For this was a man whose soul was deeply ingrained with a sense of family union and responsibility, and the strain of his decision to go to war had tortured him for years.

'You know, amigo,' he told me, 'I cannot bear to think that someone one day calls my mother and tells her I am dead. I love my work. I believe there is almost nothing of man's state which I do not record doing this job. But this thought is one I cannot deal with.'

'Death wish' is a tired old cliché – simplistic, absolute, and inept in describing our motivations. We did not want to die, but we were prepared to take a chance on it, and the odds were reassessed each morning when we woke. Death was a hooked shark to be skilfully played. My own reckless appetite for the game was cantilevered by a sense of cumulative mortal fear borne from every narrow squeak in every war I had attended. The product was far from perfect, but resulted in a tension that helped keep me alive, to this day anyway. Kurt's problem, by his own admission, was that he did not easily grasp fear. 'I just don't get it like other people,' he once confessed, sounding almost irritated to have missed out on the experience. 'My brain usually just tries to work its way around to the solution of the problem.'

Survival in war is nine-tenths logic and probability. Providing they can keep their heads together under the pressure of a fire fight, left-brain thinkers usually have the edge, so long as they are smart enough to realise that the last tenth, the unknown, is the joker that can reverse the outcome of the whole game. Kurt knew the gamble well and used his extreme intelligence to second-guess the moves several stages ahead. Yet it was the last element that fascinated him: the tenth degree.

He once told me the story of how, in the late eighties, when the war in Sri Lanka between the separatist Tamil Tigers and government troops was at its most ferocious, he had planned to cross the jungle front line alone. The Tamil peninsula was hermetically sealed from the outside world, cut off by rings of encircling government forces. Wishing to interview the Tigers' leadership there, Kurt spent hours poring over a map, analysing what he knew of the terrain and troop deployments, assessing his best infiltration route. Armed only with a photograph, taken during an earlier assignment, which showed him shaking hands with a senior Tiger commander, a picture he now carried in order to assuage the suspicions of the guerrilla army, he set off on a moped, carrying it on his back to cross trip-wires and minefields he encountered en route. Eventually, after a long and perilous journey, he realised that he had crossed the front line successfully and was in Tiger territory. But then he rode into an ambush. Gunfire shredded his moped and he tumbled into a ditch. Ragged, heavily armed irregulars poured from the jungle and, despite Kurt's protestations, tied his hands behind his back and frogmarched him off to a remote base where he was forced to kneel and have his wrists lashed to a stake. Left in this position to boil in the sun for a few hours, he was eventually approached by an English-speaking commander for interrogation. Kurt assured the man that the photograph in his back pocket would prove his past relationship with the Tigers and guarantee his release. The officer pulled the photograph out of Kurt's pocket and stared at it for a long time in silence. Then he smiled. 'Indeed this proves your past relationship with the Tigers,' the commander said. 'Unfortunately, we are government special forces.'

In the telling, Kurt was delighted by the story's conclusion, as if his honed logic bored him and its defeat was thrilling. He had found a challenge in war which could sometimes best the mental skills he possessed, talents which normally ensured that his peacetime world was a dull and predictable place.

Like his life force, his faith in both himself and his decision-making was so strong that I assumed him to be one of those rare men destined to survive while all those around him died, and at times I released my cautionary jesses and stood back to watch him get on with it. Back in the Drenica Valley, beneath the cold grey sky of another winter's day, we had driven into the tail end of a Serb assault. Desultory wisps of smoke wafted from the roofs of burning houses and there were fresh tank tracks on the road, but otherwise there was no sign of life. A single Serb jeep suddenly appeared before us, stagnant at the roadside in an abandoned Kosovar village, steam leaking from its bonnet, its four-man crew in fire positions along a neighbouring hedgerow, rifles trained nervously at the fields beyond.

'Hee, hee, hee: bad place to break down, guys,' we laughed as we sped past.

A mile further ahead the road traversed a small bridge over a river. The KLA must have only just blown it up for the air still stank of explosives, but the charge had not destroyed the structure, merely created a large hole scabbed by torn steel struts and flayed concrete in its centre. I eased on the brakes and halted well short of it. Looking left and right across the empty landscape, hearing the *kerrump* of nearby mortars, feeling the prickle up my spine, it seemed clear that someone's sights would be focused on the bridge.

'Hey, I'm going to film the damage,' Kurt announced.

'Kurt, you film the damage and you're going to get sniped.'

'I'll be really quick . . . Just wait a second.'

I knew that if I walked on to the bridge and filmed the hole I would get shot, probably in the lower stomach or groin or somewhere equally ghastly. Kurt, though, was probably going to get away with it. Besides which, there was no stopping him. I turned the Land-Rover around and reversed it down a narrow edging beside trees that allowed some cover from fire as he got out.

'You get hit, man, and I'm not running out to carry you back,' I called after him as he stepped impatiently into the middle of the bridge and pointed his video camera at the crater.

Ptinnnng! A bullet smacked into the concrete right beside him, mere inches away. He sprinted back towards me in fast, short steps, grinning like a baboon.

'I *knew* that would happen,' I scolded as we accelerated off.

'So did I,' he laughed, carelessly, ever sure of survival.

I laughed too, equally convinced.

Beyond the camaraderie, the craic and my personal desire to see Yugoslavia get a long-awaited come-uppance, I felt no great emotional attachment to Kosovo itself. The KLA were an unattractive, if inevitable, evolution of Serb repression, and their nationalistic manifesto involved none of the multi-ethnic idealism we had seen murdered in Bosnia. Nevertheless, I shared with my comrades the same angry determination to prevent, if we were able, the rampant slaughter we had seen occur in Bosnia. And as the war worsened that winter it was impossible to remain unmoved by the plight of the province's civilians. Just as they had been since the start, they remained both the targets of Serb rage and the expedient sacrifice required by the KLA to draw in foreign intervention.

'I would rather be dead in the snow than killed by the Serbs,' a young Kosovar mother told me one afternoon. She was in her twenties, her voice dull and slurred by hypothermia. Seated on the ground, she cradled her dying baby in her arms, a six-month-old girl, porcelain-skinned and comatose, her lips tinged with the first blue hue of life's end. In the woods around her death was closing in on others, too: a heavily pregnant woman, three days overdue, barely conscious on a bed of damp straw; an eighty-two-year-old man, collapsed in the mud, shivering with fever.

It was just after midday but the shadows were already lengthening across the ravine in which they were hiding. The snow, its morning flirtation with thaw at an end, started to freeze again, crisping the gelatinous ooze of mud and leaf mulch around the refugees' feet. There were over three hundred of them clinging to the edge of the gully's precipitous slopes above the Lepenac river, which gurgled far below on its leisurely run towards the nearby Macedonian border. Conversation was a furtive, hushed affair and, apart from the occasional cry of a child and the isolated rattle of a cooking utensil, the area was silent. A few of the men slid among the ravine's thin, stripped foliage trying to gather wood for fires, or wandered away nervously into the darkening shadows of the forest. Most of the women and children sat listless on their sodden bedding, tightened wet blankets around their shoulders, and adjusted the improvised bow tents they had constructed from saplings, string and sheets, trying in vain to block out the chill of the breeze. Some would not survive the night, the third they had spent in the open since they had fled a Serb assault on their village, a day's walk away in the valley beneath them.

The pattern of attack that had ejected these people from their homes was identical to scores of similar incidents occurring throughout Kosovo as the Rambouillet talks dragged on, and almost perfectly mirrored the events of the previous summer. The only difference was that whereas most of the refugees back then had survived the warm nights in the forests (although even then we had seen some small children felled by disease buried in plastic wraps in hurried woodland graves), now sub-zero temperatures were regularly stealing lives. The KLA had appeared in the area around their village a week earlier, the refugees told us. The guerrillas had ambushed a police patrol, killing a captain and wounding four others. In response, Serb troops had raked the area with anti-aircraft fire, then moved up the valley to hunt the KLA. Seeing skirmish lines of Serb infantry approach, and with memories of previous massacres in mind, the entire population of the village had grabbed whatever they could carry and fled to the shelter of the ravine, hidden in thick forest high in the mountains. And here they stayed, not knowing what to do next.

They were not willing victims. Most of the displaced Kosovars I met that winter were frightened, cold and unsure of what the next dawn would bring beyond the challenges of keeping their women and children alive as vagrants in the hills. Nor were they easily sacrificed. The KLA's own families were usually the first to be targeted by the Serbs. The insurgents bled and cried for their beliefs the same as everyone else. However, as the days went by, most Kosovar civilians began to realise that their plight was also the fuel which would propel the war towards its conclusion, as the Serbs wrote the case for NATO intervention, signed and sealed it, then laughed in the organisation's face.

There were always exceptions, victims of the war who were jettisoned out of this life as cuttings on the tailor's floor, superfluous to need, part of no one's pattern or wider vision. Gasper Karaci was one such man, an individual whose life and death meant nothing to either the KLA or Belgrade, and little to anyone except for his widow and the community in his village. I forget his name each time I close my notes.

He was thirty-six, a poor man, a primary schoolteacher. He was born and lived in the village of Ujz with his wife. Catholic Albanians, a minority religious group among Kosovo's Muslim majority, their childless state could have been something of a stigma in the remote communities of the south, but everyone I spoke with in Ujz told me only that he and his wife were exceptionally close. It was unusual for reticent, enclosed people to remark on a couple's relationship to a foreigner, so I can only imagine that they must have indeed loved one another.

Stone-walled and tile-roofed, household rubbish lay dumped around Ujz's outskirts. The high street was a rutted muddy track, the smell of animal ordure mingling with that of the outside privies so characteristic of rural homes. Shoes waited on the steps outside doorways, and the previous year's crops of corn, turnip and swede were stacked in wooden slat cages beside each house. The village was typical of those in southern Kosovo, and life there was a simple and enduring exercise in subsistence farming.

Karaci taught in neighbouring Bistražin, a settlement two miles away. On a Friday morning he kissed his wife goodbye and left for work, tramping off through the snow alone. Three days later I saw him stretched out in an open coffin in the room in which he had been born. The women of the village sat around his body, his wife at one end with her hands on his forehead. He had the lean, ascetic face of an academic.

Above him was a candle flanked on either side by a picture of Christ in a crown of thorns and Mic Sokoli, a nineteenth-century Albanian hero. Such was the tradition of death for Catholics. Unusually, the women did not weep until the coffin was carried out for burial. They had agreed among themselves that as a demonstration of respect they should contain their tears, so the atmosphere in that silent room was heavily charged with repressed grief.

No one knew who had killed Karaci. When he did not return home from work his wife became frantic with worry. Next day, some children noticed a trail of blood leading away from the edge of a track. The villagers followed it up a hillside and found Karaci there. Someone had shot him once in the upper leg. He had crawled away into the snow and bled to death alone in a field. Serb police were mounting a follow-up operation after a gun battle with the KLA in the area at the time, so the teacher could have been shot by either side.

The gravediggers toiled from dawn until midday. It was minus fifteen, even before the wind chill, and beneath the snow the ground was like rock. There were no uniforms present among the mourners, no volleys, no guns, no glory, no message to suggest this man's death was committed to anything that would leave his family stronger or safer or richer or happier than before. There was a column of Karaci's pupils, though, and they sobbed with simple, ingenuous grief for the murder of a man who had been their future in that scrubby, cold, forgotten corner of war.

I saw a multitude of funerals in Kosovo. Some, like the ceremony marking the burial of Račak's dead, were huge, almost stadium-like events replete with a sense of impending drama and symbolic sacrifice. None, though, sticks in my mind more than that frozen day in Ujz, when they buried the Catholic schoolteacher; the man shot casually in the leg who died alone and frozen; the husband without children. I forget his name again.

The war changed pace again in the gusts of a few weeks between the snows of February and the dull cold of March, preliminary squalls ripping violently throughout the province then building into a black colossus that clouded our horizon, distant at first, then closer and faster until it rushed upon us with the final spurt of a crack-addled footpad. Even Priština, the prissy little duchess of a city that had so long managed to keep her cafés full and shoes clean of the blood spilled elsewhere in Kosovo, had her dress blown over her head in the space of a few days. A series of drive-by shootings and bar bombings heralded in the city's new era; and now, with the sun gone down it was only the midnight-blue silhouettes of gun-toting cops that stalked the empty streets, ghosting through cold walkways bathed in the glowing orange soup of sulphurous smog, streetlamp and mist so unique to Kosovo's capital.

The scene at Beba's unravelled more every night as Rambouillet died its slow death, the prospect of air strikes neared, and we carried back to the old bordello the transmitted emotion of the day's events. By early evening the atrium between our rooms was usually clouded by marijuana, cigarette smoke and the dusky scent of Montenegrin wine as we unwound, delighted each other with war stories and thrilled to the thought of more to come.

'Hočel rat? Biće rata!' we chirped to one another in Bosnian: 'Will there be war? War there will be!'

Most of us believed NATO attacks were long overdue. Bosnia had put a sneer in the gentlest of our smiles, and for many of us it seemed that the years of war during which Serbia had so far escaped air strikes were a suffocating drumroll of broken parole. We had already seen the dismal, bloody failures of foreign diplomacy in the Balkans, and saw now in the prospect of military intervention a solution, even justice. It was a prejudice born from realism.

'Objective?' questioned Kurt. 'What's objective? A rock and I'm not a rock.'

Some went further. One night one of our number, a coquettish French correspondent fired up by the finest traditions of Delacroix and La Révolution, lipsticked 'Free Kosovo' across her bared bosoms, causing a small wave of outrage among those who had missed the viewing but wanted to sign up anyway. For reasons best known to himself, but perhaps wishing to emulate the statement in a more Anglo-Saxon style,

Paul, a young British former soldier who was another high-profile individual at Beba's, stuck a chocolate biscuit up his bum and invited a cameraman to film the event. Mortified in the sobriety of the next morning, 'Bisky', as he was now known, could be heard explaining the incident to his beautiful but unconvinced Kosovar girlfriend with the hopeful line: 'But it didn't go in very far . . .'

By that stage, I was involved in a turbulent relationship with Alexandra. A Parisienne, striking in looks and temperament, she was a photographer in her thirties, tall, long-haired and veteran of Bosnia and numerous other conflicts. The molecular collisions of her thought processes were dizzying to try to follow, and her love of photography knew no second place. She was ideal.

'*Viens, viens, la guerre,*' she had whispered to me across a table at Beba's one night. I was hooked.

We had a quick courtship spent hanging around the Priština morgue, a few burning villages, and were mortared once or twice as a final blessing before setting off on a chariot race of a love affair, hairpin turns, sudden impacts and rattling acceleration marking its passage in equal quota. Peace was never more than a rumour between us.

The storms of our union mirrored the precarious balance of other relationships within our small group at Beba's, an explosive mix of extreme characters, and multiple rows were frequent. Typical of the inconsequential trip-switches that propelled us into heated rages, one morning, en route to interview a KLA commander in a northern operational zone, a fervid argument broke out in the Land-Rover over the issue of whether a door should be held ajar while we smoked. Disgusted, Kurt leapt out and walked away in one direction, Yanis smashed his camera bag to the ground in lieu of punching me before striding off in another, and I yelled furiously at the interpreter, the one person entirely blameless for the fracas.

'*Hoo! Oh-la-la! Putain!* The field machines are breaking down,' Alexandra cooed from the vehicle's interior, a picture of affected innocence, pouring a little more petrol on the embers. 'I don't care what gets smashed as long as it isn't my baby.' And she clasped her Canon a little tighter to her bosom.

Days later, the dominoes fell. In France, the Albanians signed up to the Rambouillet agreement. In response, the Serb delegation walked out. All international monitors, sent to Kosovo to verify the defunct ceasefire deal of the previous autumn, were immediately pulled from the province, along with most of the aid community. The last strand of the net broke. On the ground the Serb reaction was immediate: their forces went snarling across the countryside, dealing it out in most areas, taking it from the KLA in a few. Tank columns moved south into Kosovo from Serbia; more villages flamed; the death toll accelerated to a mounting roll of gunfire. Whatever brakes had limited the scope of war to that point in time, they had just been released.

Srbica was the first major population centre to experience what followed. A predominantly Serb town surrounded by Kosovar villages in Drenica, its Albanian minority was purged on the very day that the international monitors fled Kosovo. We saw for ourselves something of what happened there. Driving towards the town from nearby Lauša, one minute the road before us was empty, the next it was filled with Kosovars streaming in their thousands out of Srbica past us, shattered and in flight. Some men's mouths were bleeding through beating; all looked wild-eyed, panic-stricken and on the run from something terrible. Behind them came the occasional clatter of Kalashnikovs. To their flank a village burned.

Passing the tail end of the exodus, as we neared Srbica we came upon two young Kosovar women weeping by the roadside, their strength spent from trying to carry away in escape their disabled father, a middle-aged quadriplegic who lolled helplessly in a wheelbarrow. Next, right at the town's edge, we came across three small girls, sobbing, lost and abandoned in the mêlée, running first one way then the other, confused by the gunfire. We jumped out of the Land-Rover and raced around after them, trying to get them to safety. Already scrambled by terror, they were not an easy quarry, and it took us long seconds to seize and bundle them into our vehicle. As we chased them, we saw ahead of us figures in police uniforms milling around the streets. They made no attempt either to help or hinder us, but instead stared in our direction, their expressions brooding and malevolent. If even one of them felt the slightest compunction in their task, it did not show.

Amid the beatings and robbery, Srbica's killings were random, even nonchalant. Survivors told us that Serbs dressed in black balaclavas and bizarre white coveralls had swarmed into a series of Kosovar apartments in the centre of the town, aided by the police, and as they pushed civilians from their homes they ordered several groups of young men to make a run for it. When these men did as they were told they were fired upon. Some were killed, some escaped. It seemed that the murders were part of an opportunistic entertainment designed with no more aim than to get the mass of Kosovars to move at speed. A truck-mounted anti-aircraft gun was used to strafe some of the runners, tearing them apart as they tried to make it to the cover of woodland at the town's periphery.

The following night Sami crept out from Lauša under cover of the darkness with four other KLA fighters to try to retrieve these bodies. We had seen little of him since the previous summer, and I had rather missed his reminiscences of firing arrows at the police, memories that were so far from Kosovo's present reality. He had spent some of the previous autumn hiding in the forest from Serb troops, but his absence had also been the result of problems he faced from his own kind. Though we did not know the source of the dispute, months earlier Sami had killed the KLA commander from a nearby village, shooting him in the face and igniting a factional feud. To avoid retribution he had subsequently kept a low profile, restricting his movements to Lauša for fear of being slain in vengeance the moment he left its confines.

Reacting to the new situation, however, he succeeded in finding the corpse of one murdered Srbica man, almost beneath the noses of the Serb troops, and carried it back to Lauša, where it was stored in a basement awaiting burial. He led us down some steps to see it the next morning, as if wanting to prove the fruit of his courage.

The basement was pitch black and cold. I could smell the corpse the moment we entered. Newly dead, it exuded the aroma of fresh meat and steel. Somewhere in the darkness a man rustled with a blanket to expose it. I clicked on a torch to see the body's face. The beam fell on emptiness.

The man's head had been blown off. Right off. There was just a bit of broken jawbone lying on his chest and a torn red rose of neck. An invisible presence beside me, Kurt's breathing shallowed. I kept the beam in place for a second or two longer, curious, I think, to know the limits of his silence. He never said a word though. We shuffled up some steps into the daylight outside and I retched.

Kurt spoke at last.

'Jesus,' he remarked dryly, 'I guess the lesson of that one is don't get shot in the head with an anti-aircraft round.'

A hideous mirth exploded from my lungs, forcing me to stagger away from the scene, trying to disguise my laughter with more retching.

Sami never noticed. He was too busy getting ready to fight the Serbs, whose troops were now gathered at the edge of Srbica in preparation for a push on Lauša. 'Real war is coming now, real war,' he jabbered excitedly as I recovered my composure, appearing to revel in his new-found liberty, regardless of the circumstances. With the Serb army almost on his doorstep, he was faced with the options of fleeing and facing revenge from other factions of the KLA or dying at the hands of the Serbs. We left him standing in the road with a score of local fighters, his head bobbing up and down on his shoulders like a fighting cock as he peered towards the direction of the Serbs, back in his battledress, a British Army helmet on his head, 'Geordie' improbably graffitied across it, an assault rifle in his hands and a rocket-launcher across his back, ready to rock 'n' roll: a man dealing remarkably well with a very short list of choices. He had come a long way since his archery days.

Moving westwards from Lauša in a loop back towards Priština, we traversed a bald Drenica hill where a hangman's noose hung inexplicably from the beam of an empty barn. Below it another Kosovar village burned as a column of Serb police looted whatever homes they could before the flames spread. They waved us away at gunpoint. Before we left, though, one of them neared us, jeering and confident.

'Where is Europe? Where is America?' he mocked, opening his hands to the skies. The words were those of the wounded Albanian in Istinić the previous summer.

Twenty-four hours later, both men got their answer.

*

All those days and weeks and months I had spent in Kosovo, accumulating knowledge and understanding by driving so many hundreds of miles and conversing with scores of people was about to result in a feast of reportage: a huge story was rolling straight towards my open hands as north, south, east and west, the conflict ditched its low-intensity rags and high-kicked its rickety bones across the province.

Yet that night, having returned from Srbica and knowing air strikes were at most a day or two away, I sat in Beba's bar, holding my head in my hands, anger and unease throbbing in time with the pulse in my temples as I fought to keep my brain together and work out a logical course of action. There was scant solace in my surroundings: the garish chrome of the bar's trim glowing in the dim lighting, the stained chintz tablecloths and lurid green of ornamental plastic flowers conspiring suddenly to mock my circumstances, empty trappings of a past normality that could no longer disguise the end of the debauched security we had all shared as Beba's guests.

Remaining in Priština was no longer an option. Western correspondents had often been regarded as a nuisance by the Serbs, on occasion targets to be harried and intimidated. Now, though, as nationals of NATO states who were about to wage war against Yugoslavia, we had become an enemy. While the clock ticked down to the first air strikes, our fortunes trickled towards the bottom of the hourglass. If we continued to use the city as a base, it was inevitable that the Serbs would at the very least deport us. It was inconceivable that they would allow western reporters to roam freely about the province during a war with NATO.

For some of our number, the prospect of being slung out of Kosovo suggested perhaps no worse a conclusion than dinner in a Macedonian hotel. For myself and Kurt, though, there existed a threat that seemed direct and personal. A series of phone calls from foreign contacts over the previous few days had warned us that we were marked men who had attracted the specific attention of the Serb security forces. A senior Serb diplomat in London had that day publicly accused me of being a spy, an enemy of the state. All this at a time when my nation was on the brink of entering the war against Yugoslavia. Even given the exaggerated paranoia of Serb imaginations and blustering war rhetoric, I knew my position was unsustainable.

Also on my mind was the fact that a major in the British Army, aide to a senior officer, had called me on my mobile phone two days earlier, seeking to clarify in great detail recent fighting in Drenica upon which I had reported. The major had seemed totally unaware that my phone was open to intercept by the Serbs, who listened in on mobile conversations as a matter of course, and ignorant of the potential context in which our conversation could be placed by the Yugoslav security forces. No matter that I had politely brushed aside his questions, telling him that anything he needed to know had appeared in the newspaper, I could not shake the memory of that call. So close to the coming air strikes, it had potentially compromised me, and I was suspicious that it might lie behind the diplomat's espionage accusations.

Kurt's position was even worse. A top NATO general had called him in person that very day, trying to confirm the scope of the fighting we had seen. Kurt had deflected his call just as I had with mine, but its possible repercussions were obvious.

Thoughts of these calls dimmed the prospect of an easy deportation to Macedonia, while far less pleasant alternatives occurred to both of us. Memories of the fate of two friends, journalists caught by Serb special forces in Bosnia years before, ran through my mind. For little reason other than being in the wrong place at the wrong time, they had been held for days in cells, hosed down with water and left to freeze in the sub-zero winter temperatures, hooded and beaten between interrogation sessions, and forced to endure mock-executions. Their circumstances seemed relatively simple compared to the ones on array before me now. Only a couple of nights earlier I had taken a punch in the face from a plainclothes cop when we had chanced upon each other in a Priština street in the aftermath of a shooting, purely because I was an English-speaking reporter. At the time, I had not taken the hit too personally. Given what was about to happen that evening, perhaps I should have done.

The alternative to staying at Beba's hotel was obvious: we should leave Pristina, travel to the interior and hook up with the KLA, indulge in real war reporting of a nature I had not experienced since Bosnia and Chechnya, living in the field with the fighters. However, this was not as easy as it sounded, for the sudden speed of events had almost overtaken us. With every hour that passed more Serb checkpoints sprung up along Kosovo's roads.

Dan was little help as I ruminated on our situation.

'I've got my call-up papers for the army,' the fat Serb waiter announced with faux-solemnity as he stood beside me, piggy blue eyes squinting from his pudgy face. 'NATO and the KLA, I'll screw them both.' His hands shot up and juddered in the imaginary grasp of a firing Kalashnikov. 'Bam, bam, bam. I'm serving no more drinks, just chopped salad and ketchup. Fuck you. Motherfucker.'

Facing this belated realisation of our changed circumstances, among our comrades at Beba's there spawned a ghastly, clawing paralysis that smothered individual initiative in favour of group instinct. Lending itself to collective inaction and passivity, it was more a visceral reaction than a cerebral one, the sense of growing dread gelling us into a herd. It was almost tempting to roll over before the pressure of this insecurity and let fate take its course, opt for the path of least resistance and allow destiny to reside in the hands of others.

The pervading sense of threat penetrated the minds of even those closest to Beba. His wife Vera, usually stalwart and unshakeable, had become quite hysterical, a black-eyed Cassandra, telling us that if so much as one NATO bomb fell on Kosovo we would be lucky to escape alive, throwing the vision of a lynch mob of angry Serb civilians to the top of the heap of potential horror scenarios.

That afternoon, in an effort to purge evidence of our company, two teenage interpreters, Kosovar sisters who had worked with foreign journalists at the hotel since the troubles began, had torn up batches of their souvenir photographs, girlish keepsakes which showed us posing together in careless happiness, and flushed them down the loo.

'Sorry, so sorry,' one told me, eyes full of tears and hands trembling, embarrassed when she saw me watching her from the door.

'It's OK . . . it's a sensible thing to do,' I said as I tried and failed to console her. But as I witnessed tiny Polaroid fragments of our grinning faces swirling down the pan I was well aware that nothing was OK any more, and that Kosovar civilians, especially those linked to foreigners, were likely to be the first targeted by the Serb response. Besides, though I had experienced some fairly severe farewell statements in my life, seeing my photo ripped up and shunted down the khazi was something new and vividly dramatic.

Even the city's mafia was falling apart, and since the assassination a few days previously of a leading Albanian underworld figure in Priština, shot down in his own nightclub, it was now only Serbs who dropped by to visit the hotel at night, craggy-faced veterans of many a criminal venture who huddled around tables with Beba, shrouded with cigarette smoke and brandy fumes, leaning close together in murmured, intense conversation.

To buy a little time and a bulwark against the threat, Kurt suggested to Beba that he acquire some security for the hotel in case it was attacked by a mob. Beba, who only days earlier had handed me his Makarov when a snowball fight with some local youths had slipped of control, suggested a better idea. Ever the businessman, he proposed that the handful of journalists staying with him form a cartel and hire protection. The rate was exorbitant but nevertheless the plan produced a flurry of wallets within seconds, conjuring visions in my mind of a private army of Serb mercenaries, loyal only to the investor.

As the night drew in, some of the potential recruits arrived in the bar, square-jawed hoods with cold eyes, wide shoulders and thin mouths that reserve smiles only for other people's pain. The fourth to enter pole-axed my budding faith in the plan on sight. Young, mean and leather-jacketed, he was the self-same cop who had struck me two nights before. We regarded each other in silent recognition.

With affected nonchalance I walked slowly up to the bar to speak with Kurt. He was standing alone, the repetitive drumming of his fingers and furrowed brow signifying an especially channelled and urgent train of thought as he figured out the best option ahead.

'The protection's fucked up,' I murmured to him, 'at least one of them's a cop.'

'If we're not out of here by dawn, we're not getting out of here at all,' he replied quietly, eyes still focused on the middle distance. And from that moment on, our fate hung above the cauldron of harm on the frayed thread of the night's few sleepless hours and Beba's word.

Our would-be protectors filed out of the bar before midnight, leaving us to stew over our fate. To have taken our chances and left in the dark of the night would have been madness. Balkan roads were full of unpleasant surprises even in daylight: come the moon and there was no telling what you would encounter. So I went to my room, but did not sleep at all, just lay there turning in the bed, wrestling with various equally hideous alternatives, waiting for the sound of pounding footsteps on the stairs. Every time I closed my eyes the walls seemed to fill with flapping wings. Alexandra was in the room next door. We were into day three of the latest of several monumental rows, and neither of us was going to back down, irrespective of the war's metamorphosis. Imagining that it might be my last night of freedom ahead of a stretch in a Serb cell on espionage charges, I was eager to talk to somebody, though, so I coughed loudly a few times, hoping she would hear and knock on my wall. I'm sure she heard, because she coughed back, but there was no knock. We lay alone.

Then, a couple of hours before dawn, a new armed group arrived at the hotel, some in uniform, some not. I peered furtively through the window shutters and saw them standing outside, talking to a couple of Beba's men. Finally, they departed.

'They came for you early this morning,' Beba explained to me and Kurt at dawn. There were tears in his eyes, a disturbing sight I could never have imagined. 'They were told that you both left during the night and had gone off to the KLA territory. I cannot protect you any more. You must go now.' He had once said that he saw me as a brother and would do all he could to protect me. I thought at the time that it was a grandiloquent statement resulting from one grappa too many, but now I saw that I had been wrong. I owed him.

Kurt and I loaded up a Land-Rover, armoured this time, taking with us our rucksacks and a Kosovar professor named Buza. He was a courageous and committed man who was both friend to Kurt and his interpreter of choice. Together we headed west for the KLA as the sun began to rise. Beneath its rays our little plan, so audacious, simple and perhaps achievable in its concept, began to quickly melt.

We were silent as the last Priština suburb disappeared behind us, each lost in our own thoughts and slightly incredulous at the apparent ease with which we had escaped the city. We never said much unless we needed to when the pressure was on. It was hardly the time to share idle philosophies and war stories. Nevertheless, I felt a deep elation as well as apprehension, imagining that we were probably the only reporters to have escaped the net. What fine adventure and noble cause, I mused to myself as the minutes passed and we progressed deeper into the countryside, and one in which I could hope for no better company.

Then, with a loud crack, the vehicle's prop-shaft broke. The three of us dismounted and stood beside the car, thunderstruck by such fateful intervention, and all but wordless but for curses.

'Shit!'

'Fuck!'

'Now what?'

An open plain stretched to our left and right, mountains north and south, and in the distance we could hear the sound of tanks.

At that moment, in the next see-sawing instalment of the day's fortunes, the distant dots of two vehicles appeared in the road ahead. Recognising their silhouettes as those of Land-Rovers, we stood in silence as they neared us, certain that they must belong to Serb troops or police.

'Well, I guess this could be the end of the assignment right now,' Kurt murmured as they approached.

But the faces behind the windscreens did not glower, but grinned instead. The vehicles belonged to friends, fellow reporters out on an early morning drive to check on the situation. Heading back to Priština, with no plans of their own to rendezvous with the KLA, they agreed on the spur of the moment to let us have one of their vehicles and towed our broken machine away with them.

I felt slightly indignant towards these surprise benefactors, in spite of their favour. Before they had arrived I had assumed we were the media's last great hope in Kosovo, intrepid and daring in our efforts to beat the beast. But their appearance, on their way back for breakfast at Beba's after a casual dawn swan around to see the sights, rather busted the buzz. Perhaps things were not as tense as we had feared, after all. Outwitting the Serbs would be sweet. But it would be sweeter still if no one else managed it.

Nevertheless, we shoved our luggage into the new transport as hastily as we could manage, fearing that at any minute a group of Serb troops or, worse still, armed civilians may turn up, and accelerated onward, our hopes cautiously reviving. They were short-lived, though, and my lack of charity fast rewarded. Minutes later we drove into the preparations for a KLA ambush. It was a big operation: dozens of fighters, armed with RPGs and Kalashnikovs, were shaking out on the high ground beneath the Berisha mountain, our intended destination. Their target, a Serb convoy, was reportedly already en route. Buza tried his best to persuade the insurgents to allow us to stay with them. But, given the circumstances, his efforts did not have the time to work and the KLA shooed us away. Having extricated ourselves from the situation, as we sped down an alternative road, Kurt's mobile phone rang. It was Elly, calling us from Beba's.

'Hey boys, whatever you are doing, don't come back here,' she told us calmly. 'Stay away from Priština on all accounts. The police have been round here this morning, twice already, and they are after you. Stay in the mountains, stay away. Goodbye, good luck.'

We grinned at each other, enjoying the sensation of escape as we drove straight into the next round of our exhausting tragi-comic ordeal. For seconds after Elly had rung off, five heavily armed men, some of them masked, stood blocking the road before us: Serb paramilitaries. It was as if the Gods on Olympus were playing speed chess with our fate, switch-blading us one way and another between each new obstacle and stretch of open road. Kurt and Buza locked the doors behind me as I got out to do the talking. As a Kosovar, Buza was liable to be attacked if he tried to communicate with such men. I felt a sour taste in my mouth as

I walked towards them, knowing that my opening gambit, an attempt at a relaxed smile, resembled instead a smeared grimace. Numerous people have boasted to me that they know how to handle Serbs. Handling Serbs is easy enough, until you meet a group who don't want to be handled. And now, though I knew their language passably well, my conversation was brief and consisted mostly of having a gun barrel stuck in my face while being told to 'shut the fuck up and fuck off back to Priština'.

The scene was repeated a few hundred metres down the road as another Serb checkpoint appeared out of nowhere. If anything, it was slightly worse. These Serbs were aggressive and pumped up, shoving me around as they questioned me, shouting accusations that I was an Albanian spy. After a minute or two, suddenly bored with harassing me and distracted by the approach of a civilian vehicle, they pushed me back into the Land-Rover and we set off again, channelled by a series of further checkpoints back in the direction we wanted most to avoid, towards Priština, defeated by the few minutes difference between what had been an empty road and what was now part of a widening Serb security zone.

'Kurt, we get back to that city and we're going to be arrested,' I began, breaking the silence that had been more or less intact since we had set off from Priština barely two hours earlier. 'How about we just ditch the vehicle and set off cross-country on foot carrying what we can? First Kosovar village we get to we find a guide on to the nearest group of KLA. Then we work with them as planned. We'd probably have lost the Rover soon enough anyway, stolen or shot up or whatever.'

He said nothing for a few seconds. I could see he had already made a decision, but it was one that he did not like. 'Listen,' he said finally, his voice strained with disappointment, 'I think we've got to accept that we've blown our chances of hitching up with the KLA and should concentrate right now on getting out of Yugoslavia without being detained by the Serbs. To do that, every minute counts. These guys are going to get more organised by the second. Sooner or later we're going to hit a checkpoint where a cop has a radio and is smart enough to call in our details to headquarters. Then our troubles will really begin.

NATO'll bomb at any moment. Probably today. Can you imagine just how much the authorities here would like a Brit and an American on trial for spying? How much fun are we going to have explaining to the DB how we ended up talking on the phone to NATO officers about the situation in Drenica just before the air strikes started? Not a lot, my friend, not a lot. Mobility is about our only asset at this point, so I suggest we keep the vehicle and get the hell out of here.'

It was unlike Kurt, in a way. He was no easy pushover. And the decision was to haunt him for months afterwards. He hated to lose. But he had realised that everything we touched that day was turning to dust. We did not need to read a chicken's entrails to know that we had lucked out. So I conceded, even slightly relieved to do so. And as I imagined sitting the wrong side of the table in a DB interrogation cell, supper in a Macedonian hotel suddenly did not seem such a bad idea.

Rather than take the obvious route out of southern Kosovo to Macedonia, a road we assumed would have police upon it briefed specifically to look out for us, we opted for the least expected path: drive into Serbia itself and cross the border by a back road. So we raced onward, heavy with the sense of pursuit and flight, cutting necessarily through Priština to pick up the appropriate road junction. Troops were cordoning off the city, apartment block by apartment block, as armoured personnel carriers took up positions on the main intersections. An air-raid siren wailed. The few people outside on the pavements hurried past with shoulders hunched, eyes down. Groups of shaven-headed Serb youths chanted and saluted. But it was the feeling more than the sights around us that augured the new stage of the war: turgid with fear, charged like the ground beneath a copse after a lightning strike, the unique atmosphere so quintessential to a land on the threshold of open conflict.

As we rolled down a Priština street, feeling elephantine in our conspicuousness, we heard the shouts of a woman, calling my name. It was Alexandra, running along the pavement behind us. 'Hey, take me with you,' she gasped by the window after we braked.

The Serbs loved the French, and she had none of the problems we faced that day. She was not under any investigation. She had her own plans, and she wanted us to return to Beba's to collect her luggage. Though I had always been happy enough to take second place in her affections behind her camera equipment, I was not prepared to go to jail for it. So we left her there, a receding figure in the wing mirror with just an echoing '*Putain!*' as farewell. It was not my most glorious moment.

Crossing eastwards into Serbia, we saw tanks and heavy artilley pieces moving on to the high ground along either side of our route, Serb soldiers digging up mountain roads and preparing bridges for demolition. A couple of MiGs screamed overhead. Every checkpoint seemed a nightmare while we waited as our documents were checked, taut for the second that a policeman may care to radio our details back to his superiors. But it never happened. Greasy with sweat, backtracking, feinting and weaving, we drove for hours on our circuitous route through Serbia until we finally crossed the border into Macedonia. The final customs post never even bothered to look at our passports.

By evening we had checked into a Skopje hotel. Across a plate heaped with calamari, a bottle of Montenegrin wine at my side, I saw on television the city we had just left being bombed by NATO. The food and wine may as well have been papier-mâché and vinegar. Whatever relief I felt at having escaped arrest was crushed by disappointment and the undignified realisation that I had been run out of town. Worse still, I knew it was our own fault. We had gambled away the huge shareholding of our knowledge and contacts in the province at the very moment when it was most needed by a few hours' tardiness in leaving Priština. We should have known better than to allow our sojourn with Beba to lull us into false security and sluggardly reaction. The sense of depression and culpability was all-pervasive and quite unmovable. Only that morning we had been kings on the edge of an epic enterprise and brave endeavour. Now we were the lowliest pawns on the board, beaten by the system. The Serb system at that. It was a colossal defeat and, for anticlimax alone, felt quite shattering.

Within twenty-four hours, in a development that improved our position no more than that of a blighted farmer who hears that his neighbours' crops are also withering, the Serb police cleared all of the remaining journalists from Beba's hotel and ejected them over the border into Macedonia. A day or two later, the security forces completed their operation, leaving the entire province all but barren of a single foreign reporter. Save for the tales of refugees, pouring in their hundreds of thousands across the border, and the occasional snippet of smuggled video footage, the door to the world's vision slammed shut on what was happening in Kosovo. It stayed that way for seventy-eight days.

CHAPTER 5

Albania, Spring 1999

'My God!' Kurt's clipped tones echoed along the corridor. 'I've seen dogs of war the world over, but this is the first time they've shat outside my bedroom.'

An unseen form beneath a pile of blankets which shifted in sudden irritation on the other side of our cell-like room, Elly cursed softly, her voice croaky with sleep and cigarettes: 'Christ, he's awake already.'

I rolled from my own creaking iron bed, pulled on some clothes and went to investigate. Dawn trickled a weak blue light through the bars of our window on to walls of bubbling beige plaster stained with mould. Sticking my head out of the door, I could see a mange-ridden street cur defecating on the floor, completing the last in a line of turds that ran the length of the corridor's scuffed matting, watched quizzically by Kurt.

'Hey, are you guys ready or what?' he asked when he saw me. He was fully dressed and burning with energy to get outside and into the mountains. He had probably been up for at least an hour and would have already begun to write.

'Kurt, try to be normal. It's half past six.'

'Exactly. Elly! Where's the tea?'

Our new living arrangements were the best Bajram Curri had to offer: cold, draughty, dirty, the squalid guesthouse in which we resided was a former bank. At night we retreated to sleep in a row of strongrooms sealed from the outside world by a grated cage door, its bars too widely spaced to keep out dogs but successful obstacle to the advance of the cows and sheep that so frequently wandered into the foyer. There were no other guests. It was a far cry from Beba's, but then Bajram Curri was a lone wolf's long howl from anywhere, and our fortunes were at a low ebb.

Taking its name from an Albanian hero who blew his brains out when surrounded by his enemies in a nearby cave in 1925, and accessible only after hours of travelling through twisting mountain roads haunted by bandits, the little town was the most northern centre of population in Albania. Crumbling, poverty stricken and devolved from any central authority, its border environs with Kosovo were a wild-west territory where the only law was that of the gun. The collapse of the Albanian army two years before had released a flood of Kalashnikovs on to the open market, and the start of KLA operations in Kosovo had sucked them into northern Albania's border zone, where a Kalashnikov could be bought for as little as eighty dollars. The arms market had also ripped the last traces of law from Bajram Curri. Nearly a hundred locals had been killed in shoot-outs in the town during the twelve-month period before the KLA had even arrived there to add their own set of tensions over the existing clan feuding and mafia wars.

Vendetta was rife. Rather than being a simple killing tradition, blood vengeance was an established part of local law, '*kanun*', in northern Albania. Complex and Illyrian in its roots, this code bore a few similarities to some contemporary Western doctrines in the fields of negotiation, mediation, conflict prevention and resolution, yet also placed emphasis on honour, loyalty and revenge. Designed originally to prevent rather than promote killing through the promise of retaliation, the *kanun* nevertheless accepted retaliatory slayings as an interim measure before resolution, albeit with some guidelines. In the first twenty-four hours after a murder any male of the perpetrator's family was liable to be killed by the victim's relatives on condition that he be shot or stabbed from the front, and that he was found outside the walled enclosure of his home. If this was achieved within the time limit, then the feud was considered to have ended. If not, then the cycle could continue for years. Mediation between the two families, both to try to establish the limits of the blood feud and to end it, was embarked upon by a *'pleqnar'*, a respected and neutral third party, usually an old man. Under his arbitration, periods of amnesty might be granted to individuals of either family, guaranteed by *'besa'*, the promise. *Besa* would be given so that male children could go to school untouched, or at times of harvest so that families locked in feud could leave the sanctuary of their homes to collect their crops. The mediation was long and complicated, and feuds often stretched on for generations.

Albania's communist rulers had largely halted the practice of vendetta, but after their demise it had reasserted itself, only without many of the historical rules of limitation. So, rather than being the scene of honourable and rigorously restricted tit-for-tat slayings, by the time we reached it, northern Albania was more reminiscent of Billy the Kid's Bean Field County Wars, hallmarked by brutality and banditry.

The largest feuding family in Bajram Curri were the Haklajs. They were fighting an on–off series of vendettas with several rival clans, indulging in a cycle of killing which had begun three years earlier when Fatmir Haklaj, Bajram Curri's police chief, murdered two men in the hills. In the spring of 1998 one of Fatmir's four brothers was gunned down in retaliation. That same day, Fatmir handed in his badge, and in the ensuing weeks killed seven men related to the family of his brother's assassin, one for each of the bullets found in the corpse. The hit list included another policeman. Taking to the hills for a while, Fatmir was reinstated as police chief later that year, a position more akin to that of godfather than lawman, and his respect for any rule other than his own was at best nominal. So the feud simmered on and crime soared, making Bajram Curri so synonymous with robbery and violence that it had become a virtual no-go zone for foreign journalists and aid workers.

In Macedonia, recollecting ourselves as ruffled birds thrown unceremoniously from their roost, the mixed blessing of our escape from the Serbs had allowed us little celebration. Our detailed knowledge of Kosovo and the KLA counted for nothing in Skopje, where the world's media arrived in a swamping mass. Our luck was altogether in decline. Nothing seemed to go as intended, and our subsequent attempt to cross the Macedonian border back into Kosovo with the KLA was aborted by the insurgents at the last minute. Depressed and disconsolate, we regrouped in Albania's capital Tirana, where we planned to try again by travelling north to Bajram Curri, the natural jumping-off point from which to enter Kosovo through the mountainous border.

At this point, the finer details of northern vendetta acquired an interest that was more than anecdotal, as Kurt hired one of Fatmir's remaining brothers – a psychopathic hillbilly named Halil – as our escort and bodyguard in Bajram Curri. Worse, as we tried to fine tune our cross-border preparations, Kurt became embroiled in his own struggle with the Halil over which of them was to be top dog. So one way or another, each morning we woke in Bajram Curri seemed a miracle of survival, dogshit or otherwise.

From the first seconds of meeting, it was obvious that tact and subtlety were alien concepts to Halil and his cronies. Arriving to collect us in central Tirana one morning, this huge, rubber-lipped man exuding thinly masked violence turned up at our hotel gates in a black-windowed Transit van wearing full combat dress, leaving a clutter of assault rifles and drum-magazined light machine-guns piled in a mechanical gateau behind him as he sprung from the vehicle with the grace of a young rhino. Chinese grenades rolled between the seats while he puzzled over which was the best of five different number plates to use for the journey north. With two Mercedes as back-up, he walked around accompanied by three bodyguards, gunmen similarly equipped with Kalashnikovs, grenades and pistols, each with extra magazines of ammunition strapped across their chests.

Sharing expressions of vague embarrassment, we loaded our luggage into his convoy and headed off. Halil's van had a siren, which wailed if anything so much as a bicycle appeared in the road, while Yllber, his lieutenant, had attached a blue police light to the top of his Mercedes. It flashed throughout the eight-hour trip in time to a pumping bassline from dashboard speakers. Someone was buying the act, though: every police checkpoint we came to waved and saluted as we sped past with our gang of provincial mafia freaks on their spring tour.

Along the route, Halil gave us his own succinct appraisal of the situation in Kosovo. 'We have been expecting evil from the Serbs for a long time,' he expounded pompously, rubber lips aquiver. 'We all know that they are the tip of the Russian spear towards the Adriatic. But the real problem here was caused by socialism. Before that there was respect for family and clan affairs.'

Kurt's immediate assessment of Halil was equally to the point: 'Great – the guy's a complete fucking moron,' he hissed to me above the throbbing bass as ahead the mountain ranges loomed. And his eyebrows began to twitch: always a sign of impending conflict.

Barely a year earlier, the mountain border above Bajram Curri had been almost silent – an empty, wild land of plunging slopes and bucolic valleys, crossed in one direction by groups of exhausted refugees fleeing south from the fighting inside Kosovo, in another by furtive bands of KLA guerrillas infiltrating northwards with mule trains of weapons. Semi-clandestine training camps had existed in the forests, temporary bases to some of the thousands of young KLA recruits drawn from the diaspora in Europe and America, but they were shoddy affairs symptomatic of a disorganised force outmatched and outgunned by the Serbs at every turn.

The territory had changed greatly since then. As Kurt, Elly, the South African camerman Mark and I surveyed the ground from the heights above the tiny border town of Tropoja, we could see hundreds of KLA fighters lying sprawled in the spring sunshine. No longer the ill-armed desperadoes of yesteryear, they leaned in uniform rows against packs laden with small-arms ammunition, grenades, RPG warheads and digging equipment. Captured Serb trucks ferried out casualties, dropping off their bleeding cargo for treatment at a front-line aid post where doctors and nurses attended to their wounds before sending them deeper into Albania. Scores of new recruits, shaven-headed and in fresh combat dress, were being instructed in weapons skills on the slopes around them, while each surrounding gully and ravine was clustered with orderly lines of tents and ammunition stocks. Mortar pits speckled the reverse slopes, some of the crews firing ranging shots at the Serbs, fire which multiplied as soon as their forward observers inside Kosovo radioed back to confirm 'on target'.

The border itself, marked disquietingly in places by the acne-scarred holes of a partially excavated mine belt, bore the further blemishes of shell impacts from the Serbs' retaliatory fire, which continued in spite of the NATO air campaign.

Halil, who had ditched his camouflage uniform in favour of the more Sicilian look of goatskin jerkin and black leather cap, was nevertheless suitably carried away by the vision for a momentary fit of Napoleonic delusion. Shifting the grip on his rifle, he stuck one hand inside the flap of his coat, allowing it to rest on his ample gut as he grunted a ruminative series of 'mhhmmm's, as if every one of the fighters were under his personal command.

Two NATO jets suddenly appeared high above us, circling in the sky. They banked and dived. The sound of their bomb strike crashed through the valleys, a distinctive, booming *kerrummmmp* of noise. The target, a Serb fire base on the Kosovar–Albanian border which acted as communications terminus for the Yugoslav observation posts stretching along the ridgelines to the south, was transformed in an instant into a blitzed dust haze topped by a grey shroud of smoke.

Around us, the KLA whooped with delight, some clasping their hands together in jubilation. None seemed more excited than Halil, who jumped up and down like a child in a playground, his beefy legs pumping with an impressive energy. 'Oh, look at our birds, see how they fly,' a voice from a forward position chattered back over a radio.

Serb mortar fire from the plateau below fired back in retaliation. After initial ranging shots dusted down the crest of a nearby slope, the mortars locked in on a single stone building and a series of shells detonated both on and around it, knocking down some guerrillas. Between blasts, their comrades scurried around to collect the casualties. Minutes later, more jets arrived. Again the sound of their bomb impacts resounded through the mountains; the KLA fired; the Serbs fired back. It seemed a three-way war of minimum coordination and maximum confusion.

Aside from the distraction of the jets, the KLA had scant reason to celebrate. In a little over three weeks of border fighting, and with heavy casualties, they had barely succeeded in pushing the smallest bridgehead from Albania across to their Kosovo homeland, and were unable to open it in order to resupply fighters inside the province with more men and munitions. In spite of their new equipment and training, they still took a hammering from the Serbs in every major clash. Moreover, the casualty-conscious, Clintonesque approach to the war resulted in NATO jets bombing from maximum altitude to avoid anti-aircraft fire. We saw pilots fly lower from time to time, but generally the order held, so the slightest deterioration in the weather had a disproportionate effect on the jets' ability to bomb with any accuracy, allowing the Serbs to shell away as they pleased.

Politically the war was also in bad shape. The unity of the NATO member states was beginning to crack, just as Milošević had hoped it would, due to the failure of the bombing strategy to bring quick results. While NATO spokesmen reeled off impressive and completely unbelievable lists of destroyed Serb military assets, on the ground the air strikes appeared neither to halt the expulsion of hundreds of thousands of refugees nor shake the Yugoslav army.

Internally, the KLA, unable to protect their own people let alone win the war themselves, was riven by bickering, with various commanders establishing factions as they vied for their slice of the amassed fortune donated by the Kosovar diaspora to fund the war. This discord added to our problems. Our best contacts within the KLA were commanders who had remained behind to fight in the heart of Kosovo, and our attempts to reach them were continually thwarted by the failure of the Albania-based KLA, to whom we were strangers, to open up a corridor into the interior.

Moreover, though Halil's clout was powerful up to the border's edge, it counted for little beyond. And only days after our arrival in Bajram Curri he began to display the first of a series of black rages, becoming increasingly unbalanced in his dealings with us as time progressed. One afternoon, in his absence, we had driven to a local KLA funeral for some fighters killed in a clash with the Serbs. It was a common enough event and not even near the front line. But when Halil heard about it later he exploded, accusing us of causing him to lose face for going without him, a serious charge in Bajram Curri. Kurt, never a man easily to acquiesce to another's authority, finally managed to calm him down, but the tension remained. As the days passed we began to feel that, rather than providing our security, Halil was a volatile and threatening liability who was sizing us up for whatever he could get. But there was no question of sacking him. Without his patronage we would not last an hour in Bajram Curri, let alone on the route out.

Our mood lowering once more, we journeyed back up into the border mountains to see the KLA, and ran into an individual whose psyche made Halil look like a paragon of sanity and benevolence.

It was a beautiful spring morning and as we trudged through the edge of a forest the war looked wonderful. From the slopes of the Reka-E-Keqe Mountains, puffs of anti-aircraft fire rose in futile attempts to meet the jets swooping in to bomb Serb troop concentrations hidden in woodland below; tracer fire lanced between contested ravines; mortar duels scored dark whorls of smoke along the crests of ridges, vivid green with the new season; teenage KLA recruits trained among blossom-heavy trees; and Albanian peasants tilled the slopes as they had done for generations, following plough-pulling horses across the soil in well-paced, resilient toil.

The impression was not without shadow. An obese Kosovar businessman from Geneva, a KLA financier, had latched on to Halil. Pasty-faced and sweating, the man had acquired a crisp new uniform for the trip and was carrying a gun. An unlikely, ridiculous figure with such alien accoutrements, he heaved and grunted his way up the ascent, motivated by the desire to see some profit from his fund-raising efforts. He did not have long to wait.

Entering a clearing, the soft scent of the forest floor changed suddenly, overwhelmed by the stench of rot. A group of KLA fighters stood over two corpses, swollen and moist, Serb soldiers whom they had dragged to the spot with rope. There were more than twenty other bodies lying among the trees, we were told, killed days earlier when the KLA had overrun the area. The Kosovars were either genuinely sick of the smell and wished to start interring them, or what followed was some warped attempt to present their organisation as a humane counterpart to their atrocity-stained foes. Either way, it was a dismal failure.

As four of the guerrillas began digging graves, their commander began a crazed incantation of hate as he leered over the dead men. 'Century after century, decade after decade,' he began, voice rising in volume with each word, 'all those who confront the Albanians will leave their bones here. We don't want their corpses here; this land doesn't want them even in death . . .'

Blond-haired and hollow-cheeked, he was was known as the 'Fighting Emir'. Beneath a jauntily angled camouflage bush hat, his blue eyes shone with a fevered glow while the taut skin of his face split before a hideous grin. He produced a photograph of a dead Kosovar child from his pocket as he spoke, claiming it was the body of a baby murdered by Serbs in a massacre in Drenica, and his diatribe continued regardless of the nearby angry chatter of small arms.

'I say this to all Serb mothers: we will eliminate those barbarians who have done this to the Albanian people. Just as I have sworn on oath to fight unflinchingly and continuously until the day when the whole of Kosovo is totally free, we will shed the blood of the hated Slav . . .'

On either side of him stood his bodyguards, self-named 'Rambo' and 'Tyson', human Dobermans of muscle, aggression and hardware teeth. Tyson seemed especially happy with recent events. Short, with the build of a wrestler, he caressed a stub-barrelled nitro-glycerine gun that he had captured from the Serbs, and claimed to have personally killed the two men sprawled on the ground a few days before, gunning them down in one of the skirmishes that were daily seizing life throughout the mountain battle zone.

The burial party's labour was slow and lackadaisical. After twenty minutes or so, with the graves still no more than shallow scrapes in the forest floor, the men broke from their work to mop invisible sweat from their faces. Halil and the fat businessman, unable to contain themselves, stepped forward and began to poke the bodies with their rifle barrels and boots. The financier's footwear was fresh from a storeroom, its leather so unblemished that ooze from the corpses stood out on the toecaps in stark relief. A KLA fighter took photographs of him as he posed like a big-game hunter, one foot upon a dead man's chest, rifle barrel pointed at the body's head, a hand raised in victory.

The Fighting Emir's burial party finished predictably. With the graves no more than a foot deep, two of his men tried to drag the dead Serbs to the edge. However, the gaseous stench that erupted was so dreadful that they stopped. A KLA doctor bandaged their mouths and noses with lint and gauze and they tried again, sweating for real now, silent and without enthusiasm. Then everyone simply gave up at the same second, as if obeying an unvoiced order, turned and went away, leaving the bloated bodies lying on the grass between the graves.

I could still hear the Fighting Emir's mantra above the shellfire as I walked back through the forest. 'These Slavs are victims of the mad war machine of Milošević,' he raved, 'but they are not worth any mercy. We must cleanse our land of them, we must destroy them.'

Combined with Halil's pathological behaviour, the incident broke our will to remain in northern Albania any longer. We were sick of dealing with the KLA. Telling Halil we needed to go back to Tirana for a few days' rest before returning, a lie aimed at keeping his eyes focused on our golden-goose potential so that we might avoid being robbed by him in the short term, we departed from Bajram Curri the next day in the same circus convoy by which we had arrived.

As we journeyed towards the capital, behind us in Bajram Curri the blood feud reignited. A roadside bomb blew up beside Halil's brother Fatmir. The blast was enormous and shredded the police chief's four-wheel-drive, toppling it down a small ravine at the edge of the town. The driver was blown to pieces. Fatmir himself, ever the Hallowe'en bogeyman, scrambled out from the twisted metal with little more than light burns and a cut face. Word of the hit reached Halil on our arrival in

Tirana. Hanging around just long enough to drop us off and receive his last down payment in cash, he raced off with his mob, intent on new retribution.

He was killed a few months later in another Bajram Curri bomb blast.

Kurt never forgot him. 'Listen, man,' he said, with a smile after hearing of Halil's death, 'if you get whacked one day, be sure to buy him a drink for me in hell. Tell him I'll be along soon.'

The others left the Balkans for a while after that trip, but I stayed on, moving back to Macedonia. It was a dispiriting experience. The war was almost impossible to cover, and in a phase of brutish stalemate. The KLA remained incapable of significant breakout from their border bridgeheads to relieve their units inside Kosovo; the Serb army, who had the ability on the ground to push the KLA back to Albania, could not do so because they were being bombed by NATO; NATO, the only organisation with the power to end it all swiftly, was constricted by its lack of will to commit ground troops. Meanwhile, inside Kosovo, hundreds of thousands of refugees remained victim to the whims of Belgrade.

One evening, as I swayed in a state of dismal half-drunkenness down a scruffy Skopje hotel corridor back to my room, a voice called out from behind me. Turning, I saw a young Kosovar whom I had last seen standing outside Beba's several months before. He spoke good English and was in the hotel touting for work as an interpreter, having recently been purged from his Priština home by Serbs. Beyond the need for politeness, I did not wish to extend the conversation. I was tired, wanted to get to sleep, and had no more room in my head for another refugee story. But the man seemed charged, aggressive even, with the need to tell me something.

'Yes, I see you many times outside Beba's hotel,' he declared. 'My home was in that street. You are a friend of Beba, I think.'

I paused, trying to second-guess his next line, then told him simply that Beba had always looked after me well. The hotel-owner had frequently come up in conversation between Kurt and me since we had left Kosovo as we wondered about his present circumstances. Both of us knew that, whatever his fealty towards us, and in spite of his network of Albanian friends, like every other resident of Yugoslavia his ethnicity demanded his primary loyalty in war. I had often tried to imagine how his gangland status would factor in to the new power eruptions occurring in Kosovo. The Balkans were filled with the graves of men who had risen one morning as influential gang leaders, only to be in a coffin by dusk. However confident and assured Beba had always appeared, none knew better than he the precariousness of his status. Months before we had last seen him, in the middle of the night an expensive armoured car belonging to a guest had been stolen from outside the hotel. Told of the theft at his home, rather than simply drive to the hotel to placate the car's owner and inform the police, Beba had first checked his pistol and ammunition, then left by a back exit, gathered some of his men, and walked with them to the hotel on foot via darkened alleyways.

'It was the kind of event guaranteed to provoke my arrival at the hotel,' he had told me later, laughing a little. 'So rather than assume it was just a car theft, I thought it was probably a provocation designed to lure me out to be shot. Little things like that, Anthony, I have to look at them in many ways before I decide how to react.'

'You know what he is doing these days?' the young Kosovar continued, and the tension in his tone, slightly triumphant, informed me that, though I would not want to know, I was going to be told anyway. 'Your friend Beba is coordinating the expulsion of the Albanians from Pri\u0161tina and the looting of their homes. There were only eight Albanian families in our street. His men left us alone for a while. Then, a few days ago, they came and kicked us out.'

I shrugged emptily and closed down the conversation as quickly as I could, desiring this bitter messenger to be far away. Then I stepped into my room and poured a glass of cheap whisky. The news did not even surprise me. A man in Beba's position was bound to have become embroiled in the war's darkness one way or another. He had stuck to his word and saved me when doing so gained him nothing but my gratitude and could have cost him dear; and I knew for a fact that he had also saved a Kosovar friend, helping him to escape Pri\u0161tina by dressing him in a police uniform and escorting him to the border. 'Bal kan': the very name was an Ottoman legacy, a union of the Turkish words for 'honey' and 'blood'. The paradox was never going to leave much space for heroes.

CHAPTER 6

England, Summer 1999

Voices from past wars had whispered throughout my childhood, calling from a place that was at once the source of my most treasured memories and home to the quiet echoes of a previous era. Although merely a small, rural cottage, to my mind it was as impressive as the grandest stately home, and it evoked feelings of great security and belonging. Seated above a rambling garden, its three-acre confines comprised an eclectic mix of ancient apple orchard, woodland, marsh and stream. Other than a neighbouring dairy farm, it possessed views over fields and trees that afforded no other glimpse of human habitation. The varying hues of the building's higgledy-piggledy brickwork, pulled at by burgeoning green clouds of creeper and clematis, reflected different stages of construction over three hundred years, yet it had remained largely unchanged since my grandparents had purchased it just before the start of the Second World War.

Leaving Macedonia just a few days after I had been updated on Beba, I returned to England to see this place once more, to bid farewell. It was a summer's afternoon when I arrived, my head still full of Balkan war, but the moment I turned off the car's engine and stepped into the gentle drone of insects and birdsong I was consumed by a sense of absolute tranquillity.

'Darling, if the worst happens, it is so that you and your children can still be enchanted by banks of foxgloves, the green of the birches in spring and all the other lovely things of the world around you . . . The children must grow up to love these things, they are the best tonic for frayed nerves,' wrote my grandfather, contemplating the likelihood of his death in one of his wartime letters to his wife. It was not a surprising final request for the man to make. Though usually too reserved for sentimentality, he was enthralled by natural history, and this academic, introverted character, who studied the life cycle of bees and the cell structure of plants in his spare time, became as lost in the cottage's world of hooting owls, immodest songbirds, wildflowers and barking foxes as a child in a magic garden. Small wonder that in this place of peace he had hidden away his war medals, shutting them from the loves of his life like a sordid past indiscretion.

Though he never spoke to me of the war and his experiences as navigator in a bomber crew, and I learned soon enough not to ask, glimmers of those days still remained in the house. His pilot, an Australian named Bill Brill, had cropped up there in conversation with the frequency of a cherished neighbour, though he was dead even by the time I was born. And a photograph in the drawing room of a beautiful boy in flying leathers, standing alone in a meadow of long grass, had its presence partially explained to me in private by my grandmother. 'Nicky Ansdale,' she said conspiratorially. 'Tail gunner. Bloody swine crept up and killed him as they were coming in to land.'

Here, too, I had first eavesdropped on the details of a war crime. A Polish woman, one of the many Poles who lived locally having somehow escaped the wartime occupation of their country, was in intense conversation with my grandmother in the garden one afternoon as I lingered unseen nearby. She recounted, in a few stabbing sentences, the memory of seeing a German soldier in Warsaw, unhinged by fighting, grab the heels of a screaming Polish infant and dash its brains out against a wall with the remark: 'That child will cry no more.' I was six. The words have never left me.

My grandparents' marriage had been far from tranquil, and though the union between this impoverished son of an English doctor and an ousted aristocrat of Austro–German and Belgian–Egyptian descent survived the passage of time, the war encroached upon it in moments of domestic conflict. Beneath my grandfather's quiet exterior lurked a heated temper, and my mother recalled terrible rows between her parents in which my grandmother, ostensibly the more passionate of the two, fielded with a fire poker the china that her husband hurled at her, missiles accompanied by the accusation that she was a 'bloody German bitch'. Wars seldom stop with mere peace treaties, at least not in the minds of the men who fight in them.

The taunt, at least so far as it pertained to my grandmother's wartime sympathies, was deeply unfair. Though her loyalties must have been tested during the conflict because many of her family, including cousins, fought for the Axis forces, she harboured a deep hatred of the Nazis; and while certainly not regarding herself as 'English', she aspired definitively to being 'allied'. Even thirty years after the war she liked to play an old 78 record satirising the Nazi leadership for our amusement. 'Heil Hitler/Ja, Ja, Ja/Oh what a ghastly little man you are,/With your little moustache and your hair all bla,' went the chorus, and we jigged, goose-stepped and stiff-arm-saluted around the drawing room in unfailing hysterics.

Little concerned with adult affairs, my visits to the cottage as a child, so frequent after my parents' divorce, progressed through chapters of unwavering joy and discovery. While still on all fours, I was encouraged on snail hunts through the fruit cage and vegetable garden, seizing quarry that appeared the size of apples in my hands. When I was just big enough to walk, my grandmother, a woman ever in awe of the super-natural and one whose intense superstition I was to inherit, took me out in night-time searches for the ghosts of a white woman and horse-drawn carriage that legendarily haunted tracks on the surrounding common land. We never saw them, but the rustling of the trees and animals embarking on their nocturnal patrols filled every venture with the certainty that next time we surely must.

And at an age when the tallest of the marsh's foxgloves still swayed knowingly above me, I caught my first wild trout from the stream. Standing alone on the bank, armed with a hazel sapling and length of nylon as a rod and line, dapping one of my grandfather's flies on to the surface of a pool, I fell backwards, incredulous with surprise, at the arrival of this beautiful, perfectly constructed, red-spotted fish barely four inches long, which flipped and shivered at my side, having been hoisted from the water to the complete amazement of both parties. Seizing the fish with both hands, I abandoned the rod and rushed up to the cottage yelling in triumph. We put it in the bath for a while and admired it, then bashed it on the head and ate it, after which I went into brief decline, miserable at the realisation that I was architect in the death and digestion of such an amazing creature.

The cottage environs had other equally fascinating human elements during those years. An elderly Shetland hobo named Gear lived in the grounds. A former fisherman, he had appeared during the war looking for work, been given shelter and had never left, inhabiting a large wooden tool shed at the forward edge of the garden. Taciturn and remote, with hairy ears and work-roughened hands, he appeared sporadically in the pantry to boil a kettle or perform some token odd job, and his entire wardrobe seemed to consist of a set of frayed grey overalls and peaked tweed cap.

'Mum, where does Gear eat and crap?' I asked once, aware that the tool shed had not so much as a tap, let alone a loo or a cooker.

'Darling, it's been a mystery ever since he arrived,' she replied. 'He's very discreet.'

Wherever Gear ate and crapped, one morning in the mid-seventies he died where he had lived, alone in the dusty tool shed among the hoe, rake and shears, and with the sleeping bats, spiders and nesting bees as the only witnesses.

In woodland beyond the marsh, amid firs, silver birch, oak and alder, lived a character with a fuller history and more open heart. Tink Jones was a former Japanese prisoner of war. As a young infantry officer, he had been shot in the legs and captured during the fall of Singapore, and later incarcerated in one of the infamous PoW camps that constructed the bridges over the River Kwai. I was told that, just like my grandfather, he never spoke of the war. Except that he did, to me at least.

As an old man, ponderous and reflective, with half-moon spectacles and an impressive white moustache stained yellow at its edges by tobacco, his almost every move seemed to be devoted in some way to preparing his pipe for smoking. The instrument was forever being tapped, scraped, poked, pushed through, filled, prodded, tamped, lit and relit. The moments when Tink would at last emit a contented sigh beneath billowing smoke seemed minuscule compared to the time spent to achieve them.

He taught me to play chess and draughts, and how to drink alcohol. His wife was often away travelling, and in her absence I would wander down through the vegetation of the marsh, leopard-skinned with sunlight falling through the canopy of alders overhead, push through the undergrowth of the slope beyond and make my way across the moss-sponged lawn of their isolated home.

'Hello, old boy,' he would greet me unfailingly, 'fancy a snifter?' Pouring a potent cocktail comprising two measures of white wine to one of whisky, pipe never far from his side, he would sink into his armchair with the harrumph of a wise walrus, lay the board for a game of chess, then discuss uncaught fish, the latest sighting of badgers and other pressing issues of my childhood world as we played. Just occasionally, as the third glass neared its end and a bloodshot mist settled around his cataracts, the war would arrive.

'Hmmmm, bloody Japs,' he would announce, and pause moment-arily, eyeing the board as I waited with held breath for whatever fragment might follow. At times the Sesame door on the past would shut again immediately, with a concluding sigh of 'Bloody cruel. Tough, though, but bloody cruel,' as closure. Some afternoons, however, especially if the ratio of whisky to wine was more even, further information would emerge.

'Once on that railway – no good trying to escape. The Japs'd cut your head off, you know,' he told me, pipe smoke wreathing around his face. 'I remember a guard giving one of our chaps a frightful beating. The poor fellow was sick, of course, absolutely through . . .' He leaned forward, took a rook, and was silent for a while. 'I stepped towards him. I wasn't going to do any more than that or it'd be my turn next. But as the guard turned round he tripped over a sleeper and fell on his back. Everybody looks up and sees me standing over a fallen Jap and thinks I've thumped him. Huh! Thumped him! The Jap is too proud – they were very proud people, you know – to say that he had just fallen over, so they put me in the sweat box for a few days. Awful place. Can't stand up, can't sit down. Can't see anything. Bloody hot. They let me out eventually. I was lucky. Hmmm. The deer were here yesterday, damn them, they eat all the bloody plants . . .'

And that would be it for the day, the war's brief appearance over.

He was a kindly hero in my eyes and I was sure then, and remain so now, that much of what he told me was filtered through contrived self-deprecation. But once he recalled an event concerning a type of courage that was difficult for me to grasp.

'A lot of brave chaps around, you know,' he started with typical suddenness as we sat drinking one dusk on the lawn. 'Like your grandfather. No whizzing around or looping the loop in a Wellington or Lancaster. Straight there, loaded with bombs, straight back, Jerry shooting at you all the way, hope you bloody make it. Hmmm. Yes, lots of brave chaps around.' He halted and took another sip from his glass. 'Sometimes, though, we're not all brave.'

The light settled around us, warm in the summer day's end, and from the woods came the first clumsy screech of an owl.

'Just before the war ended,' he continued, 'when the show was nearly over and it was obvious the Japs were through, one of the guards, a Korean – there were lots of Koreans with the Japs then – handed me his rifle. Handed me his rifle! Our chaps weren't far away, we knew it'd only be a few more days until we were liberated and the bloody man hands me his rifle! "No thanks, old chap," I told him and handed it back. Would've been bloody stupid for me to take it, you know. Brave, but bloody stupid. You see, we thought we'd survived so much by then, the few of us left, that we didn't want to take any chances. Just wanted to stay alive. Get home. Hmmm.'

After my grandfather's death, his wife remained alone at the cottage, comforted in her intense grief – for whatever their fights she had loved him well – by the presence of so many memories and so much familiarity of surrounding. She still remained an enigmatic figure, unconventional, difficult, hilarious, selfish, loving, a bundle of paradoxes vying within her slim figure and challenging brown eyes, yet after he died there was always an aura of sadness about her.

Sure of safe reception, it was to the cottage that I made my great escape from the homesickness of boarding at prep school, 'running away', when I was ten, after a careful logistical assessment of whether to wear my school cap for the breakout.

'Ant, how lovely to see you,' my grandmother greeted me in the garden as I arrived, breathless with nerves and effort.

'I've run away,' I confessed immediately.

'All that way by yourself? My God, how clever! We had better go inside and have some tea.'

She sent me back, of course, but the grim tread of term time had lost much of its threat after that, punctured by the knowledge that escape was always possible and sanctuary certain.

She died quite suddenly, or so it seemed to me, four years later. I was at public school by then, an experience far more twisting than the comparatively banal suffocations of my earlier education, and had failed to notice the details of her worsening health. My mother arrived on a surprise visit to take me out for tea and broke the news. I was of no comfort to her and could barely register what had happened. Returning to the school later that afternoon, I remember shrugging off the event when asked to explain my absence by my peers with the louche, throwaway line 'My bloody grandmother died.'

It was uncharacteristic too, for just as my grandmother had been an influential figure in my upbringing I adored my mother more than all. A source of constant intrigue and enchantment, I found her the funniest, most companionable person I had ever met. Her parentage during my childhood was one of selfless love and devotion, gentleness, wit and honesty, rare clouts and moderated shouts: all the things a child could hope to find in a parent. Whatever the harum-scarum nature of our family's existence, she was always a figurehead of grace and composure. Possessing a unique ability to engender a sense of calm in almost everybody she encountered, she was also tough. Tried by different ordeals, her understated courage was more esoteric than that of her forefathers. Pregnant as an unmarried teenager in the fifties, she had given up her daughter for adoption. The bitter end of her first marriage, as well as the loss of her parents and her only sister, she endured with stoic resilience.

Her wartime upbringing had been a typically raw experience under rationing and relative poverty. The cottage at the time had been without electricity. Infrequent baths were had in a tub by the hearth, using water hauled up in buckets from the stream. The legacy of those years allowed her familiarity with hardship, both physical and mental. Later, for a time in her adult life, she was a single mother bringing up two young children, then she became a nurse specialising in the care of elderly and terminally ill patients. Enduring, hardy, generous, but very tender, pain was an anomaly in her self-description, and though there were sometimes private tears at home when she lost a patient or witnessed particular suffering, she would fast recover and collect herself with altruistic resolve.

The contradictions of her life showed in her hands. They were incredible, among her most beautiful features. At a distance her straight back, slender figure, dress and deportment suggested privilege, even wealth, but her hands were callused and hard, swollen-knuckled and scarred; legacies of hard physical graft, chopping logs, scrubbing floors, bathing patients.

There were plenty of rows. We were confronted by complex problems, challenges that in later years included my heroin addiction, questions over my sister's paternity, and the discovery in my mid-twenties that I was not her first-born child. The period between the end of the Bosnian war and the start of my rehabilitation programme at Core saw our relationship pushed almost to breaking point and at times I was exiled from appearing at the cottage. But we never skirted around the important issues, nor colluded in ignoring them. The bonds that linked us allowed free range and independent choice, though neither my sister nor I ever found much forgiveness for anyone who insulted or crossed our mother. As her son and daughter, we often gravitated back to visit the cottage as adults simply because of the sense of family union the place afforded us, and the natural delight we had in our mother's company.

She had remarried a few years after my father left, and following my grandmother's death the four of us – my mother, her second husband, my sister and me – moved to make the cottage our home. The place had lost none of its earlier attractions. A ménage of animals accompanied our occupation. In the nineteen years my mother was to live there various generations of dogs, horses, ponies, cows, goats, chickens, doves, an owl, squirrel, cat and a crow competed for space alongside the humans. Though their living arrangements were supposed to be separate, under the easygoing and slightly Bohemian nature of my mother's rule the boundaries often became confused. Naturally, the dogs assumed the beds and furniture to be their own; somewhat more unusually, the owl had its perch for a time in my mother's bedroom. Other animals explored the cottage whenever they chanced upon an open door.

'Oh, bloody hell! Get out of here! What do you think you are doing?' my mother would cry out in exasperation from within the cottage. The next minute a Dartmoor pony would wander nonchalantly from the dining room and out through the porch, an apple stolen from the fruit bowl clamped between its teeth; or a posse of chickens would flap down the stairwell and exit through the back door.

Towards the end of my teens, my public school experience prematurely over and education haphazardly concluded in a local college, I had a car and temporarily moved from my bedroom to make way for a lodger, living instead in the cottage's semi-converted barn. It was an idyllic time. Characteristic of our lifestyle, the barn was falling slowly to pieces, its beams filled with dry rot and woodworm. Yet it was the only space large enough to hang our chandelier, one of the few visible assets remaining from my grandmother's affluent past. So I spent my final summer there before joining the army entwined in the arms of my first love, a girl lured from distant Lambeth, on a bed squashed between bric-a-brac, junk-stuffed trunks, old toys, my grandfather's microscopes, unused furniture and dustsheets, on a floor of butterfly wings and crunching beetle carapaces, the unlikely cobwebbed twinkle of the chandelier glowing above us.

The pressures on the cottage, long dormant, awakened soon afterwards. A maverick of her generation, the men in my mother's life had always been more conservative than she. Perhaps for this reason, or for the simple capriciousness with which time can treat relationships, her marriage to my stepfather began a slow but steady drift towards division.

A separate concern was money, which had always been a problem. Though not poor in the true sense of the word, there was never enough cash in spite of my mother's work. On leave from the army once, I noticed that she had begun to sell my grandmother's jewellery, a progressive affair that continued until the little velvet-lined box was all but bare. Her crowd of animals began to decline too as the financial squeeze reduced their numbers.

Now these tensions had peaked at the very point when the war in Kosovo was stumbling to its conclusion. Her second marriage at an end, my mother had put the cottage on the market, unable to maintain it any longer in the changed financial circumstances created by her separation. The sale's completion came at the very moment when the Serbs – realising at last that NATO was unified more by a desire to avoid failure than a belief in their mission, and bowing before intense diplomatic pressure – started to pull out of the province, withdrawing nearly intact the forces which spokesmen in Brussels had claimed had been decimated, allowing the vanguard of NATO troops to enter unopposed.

Few events or individuals could have interfered with the single-mindedness of my purposes at the time. Yet, though disappointed, for it would have been gratifying to see the conclusion of a war in which I had invested so much time, I realised that my mother was alone and needed help to pack and move out. I also wanted to take the chance to say goodbye to the place which more than any other I called 'home'.

So, as the news on a background radio announced the arrival of the first NATO troops in Priština, just behind a Russian column that had secured the airport, I found myself wrapping pictures of my family's soldiers in newspaper, and stacking them on the floor among the packing crates. I looked at each picture again as I did so, at the faces above the medals: William Orpen's First World War portrait of my great-grandfather, severe and proud, seated against a backdrop of khaki tent canvas, black eye-patch and empty left sleeve scaled by the pale lines of wound stripes; a photograph of my grandfather in his RAF uniform taken during the Second World War, showing a gentler, even shy gaze underscored by shadows and stress lines around his eyes; a portrait of a great-uncle, a decorated King's Royal Rifle Corps captain, his right cheek scarred and his eyes rimmed by the bruises of exhaustion, painted not long before he was killed at Cambrai.

Between them, their war experience charted every nook of personal courage and depraved strategy, from the Great War's sacrificial human-wave attacks through to the massed destruction by bombing of German cities. And I wondered again: did you find what you were looking for?

We took our last walks together through the stream and across the fields, caught the last small trout from the stream, saw the final badger in the woods and ran our hands over the flaking bark of the orchard's two remaining apple trees. We packed away all the family belongings, including the still faces of the dead and silent men, and dusted, swept and cleaned.

Our old mare, the last of the larger unsold animals, we considered too ancient either to sell or to make the move. Besides which, my mother's new home, a semi-detached cottage in Somerset, had no paddock. So we brought in the vet to give her a lethal injection in the field, then watched her shiver back on her haunches, collapse and roll over with a final sigh. We loaded the remaining animals – two dogs, the cat and three bantams – into the car and pulled out of the drive for the last time, leaving the cottage empty behind us. Sixty-one years our family had been there. The cottage was our home and now it had gone.

Returning to London, I felt no need to call Cathy before catching my flight to Macedonia, staging post back to Kosovo. It had always been a strange feature of my addiction that when confronted by outside setback I could reassemble myself and clean up, at least until the pressure subsided, when I would relapse. In loss, it seemed, I was somehow strong.

CHAPTER 7

Kosovo, June 1999

It seemed such a small theft, justifiable, necessary even, one I was sure God would forgive, and my fingers hovered magnetically by the icon, a magnificent portrait of an Orthodox saint, black-eyed and serene, dark robed, and hallowed in the rich orange of an ancient century's oils. The picture hung at neck height on the wall of a small Serb Orthodox church we had chanced upon up an anonymous track north of Dečane. Isolated, cloistered from casual view by the thick summer growth of trees which sprang beyond the graveyard's low stone wall, the church was empty, the priest gone and his flock fled. The building was unmarked by violence, with even its stained-glass windows still intact. Only the broken chain leashing together the building's heavy oaken doors suggested some ominous recent event. Yet, whoever had forced their entry into this holy place, they had departed without loot, leaving the sanctum's rich pickings for the mobs that would follow, as follow they surely would. For southward across the valley, past fields lurid with the season's greenery, the smoke from burning Orthodox churches and Serb homes curled lazily into the sky as mobs of returning Kosovars, drunk on vengeance, did as had been done to them.

'Come on, man, if you gonna do it, then do it,' Alexandra urged beside me, eyes glittering, her own hands already clasped around a picture, one of the many tapestries and oils which clustered so thickly on the walls that it appeared as if we had walked into a theological museum. 'You're not gonna go to hell for it. And if you don't take it, the Albanians will smash this place to pieces. *Putain!* Are you going to save it or what?'

My gaze skittered once more around some of the other church artefacts. The cross on the altar, perhaps? No, that would be damnation for sure. The altar cloth, glowing with brilliant golden weave? Too near profanity for comfort. Maybe a tapestry or one of the purple velvet hangings? Too large, and I did not like the colours. I turned my attention back to the icon and tried to read the expression on the saint's face for a clue. Did he want to be stolen or torched? The black eyes gave away nothing. It would be so easy, and yet there was still torment in my mind, a wrestle between desire, superstitious dread and moral uncertainty. To seize the icon for myself would be theft under the guise of salvage, and theft of a spiritual symbol at that, one held in reverence by generations before me. Leave it and it would be destroyed for certain, for the Kosovars were little interested in plunder: they wanted to exterminate, to smash, to burn, to erase the Serbian core at its most profound level. Furthermore, it was beautiful. I wanted it, perhaps no more than on the level of a magpie wanting a silver spoon. And yet . . .

'It can burn. Let history decide.' My words sounded decisive, but as I turned and walked from the church, with Alexandra tutting dismissively beside me, I remained wanting and unconvinced.

The church was wrecked a few days later, becoming a roofless, smoke-stained shell over a carpet of smashed glass, ash and blackened timber. Shuffling among the rubble, I spotted the occasional portion of a wooden frame and some tiny pieces of soot-crusted fabric.

The fate of the Serbs in Kosovo was being sealed more by their own history of violence than by the presence of foreign troops. NATO and the United Nations, the self-styled defenders of human rights, should have played a greater role in their destiny; after all, the whole war had been billed by the West as a 'humanitarian conflict' designed to end abuse and killing. 'Intervention' is a phrase that suggests the overriding of a nation's internal tumult. However, having arrived, the NATO troops either could not or would not defend the Serbs effectively. Whatever their culpability in the orgiastic violence that had coincided with the NATO air campaign, the Serb civilians deserved better than the payback they received from the Kosovars as a result.

I reached Kosovo less than a week after the advance of the NATO forces, who had entered the province with Belgrade's agreement as the Serbs withdrew their army, and just ahead of the returning exodus of Kosovar refugees, more than three-quarters of a million of them, going home after their exile in Macedonia and Albania.

Unlike the countryside after long-term conventional conflicts, the landscape was scarcely marked by the scarred trench lines, bunkers and no man's lands that define, should time allow, the tectonic stand-off in man's efforts to slay his fellow-man, the idiosyncratic kill-and-survive burrows cluttered with crushed cans, torn ration packets, barbed wire, spent ammunition; sour with piss stink, old boredom and fear. However, it was still scourged. Priština had become a temporary ghost town emptied of its population, though it had been more or less untouched by violence, preserving the same inexplicable amnesty that had guarded it from harm during the build-up to the air strikes. Elsewhere, though, it seemed a hate-filled and pyromaniac djinn had been at work. Almost every Kosovar village had experienced some form of destruction: from the torching of just a few houses in some to the consummate and deliberate annihilation of every home and mosque in others. Not content with merely driving the population out of Kosovo, the Serbs had gone to great lengths to ensure they would never come back.

And there were numerous massacre sites, although there was no consistency in how the dead had been dispatched: the Serbs' treatment of those they executed had changed as time progressed. Some lonesome cadavers lay in the foliage of roadside verges, their hands tied behind them, part of no particular plan, victims of simple opportunism. Others, reflecting a more calculated approach to killing, lay in groups in fields, green-slimed and swollen beneath the summer sun. In places in Drenica bodies were stuffed down wells, poisoning village water sources. Others were little more than carbonised lumps, gaping jaw lines their only discernible human trait, incinerated in the homes of their burning villages.

Larger groups had gone through a processed killing structure. Corralled together and executed, their bodies had been loaded by gypsy labourers on to trucks, transported and interred in pits dug by bulldozers. Wary of war-crimes charges as their fortunes declined, the Serbs had then dug some of these up and moved them into Serbia. Several groups of dead Kosovar civilians were later discovered in mass graves near barracks outside Belgrade, and in the River Drina, far to the north of Kosovo, a local Serb diver called to investigate a large refrigeration truck found floating down the river opened its doors to find the lorry stacked with executed Kosovars.

Local Serb complicity in these crimes was widespread and included numerous units within the Yugoslav Third Army, which had been a willing participant in the strategy of fire, blood and ash. They, in turn, had been backed whenever necessary by the usual zoo of Serb paramilitary units as well as the police and civilians. The pendulum of their purgative spree had swung to its fullest extent at the point when Milošević agreed to pull his forces out of Kosovo. Now, in spite of the presence of NATO troops, it was swinging back in an accelerating arc that began with a few murders, then grew daily in size and scope as more and more Kosovar refugees returned, found their wrecked homes, and exacted retribution on any Serbs who remained.

Beba, a man finely tuned to anticipating the change of every breeze, had upped sticks and moved to Serbia as soon as NATO entered. Most of his hotel staff had left, too. His wife Vera had stayed on. As an Albanian-speaking Muslim woman whose exact origins remained intentionally unclear – for though she said she was from Bosnia her tongue was pure Kosovar – she continued to run the hotel on her absent husband's behalf, filling the jobs left by her departing Serb staff with returning Kosovars. Business was business, after all, and as a couple they had always been skilled in realpolitik survival.

Members of our old gang regrouped there in the war's immediate wake, Alexandra and Elly among them. Kurt was temporarily absent. Waiting to enter across the Macedonian border, he had taken one look at the droves of international media queuing to follow in NATO, stated, 'Not my scene at all, man, not my scene at all,' and, playing by no one's rules but his own as usual, went off for a holiday. Mass-media stories were never his thing.

'My God!' he expanded to me over the phone afterwards. 'I've seen it all before, after the war ended in Bosnia – scores of cameras packed around mass graves held by people who mostly didn't even know the place existed until it was all over, acting like they're kinda surprised at what happened. Forget it.'

In Lauša, reduced by the Serbs to a husk of walls and burned beams for the second time in a year, I found Sami. A little thinner and less stable than when I had last seen him preparing for battle barely three months earlier, he had somehow survived both the Serb attack and his central position in the KLA blood feud.

'I went a little hungry in the hills and forests, but it was not too bad,' was all he had to say of his latest outlaw experience, before entertaining us with tales of how a male relative had escaped a massacre in the Second World War disguised in a woman's dress. My interpreter for the day, an educated young Priština woman, was so taken with this wild Drenica guerrilla that against my whispered advice she asked him back to the city with us to meet her family, middle-class urbanites who knew nothing of the KLA and included in their circle a number of Serb friends, absent since NATO's arrival, whose apartments they were safeguarding. Sami was delighted with the offer. Donning a mismatched suit jacket and trousers, his wrists and ankles sticking out at either end of the short cut like those of a scarecrow, he gave his bushy red beard a brief finger twiddle, dropped a pistol into his pocket, explaining, 'This is in case I meet some people who have a problem with me,' and hopped into the back seat of our car, a disaster waiting to happen.

Sure enough, the experiment with philanthropy had ended by the following morning. The young woman appeared for work looking shocked and distressed, saying that, having devoured the supper placed before him by her family like a beast, Sami had told them a series of revolting, gore-spattered war stories before kicking in the doors of the neighbouring Serb apartments and looting them. After an uneasy night, her father had asked him to leave.

This new era for a time provided easy pickings for the crows and journalists alike, filled with the old debris of the departed war and its victims, and the new dynamic of revenge. Even Priština was momentarily exciting as its empty streets refilled with emotion; and British paratroopers, disappointed at the lost chance of getting to grips with Serb units, turned their rough and ready enthusiasm upon score-settling Kosovar gangs.

Yet their efforts were not enough to save the city's Serbs. In every peacekeeping operation involving British troops some or other officer explains their army's aptitude for the job as having resulted from the 'Northern Ireland experience', as if that had been a roaring quarter-century success. In Priština it was no different. Our soldiers, we were told, so versed in the intricacies of West Belfast and South Armagh, would save the day. However, under nominal British control the city's twenty thousand Serbs dwindled to little over a thousand in a period of a few months.

Outside Priština, Serbs and gypsies were slain in their dozens and their property burned. Once the dominant minority, in the months following NATO's arrival most of the province's Serbs simply packed their belongings into their vehicles and fled north to Serbia, preferring the uncertainties of life as a refugee than the local mercies of those their government had once persecuted.

Dan, however, stayed on. His final promise to me on the eve of the air strikes – to screw NATO and the KLA – might have proven desperately overambitious, but he had indeed served his last drink at Beba's. No one was sure as to the exact details of his role during the NATO air campaign, but a few of Priština's remaining Serbs recalled him appearing several times at Beba's in uniform, armed, drunk and belligerent, a description which probably put him securely in the majority of Serb males during the conflict. Nevertheless, he had survived the war. But the peace killed him quickly enough.

Rather than flee to Serbia behind the withdrawing Yugoslav army, Dan had gone home, to his birthplace in Kosovo Polje, the poor, smog-choked suburb at the edge of Priština where he lived with his parents. A month after NATO arrived, dressed in a T-shirt and shorts, he got on his moped and wobbled fatly off to meet some friends in Priština. At the edge of the city centre a gang of Kosovar youths blocked the road. It was broad daylight and the streets were busy. Dan did a quick U-turn but found members of the mob behind him. He ditched the moped and ran up the stairs of a nearby apartment block, banging on doors as he did so, gasping for shelter. None was given. The mob caught him at the end of the corridor on the building's top floor and beat him to death with an adze.

His parents collected his body from the morgue and buried it in a cemetery two hundred yards from their house. Once one of many Serb residences in the street, when I found them it was one of just three homes there still occupied by Serbs. An American flag was hanging from the window to deter intimidation, and a US police officer lived in one of their rooms. They could not even visit their son's grave unless escorted by United Nations police for fear of Kosovar attack.

The list of the international community's excuses for failing to protect the Serbs was endless: there were not enough troops or police or judges or courts or prisons or resources; take your pick. When, after Kurt's eventual return, we followed up Dan's murder with UN police officers in Priština, we learned that it had not even been allocated a file number. His podgy face, dirty, bruised and cleaved by the adze that lay casually discarded beside him, was one of many in a thick file of John Does. No investigation was pending.

So many of the war's good intentions died in the peace, as the result of the failure by Western powers to anticipate the level of hate that would remain in Kosovo after the arrival of their troops there. NATO thought that in the worst case it may have to protect a largely passive Albanian majority against an aggressive Serb minority. The reality was instead the reverse, and it overwhelmed the organisation. British troops may have been considerably more experienced than any other of their NATO allies, but the glib logic that assumed Northern Ireland was some sort of comparison for the challenges NATO troops faced in Kosovo was part of an arrogant myopia that led to a lot of people being killed.

'I have never experienced the levels of hatred that are here anywhere else,' an American police officer told me as we stared at dead Dan. 'It makes the race killings I have worked on at home look like playground spats.' He said that one of his recent investigations concerned the case of an eighty-year-old gypsy woman who, on account of her ethnicity, was pulled to the ground by a gang of eight- and ten-year-old Kosovar children, who then beat her to a pulp with bricks.

Some justice. It was difficult even for a believer in NATO's intervention such as me to swallow. I watched the conclusion of the war in which I had placed so much hope with the same frozen smile as a father beholding the birth of a tailed son.

There was no sudden farewell from Kosovo. My assignments there started to dwindle as winter neared. The stories began to dry up, and people's interest in the place faded.

The gang at the bordello, once our own private Casablanca, peeled off to look elsewhere, leaving it unfamiliar and sad, the echoes of our laughter and fights thin, distant and diminishing.

The last time I was there, traipsing around two years after the war had finished, clutching at the wisps of memory, the bar was empty of guests and I was alone apart from a clean-cut Kosovar waiter who was polite and deferential whenever I ordered a drink and never included 'fuck you, motherfucker' in his repartee. Vera, with whom I sat smoking in peaceful understanding, broke the silence only to say, 'Anthony, I'm very sorry about Kurt. I am so, so sorry.'

I stared through our smoke and wondered if I should have taken the icon from the church after all.

CHAPTER 8

Ethiopia, May 2000

Midnight in Addis Ababa and sleep eluded me. There was no presentiment intruding on my thoughts, no subconscious awareness that somewhere that day the cosmos had just made a huge mistake. Instead, as I lay on my hotel-room bed, smoking and watching MTV to pass the restless hours, my mind rattled around in the manner of a flea-market trader trying to match styles from a stall of eclectic junk, searching for a full set among the incomplete array of worries, hopes and memories of the previous weeks.

I had left Core just over two months before, and as with any addict recently out of rehab, my place in the world was akin to that of a newly fledged bird wary of heights and strong gusts of wind. It had been an imperfect farewell. With life still seeming to be a quest for event and happening, the periods I had spent at Core had continued to baffle me with their sublime, ethereal rhythms. Yet, as time had passed so had emerged realisation that just being there was itself the key ingredient in the alchemist's recipe, and that time itself, my oldest enemy, was in Lisson Grove a temporary ally. The patience of the staff, the sense of shared understanding I had experienced with Core's other clients, the familiar holding structure of acupuncture and meetings, even the sessions with the shrink had finally mortared the crumbling walls of a disconnected life. There had been no eureka moment of enlightenment, just the slow-grown but hard-fought awareness that whatever once had been missing was now there, that choice was again possible.

'Are you all right now?' the ill-informed would ask, as if I had just had the plaster removed after breaking an arm.

'Uh, yeah, thanks,' I would answer, not wanting to try to explain something that the questioner clearly could never understand. And I *was* all right, as long as being all right allowed for one drink never being enough, chain-smoking, an inability to accept the end of each day by going to bed, kaleidoscopic concentration patterns, terror of relapse and a more generalised fear that life may tip some surprise slurry-load of problems my way that might make heroin a viable alternative once again.

Because heroin was still there, lurking at the perimeter of my days with the same half-possibility of reality as the rumours of gathering rebel horsemen in Afghan hills that haunt a Kabuli bazaar. I had even relapsed a couple of times since leaving Core: desperate, fast and furtive events conducted like backseat fucks in a car with an illicit lover, from which I shook myself free in clean clothes and with racing heart, hoping that no one would ever know. But I was in with a chance. Providing I tried to avoid too many challenging situations, and cut myself enough slack to preserve the hope, fragile but developing, of a life without heroin, I knew that maybe, just maybe, I might make it.

Now, though, not even the facile distractions of MTV could mask my irritation at being in the Ethiopian capital. I did not want to be in the country at all, and but for the chance overlap of two African wars I should not have been there. In Sierra Leone, in the west of the continent, the Revolutionary United Front, possibly Africa's most infamous rebel army, had routed government troops, killed numerous United Nations soldiers, taken others prisoner, encircled many more, and was moving on the capital, Freetown. British paratroopers had deployed to secure the city ahead of their advance. It was where I wanted to be, not least because Kurt was already there.

Receiving a call from my boss, I had collected my Sierra Leonean visa in London and prepared to fly the following day. Yet, at that precise moment, Ethiopia finally invaded Eritrea after months of threats, causing the office to divert me to Addis Ababa, where I now waited petulantly for clearance to fly up-country to link with the Ethiopian army. The war in Sierra Leone seemed a far more exciting prospect. Ironically, though, Kurt was dissatisfied with his experience there. Assessing that the story had peaked and was fading, he wanted to join me in Ethiopia. The previous day we had argued over the telephone about who had the best African war, each haranguing the other to remain in place and wait to be met. This time I won. I was convinced that the Ethiopian offensive would be limited in scope and over within a week, allowing me to move on to Freetown. Kurt acquiesced.

'Well,' he had agreed reluctantly, 'then I guess you come over here and have some fun down the road with us.'

Those were the last words I was ever to hear from him.

When the phone rang, the video clip on the screen showed a French singer, a woman. It was quite funny. Hidden in a bank of rushes, she was indulging in some salacious voyeurism, spying on two handsome men who were swimming in a river. Suddenly the men turned to one another and kissed. The woman looked horrified. Maybe she fainted. I cannot remember. I reached for the phone, curious to know who could be calling me at such a late hour, welcoming the distraction from my insomnia.

'Is that Anthony Loyd?' the voice asked, formal and slightly hesitant. I mumbled confirmation. It was a journalist from Kurt's agency, a reporter based in Addis whom I had met coincidentally the day before.

'Listen, Anthony,' he began, 'I know that you are a good friend of Kurt's. We are getting word that two journalists have been killed in Sierra Leone. There was an ambush. An American, a Spaniard, a Greek and a South African are among the casualties. We're hearing two are dead and two wounded. We don't know for sure yet, but Kurt may be one of the dead. I'll call you when I know more. I'm sorry.'

An American, a Spaniard, a South African and a Greek. I knew there was only one crew that could be. I got off the bed and pulled on some trousers, poured a glass of whisky and made a couple of phone calls to get friends in London on the case. Then I waited for them to get back to me. I was cool, clear headed, icy with shock and disbelief. One thing was for sure: it was impossible that Kurt was dead. Two out of Yanis, Mark and Miguel were dead, but not Kurt. Kurt was immortal.

About an hour later the phone rang again. I stared at it for a while before answering, hoping to preserve that conviction for as long as possible.

The line crackled, the voice on the other end distant and disembodied. It belonged to a staff correspondent from my paper, calling from Freetown. An urbane and gentle man, the information he imparted with a few carefully chosen words sent an express train crashing through the walls of the hotel room with shrieking siren and the roar of metal on track. Kurt and Miguel were dead: our best and bravest champions felled by war's muleteers, rebel soldiers who had blown them away in a few idle seconds of chattering Kalashnikovs on a forgotten jungle road.

For a few seconds my brain attempted to process the news, then it switched off and blinked out, leaving me with only the practical awareness, pared of any emotion, that things needed to be done. The bodies would soon be flown from Africa to Paris. Sabina, Kurt's girlfriend, was arriving in London from the States the following day en route to collect his coffin. I needed to be there.

I packed my gear, checked out of the hotel and took a taxi through the sleeping city to the airport. It was four o'clock in the morning by the time I arrived, the desks were closed and the building empty, except for a few cleaners sweeping the foyer floor.

'What do you want, man? This place won't be open for another few hours,' a thin figure in blue caretaker-like overalls asked.

'I need a ticket to London. I need the first plane out of here.'

The man looked at me for a couple of seconds, working out the intensity of my need. 'How much you got?'

'I can give you five hundred bucks. Don't rip me off. My friends are dead and I need to get home to sort things out.'

He took off his overalls, put his brush aside, accepted my money and disappeared down a darkened corridor. He reappeared ten minutes later with a first-class ticket in his hand.

'Here you go. Eight a.m., via Nairobi,' he said. 'You'll be in London this afternoon.'

For a few more seconds his thin black face stared at me. Then he picked up his brush and began to sweep once more.

*

A storm was about to break inside the characterless suite of the Gatwick hotel room. The pressure of expectant grief, as it strained against bonds frayed by exhaustion and jet-lag, hung from the bland paint of the ceiling darker than any gathering cumuli. Sabina, Elly and I sat there in virtual silence, pale and glassy-eyed, and it seemed that any words we did exchange were hushed by the dragging effort of merely speaking.

It had taken us barely twenty-four hours from the time of the killings to rendezvous in England from three different continents in preparation to fly to France to receive the two bodies. But first a survivor of the ambush was due to arrive in Gatwick direct from Sierra Leone. Mark had been sitting in the front of the car next to Kurt when they were hit. He had escaped into the jungle, shot through the hand, and was on his way to a London hospital for treatment. He was our friend, he was alive, he was wounded: we wanted to be there to give him some support, but we also wanted to know what had happened, how the impossible had become reality, how it was that Kurt and Miguel had been slain while others survived.

Time stretched in a grey cocoon of shock and fatigue as we waited, chain-smoking and sipping cold coffee for something to do. Finally, we heard a door opening at the end of a corridor and soft footfalls. Mark had arrived. Elly and Sabina stood up and walked out of the room to meet him. There were whispered greetings and through the open door the sound of uncontrollable sobbing bit into the silence. It was an explosive sound and marked the second when reality hit home, the black hole opened inside and pulled everything through it in a silent cyclone howl. Grief for the dead: the start of the unique pain that subsides only when the afflicted are too drained by it to feel any more, a pain which returns as soon as they regain an ounce of strength; a torture so refined and unremitting that it holds a person gagging under the waves but refuses them the relief of drowning. Gone. Those we loved were gone. And I heard the heart's forlorn shout, desperate in its hope, echoing unanswered into the infinite, and I damned the savage God.

Eventually, Mark walked through the door. He stood in front of me, very composed, his hand bandaged and his face the colour of putty.

'I'm sorry I didn't bring your friend back with me,' he said. His eyes were dry, but blinking quickly, and he stammered a little.

We sat down.

'I can tell you exactly what happened, now or later.'

'Tell us now,' we said as one.

We collected our two friends in Paris the next day. They arrived in crates as freight. Miguel was taken on to Barcelona to be buried in a family plot on a dusty hillside. Together with Sabina and Yanis, who had also been in the lead ambushed vehicle but incredibly had survived unscathed, I flew to Washington with Kurt's body. I had never realised the strength with which Kurt had felt his own mortality until I arrived in the city and learned that I could answer questions regarding the funeral to which his family had no answers. Forgotten conversations we had shared returned. I found myself saying with conviction that Kurt wanted to be cremated. He wanted to be cremated because he disliked the process of decay in a human body.

I felt like a cheat to have such knowledge, though, as if I were there under false pretences. I had walked in from another world, in which together he and I had revelled in trouble, courted terminal risk and colluded in the secret thrill of war, to attempt to comfort his shattered family while advising them on how he wanted his body to be treated. Only a few days before I had been telling Kurt to stay in Sierra Leone. Now heartbreak and misery were their reward and I was the small-time emissary, wearing the scent of sympathy to cover the smell of rot, stepped up from Hades to make sure Charon got his coin. I performed my task dulled by alcohol. It was easier that way.

I did not have all the answers. Kurt's family wanted to see his body. I knew from Yanis that Kurt had taken a bullet in the head and two more in the chest. He had lain dead in the roadside dust under an African sun for a while. Our man was not looking his best. I did not want his family brutalising their memory of him by seeing his disfigurement, and somehow imagined that I might be able to prevent them from further hurt, as if that possibility existed. Not knowing the right solution, at first I tried to dissuade them from the idea by explaining that what lay in the coffin was not Kurt but the broken vessel that had carried him. That did not work, so I gave them the straight-up fact that he had multiple gunshot wounds. That did not work either. We walked into the chapel of rest together. They gasped at the machinations of lead, heat and the clumsy theatrical make-up of an African morgue upon a once handsome man. The sound of their indrawn breath was the brand-iron hiss on my own sense of complicity.

Seeing Kurt's body sundered my belief. People have on occasion asked me to reveal the most shocking sight I have seen. They want a little vicarious hit off a war correspondent's memories. I never really used to rankle at the question until I saw Kurt stretched out in a coffin. It was not the indignity of the mutilation that astonished me. It was not the coldness of his hands. It was not necessarily the proof of his death and the beginning of a void in my life that could never be filled. It was not even the small stabbing skein of terrible envy that twisted in my stomach and pursed my lips. No, the depth of my shock lay in the fact that I was seeing something I had never believed possible. And every day ever since I have wondered at it. The man was the embodiment of purpose. He was vital. And his death, every bit as cheap and random, even mocking, in its award, as the splatter of a roadside puddle from a passing car, threw my entire concept of pattern and meaning into the arena of doubt. I sought some sense in death and found none.

Kurt was cremated and his ashes were divided. Part were interred outside Washington. Part were later buried in Sarajevo's Lion Cemetery. Seven years earlier Kurt had written probably his best-known story, concerning Boško Brkić and Admira Ismić. A Serb and a Muslim, the young lovers had been shot dead as they tried to flee the besieged Bosnian capital by crossing the front line at night, their bodies left to lie beside a bridge in no man's land. In death they became known as the city's Romeo and Juliet. Their killings, illuminated to the world by Kurt, provided the perfect metaphor for the merciless divisions of Bosnian war. Their families were so appreciative of the respect and sensitivity which Kurt had shown them in telling the story that they agreed now to have his ashes interred in a plot beside the slain lovers' tomb.

A remaining part of his ashes, held in small brass vials, were given by his sister to each of a handful of his closest friends. I was wary of accepting mine, feeling that Kurt in death should perhaps remain as undivided as possible; besides which, no possible vestige could temper his loss. But I took the vial for the generosity of heart with which it was given, and in the realisation that I could carry no more powerful a talisman.

For a week or so, scores of Kurt's friends from around the world were drawn to Washington. It was a unique moment as the small international band of war correspondents, their restlessness so suddenly stilled by the loss of two such pinnacle figures, united to pay tribute and share the heavy burden of memorial. Not even a big war could have brought so many of us to the same city. Alexandra appeared among them from a job in Indonesia. She had been working in a particularly inaccessible region and I had not been able to contact her until a few days after the killings. The combination of this time delay and our differing reactions had the effect of uncoupling us completely.

She was as much frightened as upset, wondering who among us would be next. I was remote and cold, disinclined to engage with anything beyond the next few hours and the administrative details of Kurt's memorial service. Our on-the-run relationship had survived that far due to our states of perpetual motion. Now a fixed station had arrived and we found ourselves totally ill-equipped to deal with it. Mutual bereavement cleaved us. We split up not long afterwards.

Our crowd eventually began to disperse. I stayed on for a day or two with Sabina after most had left, then flew back to London. For a few days I wandered around the streets waiting for something to happen, as blank as the pavements over which I trod. Adrift from the world, spinning with disorientation, I barely thought about Kurt and felt very little, beyond wondering at the right to life of the strangers walking around me. Then, reminding myself that I still had freedom of choice, I decided to use it by getting wasted.

Stepping back into addiction after a period of abstinence, however long or short, is the same as opening a door to a burning room in a house that may otherwise be untouched by fire. Rather than ebbing since you last stepped inside, the flames are higher and hotter, as if somehow the addictive appetite has progressively raged on without fuel, parallel to whatever efforts you have made to reconstruct your life and clean up.

Wanting as much of a grand slam as possible, I rang an old friend who had the double-barrelled distinction of being a crack and a smack addict. Like some ancient Japanese soldier living on a remote Filipino island unaware the war is over, Jago had somehow clung on to his habit while over the years the rest of us had burned out and opted for surrender. This took some skill, for though some heroin addicts manage to turn drug use into a decades-long affair, good-quality crack is a fast-burn short fuse to total meltdown, its extreme addictive properties, potent effects and fleeting highs guarantors to a mayhem that usually hurries even the hardest-bitten addict in a quick-time shuffle down the corridor to rehab, death or destitution. Crack-heads don't do age. As a high, though, it is unbeatable.

A tall, heavily built man with a shaven head and goatee beard, Jago had once been the party king in the court of our early nineties London gang of revellers, able to work and play on minimal sleep and seemingly oblivious to comedown, until finally the grade As took their toll and felled him in the slow descent of a huge oak, to crash and creak to stillness in his dusty west London house, all but alone other than his rocks and wraps. He was pleased enough to see me. A naturally kind-hearted and gregarious man, my appearance momentarily broke the pattern of his artificial isolation. Besides, using addicts usually welcome the visit of a relapsing comrade, another guest on the island with whom to share the view of empty ocean waves. It reinforces the idea that escape is impossible.

We called a dealer round to deliver the goods, took a quick hit of heroin to tide us over in advance of the crack comedown, then charged the pipe, an improvised affair comprising a half-filled water bottle, tube and foil. I placed the rocks on a bed of ash upon the perforated foil cap at the bottle's mouth, then fired them up with a lighter while drawing the smoke down into the body of the bottle with a single steady inhalation. Once the density of the smoke in the bottle was at its thickest I paused, gathered another breath, steadied my nerve, removed a finger from the bottle's second stop-hole and sucked every last trace of the smoke straight into my lungs. Then I held it there for as long as possible.

Having taken my haul I waited, chest bursting. After several long seconds a slight and rustling hiss gathered at the edge of my horizons, intensifying into a roar, paced at first, then louder and louder until it crashed through my body and into my brain in a huge breaking wave of fragmenting peak, scattering my senses like fleeing angels to the skies, each ripping and re-forming in ecstatic oblivion, as my chest contracted in an almighty spasm that jack-knifed me to the back of the sofa, sending smoke blowing from my mouth like a steam-valve eruption.

The frantic peal of bells lessened after a while, some minutes perhaps, so I took another quick run of heroin to prevent myself from falling into the terrible gulf of crack aftermath I knew would quickly follow before lurching to the loo to throw up, head lolling against the sides of the bowl between purgative sprays of vomit. Then we charged the pipe and did it all over again.

I spent a day and night like that. Never had getting wasted seemed so utterly deserved. Surely no one could begrudge me this one, I thought, this one last desolate clinch. And Kurt's words reverberated through my mind in a beckoning chorus:

'Come over here and have some fun down the road with us . . .'

CHAPTER 9

Sierra Leone, May 2001

I had been in-country for a few days. Prickly heat blotched my pale skin with angry red rashes. My hair felt as though it had been washed in a fuel sump. Sodden, my clothes clung to my body. A permanent sheen of sweat coated me from head to toe, occasionally forming on my forehead into a stream which ski-jumped from my nose to spatter upon my notebook whenever I leaned forward to write. The crisp map of Sierra Leone which I had bought in London a week earlier had wilted within hours of arriving like an overheated flower, its reassuring definitions of uniform shading, gentle contour lines and careful scale now barely legible beneath a coat of smearing stains and dirt. Acclimatisation to jungle heat is a long process for a white boy and is a state without joy. The physical adaptation is the least of it: more than your pigment darkens beneath West Africa's sky.

Staring out into the deep blue shadows of the night, I could hear the jungle throb with an orchestra of insects. Sporadic bursts of lightning illuminated a distant towering cloud bank. Revealed, too, in those brief flashes of light were the dishevelled outlines of Makeni. Deep in the centre of Sierra Leone, the general dilapidation of the town's crumbling buildings left me uncertain as to whether it was emerging from the ever-creeping press of encircling foliage, the paddle-sized leaves and twirling tendrils, or sinking back into it. Beside me, teeth glimmered through the darkness. A young Nigerian intelligence officer, Lieutenant Tanku, was enjoying my naivety.

An hour or two earlier, just before dusk, I had watched a masquerade tramp along Makeni's main street. Tootling and wheezing in demonic fanfare, some thirty men playing drums and flutes had followed behind a figure at once intriguing and monstrous: the bush devil. Central to the ceremonies of the Poro secret society, an occultist sect at the heart of voodoo, it was covered in a ground-length shroud of snakeskin and furs, its grotesque eyes halved coconuts painted purple and red. Animal horns sprouted from its head; porcupine quills sprang from its neck; sea shells and tennis-ball-sized seeds rattled down each side of its body as it sashayed and pranced forward, trailed by the procession of wide-eyed musicians. The column had moved slowly through the town before finally circling the house of General Issa Sesay, the twenty-seven-year-old commander of the RUF, where it halted as the devil rustled and shivered, performing some kind of spell.

Bad magic: the scene fitted in with everything I thought I knew of the RUF and its reputation for sorcery and jungle rituals, ceremonies which on occasion involved cannibalism and sacrifice.

Tanku was chuckling at my assumption, though. 'That's not just the RUF,' he told me as we gazed into the jungle, across the low perimeter wall of the Nigerian base, 'that's the heart of West Africa. You shouldn't laugh at it, either. People can disappear here. *Disappear* . . .' He let the word float off into the night.

I could not see his face at that moment, but I knew he was serious. Not that I was laughing anyway: whatever had taken Kurt and Miguel must have possessed something beyond the powers of the world I knew. I stared ruminatively over the perimeter into the inky void beyond, twisting the vial of ashes around my neck. I was close to my friend's killers and closing.

Barely a fortnight short of the anniversary of Kurt's death, my reasons for being in Sierra Leone were manifold. Shame was one. Though I had known him well enough to realise that his decisions, even should they incorporate the advice of another, were always based on his own assessments, that had been of scant consolation over the past year. Not only had I agitated for Kurt to remain in the country which took his life, but I had not been there myself when he elected to drive up the ambush road. He had never received more than a beating when he was working with me. It was not that I necessarily blamed anyone else for his death, but I felt that, had I been there with him, I might at least have provided some sort of cautionary input to prevent disaster.

I was curious, too. Was the account of the ambush which I had been given true? What was it about the place, what force lurked there that had been so effortlessly able to sneeze out the lives of two such skilled survivors as Kurt and Miguel?

And I wanted to say goodbye, to stand at the ambush site on the appropriate hour and day to say the farewell denied to me.

The morning of his death, Kurt had left an unfinished story on his laptop in Freetown. Datelined 'Rogberi Junction', a place he had visited the previous day, it concerned the corpses of eight UN troops killed by the RUF and later found by advancing government troops from the Sierra Leonean army, the SLA. Kurt had travelled back to the spot to collect a few last details just prior to being killed.

'It took nearly twenty-four hours for a UN team of investigators to arrive at this site just two hours north-east of Freetown's capital where eight badly decomposed bodies wearing UN uniforms were discovered this week,' he had written, before quoting an SLA officer, a Captain Dumbaya, at the location as saying, 'I am surprised that the United Nations has not been here. These are their men. They died for the UN and yet no one has come for them. As a soldier, it offends me.'

Emerging through the sorrow and guilt had come the idea that if only I could complete Kurt's last story, including the details of his own death, then I could somehow deny the event its total victory by giving Kurt a voice from beyond the grave. In order to do this I knew that I must try to track down everyone who had encountered him living or dead that day, from any soldiers who survived the ambush, to the rebels who killed him. It would be, I felt, a fitting tribute to the ultimate journalist.

A heaving port of steaming streets beneath a cluster of coastal hills at the edge of the Atlantic, Freetown took its name from the 'Province of Freedom' established near the site by British philanthropists at the end of the eighteenth century. Repopulated by emancipated slaves, at the time I encountered it the capital of the former British colony was a vibrant linear smudge, shanty-style ghettos merging from its eastern side into the more affluent zone at its western end.

Arriving there in early May, my first point of contact had been Corinne. Among the bravest and most talented women I had encountered in war, in a tribe which attracts many pretenders she was the real deal. An American, as a war photographer her predilection for ending up in situations of ultra-violence was unsurpassed. We used to joke among ourselves that even as she travelled from assignment to assignment the very shadow of her plane left death and fire in its wake. I had worked on the road with her for a year in Bosnia as her wartime protégé, so we were bonded by many shared memories. Indeed, it had been through her that I had first got to know Kurt, who during the Bosnian war had been both her colleague and her friend. At the end of the nineties, though, after many wars, a wounding and a multitude of near-death experiences, Corinne had suddenly quit journalism and moved to Freetown, where she repaid her karmic debt by collating reports on abuses for an influential human rights organisation.

It was a good reunion. At first, sitting in a restaurant eating fish on the shore of Man o' War Bay, the night sea twinkling beside us in a cosmos of fishermen's lights, our friendship had reignited with instant ease. We updated each other on mutual friends, and laughed over shared experiences in the Balkans. Then came business. She gave me some local contacts, and filled in the details of the country's current situation. Sierra Leone's war had halted, for the time being at least, quashed by a huge deployment of African and Asian UN troops in the country following their much smaller force's debacle during the previous year's fighting. A peace agreement seemed to be holding, and there were ongoing efforts to disarm the rebels. However, much of the country's interior remained lawless and unstable, with isolated UN bases surrounded by vast tracts of jungle in which former militia and rebel commanders still held sway.

We spoke of the RUF. They were a phenomenon even by African standards. In the decade since their inception, they had fought the government army, civil militias, Kamajor hunters, Gurkha and South African mercenaries, the Guinean army, Nigerian and UN forces and British paratroopers. At times they had controlled the majority of the country, and had held the capital twice. Not bad going for what amounted to a few thousand men, lacking any cohesive ideology or strategy, and relying primarily on teenage abductees for their manpower.

Drawing on the brutal historical precedents of West Africa's slave trade and the region's imperial and Cold War experiences, the RUF was about as raving and insane as rebel groups get, its operations hallmarked by savage and wanton cruelty, utilising terror as a delight rather than a tool. Funded by both internal and exterior backers, principally Liberia, to seize control of the country's rich diamond fields, Sierra Leone's only substantial economic asset, the RUF had developed from a small rebel cadre trained in Libya, swelling across the bedrock of the country's impoverished and dispossessed youth. But any claims they made to be the guardians of liberation were as cracked as the organisation's founders. The RUF's political leader was Foday Sankoh, a clinically mad former army corporal, by 2001 in jail on war crimes charges, whose manifesto was a mix of archaic Marxism and voodoo, and whose forces' battle honours included class acts such as 'Operation No Living Thing', in which thousands of civilians had been butchered. The cutting off of prisoners' hands with machetes was so commonplace that the rebels even had a terminology for it: 'long sleeve' and 'short sleeve' describing whether victims received their amputation at the wrist or elbow.

Driven back to the country's furthest environs by foreign troops on several occasions, the RUF bounced back in vengeful resurrection whenever the pressure was reduced. Rather than being a pearl of guerrillas who had evolved around a cohesive grain of doctrine and could thus be contained, or even defeated, by conventional counter-insurgency methods, the RUF was more an enduring manifestation of the general West African malaise: a lumpenproletariat of angry, ill-educated young men produced by the extreme poverty, rampant government corruption, spiralling disease and exploding population of the region.

Though in the process of being retrained and reorganised by British officers, rather than proving itself a worthy adversary for the RUF, the Sierra Leonean army had been soiled by its own reputation for pillage and murder. Underpaid, ill-led, drunken, drugged SLA units had embarked upon sprees of killing and robbery numerous times throughout the ten-year war, many soldiers morphing with the rebels whenever expedient, earning themselves the nickname 'sobels' from the villagers on whom they preyed.

Then our conversation turned to Kurt and Miguel, and I saw that, however warm our friendship remained, Corinne had changed, pulled herself back from the war trip, ended the dream. Maybe it was motherhood: her two-year-old daughter was living with her in Freetown. Maybe it was the daily litany of interviewing massacre and torture survivors that had finally got to her, making war too real and implacable an entity to court by choice. Maybe she had become sickened by the moral vagaries of journalism. Or maybe it was just something within Corinne herself. She had always had a unique ability to live her life in strictly defined eras, committing all her energy and talents in one direction, then ceasing with an admirable and almost total finality before heading somewhere else.

'I'm finished with that whole war thing,' she told me as our plates were cleared and we slouched backwards, bellies full, in the evening's conclusion. 'I did it, I had it, and now it's different. That's just the way it is.'

'Do you think the guys made an obvious mistake going up the road that day?' I asked, curious to know the perspective of a woman with whom I had driven up so many empty war roads, and whose face was scarred as the result of driving over a mine buried in debris on one of them in central Bosnia.

She paused for a moment, uneasy with the question. 'I think they were crazy to go up the road that day,' she said finally. 'This isn't Bosnia or Kosovo or Chechnya. Driving up a road here when there's ongoing fighting? You have no idea who you're going to encounter or what frame of mind they'll be in. You know how it is, how wacko they get. Remember what happened to you the last time.'

That night, back in my accommodation, a small thatched bungalow not far from the shoreline, I collapsed on to the bed, lit a damp cigarette as the heat and humidity of the night air cloyed around me, swatted ineffectually at the whine of an invisible mosquito, and thought about Corinne's words. I was not overly surprised by her reaction to my question. Like many affairs, war has a reversible psychology. Decisions that appear acceptable, perhaps unquestionable, to its devotees can seem unjustifiable, even reprehensible, to those who have stepped from behind the veil. If Corinne and I shared many of the same memories, I realised that we looked at them now from different sides of a river.

And I *did* remember what happened the last time, though I might have preferred to forget it. It was an old bill against my fortune which I feared one day must be repaid, and it had left in my mind an imprint of trepidation for the rebels, the war, the people and the country itself long predating Kurt's death.

Four years previously, I had climbed aboard a Nigerian army transport helicopter in neighbouring Liberia, an ancient grey Hip already mottled with bullet holes. Crewed by foreign contractors – an American loadmaster and two Russian pilots – it was delivering fuel drums to a landing strip held by Nigerian troops in the jungle outside Freetown. A fortnight earlier a military coup in the city, the latest in the nineties series, had ousted the country's president and government. The coup leaders had immediately formed a tense coalition with the RUF, who swarmed from the jungle into the capital to indulge in their usual looting and burning. This new alliance then clashed with the Nigerians, who had bases throughout Sierra Leone as part of a regional intervention plan.

My boss had sent me in specifically to report from Freetown, and as all border crossings were closed due to the fighting, and I had no time to find a fishing boat for a coastal entry, the helicopter had seemed my best option. Yet, before it had even taken off, I realised the mission may be a chancy affair when I noticed Nigerian soldiers drawing lots to see who among them would be flying with us. Next we lost radio contact with the ground troops as we approached our landing point. Unknown to us, they had been engaged by the rebels and fled into the jungle, pursued by their foes. Nevertheless, the helicopter started its descent, to find the strip deserted.

'Can't see nobody down there,' the loadmaster's voice came through my headphones as we circled. 'We're going to corkscrew down for the drop-off and abort if we take any fire. You want to jump out, you can, but just remember we ain't leaving nobody with you.'

The helicopter dropped momentarily on to the strip, its wheels barely touching the ground, and I leapt out with the rolling fuel drums. As it pulled away into the sky, leaving me alone in the ripple of heat and shimmering green, I reasoned optimistically that though the place was deserted, at least no one had shot at me. Perhaps the soldiers based there had just fallen asleep.

I stood around for a few minutes, working out what to do, hoping for some clean-cut Nigerian fatigue detail to arrive on the scene. The silence rang in my ears. Then I heard the sound of whooping and running from among the trees. About forty rebels crashed through the foliage and on to the strip. Armed with Kalashnikovs and machetes, they were dressed in a variety of raggedy combat gear, shorts and T-shirts; one or two wore wigs. They beat and robbed me without a word, hauling me around the ground under a rain of kicks, rifle blows and punches, though too clumsy in their haste to land a really telling strike. Seconds later a rival group arrived in a jeep. The fighters began to scream and shout at each other as I was pulled into the vehicle, which sped away into the jungle.

'Thanks for saving my life,' I stuttered to the youth sitting beside me.

He looked at me for a second, his face an expressionless mask of beaded sweat. Then he punched me in the face. As I tried to control my shaking I felt certain that I was about to die in that lonely place, and found little consolation in the thought that it would probably not be quick, and that no one would find my body. Strangely, amid those extreme moments of mortal fear a sudden calm had befallen me, together with the inexplicable sense of unseen presence. Not an individual presence either, but that of a group of invisible allies. I have met any number of combatants since who claim to have felt something similar in a fire fight. Some claim it is the presence of God and go so far as to renew the vows of their faith. Spiritual entity or the transcendental snap-out of hyper-adrenalised senses, I know not, but the sensation certainly helped.

Shortly, the vehicle stopped beside a group of mud-walled shacks that appeared to be some sort of base. The fighters pulled me out and stood me under a jug-trunked tree. At the periphery of my vision I could see vultures pulling at two or three bodies, by then little more than flesh-ragged bone and khaki strips.

'Look! Da man fear, da man fear,' a young fighter triumphed, pointing his finger at me and jigging with delight. The others called him the sergeant major. He looked about twelve years old. Then their commander, the 'major', a gargantuan man bearing an uncanny physical resemblance to Idi Amin, approached and stood before me, flicking through my passport, which had been taken from me along with everything else on the strip.

'Don't worry, Mr Loyd,' he stated suddenly in impeccable English. 'Don't you worry about a thing.'

The mood changed in that instant, and a wooden stool was produced for me to sit on. A small crowd pressed in around me, jostling each other, revved nearly to the point of hysteria, shouting above one another in an unintelligible lecture on revolution. Some appeared to be Liberians belonging to a faction once loyal to the Freetown government but now allied to the RUF, while others were locals simply along for the revolutionary ride. Many were wasted, completely off their heads. At the fringes of the scene a few fighters danced around, slugging back palm whiskey and popping pills from looted medical packs. Standing over a plastic table – red, I noticed with a sense of surprised curiosity, as if the colour were somehow significant – I saw two rebels breaking apart bullets with a bayonet, and snorting up the gunpowder from within.

In the middle of this crazed spectacle a fight broke out. Exploding for no apparent reason, the major grabbed hold of a uniformed youth, one of my original assailants, and laid into him, joined by a few other fighters. The victim fell to the ground, where he was stripped, with the beating continuing all the while, until the major grabbed a Kalashnikov, cocked it, and smashed its barrel through the boy's front teeth and into his mouth. Some of the group stood back at this point, waiting for him to pull the trigger, while two or three others grabbed the major's arms and tried to wrestle the gun from his grasp.

'Don't kill him, Major, don't kill him,' I found myself pleading, for little other reason than I feared that if they started killing one another, I was certain to be the next to get it.

The major relaxed of his own volition. Free from his sudden rage he pulled back the Kalashnikov while other rebels took hold of the youth's arms and legs, swinging him into some low bushes with the nonchalant disregard of abandoning a chewed barbecue rib. There was no aftermath of silence or anticlimax. The group simply re-formed, dancing and shouting around each other as, behind them, the beaten youth lifted his head, toothless and bleeding, to peer at us from the greenery for a second or two with an expression of aggrieved puzzlement before collapsing beneath the fronds. A rebel offered me a bottle. I took it. The liquid inside was raw but soothing.

'OK, we save you now,' the major ordered, laughing.

Without further explanation, I was bundled into another jeep, the fighters clinging to its sides, bonnet and roof, chanting, 'Operation, operation,' as we headed off down the road towards Freetown. Behind the wheel, the major danced to the reggae blasting from the stereo, his hands raised heavenwards in favourite moments as the vehicle careered around the bends. Beside me, his deputy, Lieutenant Lion, suddenly collapsed across my lap, fast asleep. A half-hour later they dropped me at the door of a hotel beside the sea, the Cape Sierra, which was miraculously untouched by the fighting, but apparently empty.

'We like you, Mr Loyd,' the major said as he shook my hand in farewell. 'Hmmm, this is a new day.'

Then they raced away into the distance as bizarrely as they had arrived, while I hurried inside the building, keen to consolidate my escape before they changed their minds and reappeared. On the left side of the foyer was a bar, fully stocked as far as I could make out, its walls almost medicinally whitewashed, complete with a barman in a bow tie.

'What would you like to drink, sir,' he asked.

I thought I was going insane. Footsteps approached from behind me. It was Corinne, who together with Miguel and five other journalists had made it into the city by fishing boat a few days earlier.

'Oh, Anthony,' she enthused as I turned around, 'how lovely to see you! Hey, you look green. And what's happened to your face? My God, you're all dirty. What's happened to you?'

That was my first trip to Sierra Leone. How could I ever forget it? I remembered that my survival that day had rested on the whim and chance of each moment, completely devolved from my control. I remembered the fighters' madness as the sound of an enraged bee swarm. I remembered the glitzy spangle in their eyes, and the impossible speed and volatility of their changing moods which allowed no possible prediction. I remembered encountering another rebel group a day or two later, child soldiers one and all, and asking them why they cut off people's hands. I remembered the way they just laughed, snickering away wordlessly between one another, West African Midwich Cuckoos participating in a living nightmare. And I remembered that I already owed Sierra Leone; that the place had always seemed cursed.

As my recollections receded I became aware once more of the room around me, and the whine of another mosquito. My energy began to fade in the shroud of humidity. Eventually I slept, but my dreams were bad and I awoke several times calling out. Huge insects crawled over my face. The jungle closed in to drown me. And at one point Kurt and Miguel, undead, walked through the door covered in dust to stand by my bedside and stare at me in silence. Then it was morning. Getting up, I felt like I had not slept at all. Worse was the feeling that I was not fully awake either, that somehow I had left my world of the previous evening, departed from its certainties, and risen to find myself unreturned, still in the dreamscape of a West African night.

A couple of days later I flew up-country from Freetown, hitching a helicopter ride in the bright, clean sun of early morning with a senior UN delegation who were to meet the rebel leadership in Magburaka, a town deep in the interior that lay not far from Makeni. It was a confidence-building measure by the UN, intended to smooth the way ahead of a disarmament agreement due to be signed a week later. It was not the first time the rebels had signed up to a peace deal. Indeed, Kurt and Miguel were ambushed in an upsurge of fighting which followed the collapse of a previous accord. But this time, having recently suffered heavy casualties fighting the Guinean army, with their Liberian allies under pressure from their own internal insurgency problem, knowing that the British were retraining the government army, and with Foday Sankoh jailed incommunicado at a secret location, the RUF had been forced to opt for another political solution.

Aboard the helicopter the mood of the delegation, senior officers and high-level diplomats, seemed relaxed. Although as they laughed and joked among themselves, I could see the sweat soaking through the well-pressed creases that ran horizontally and vertically the length and breadth of their every sleeve, trouser leg, collar and cuff. They were serious men with many worries. Their peacekeeping operation in Sierra Leone was the UN's biggest in the world. They still smarted from the humiliation of the previous year, when the RUF had taken hundreds of their soldiers hostage and killed an undisclosed number, leaving the original treaty in tatters. They could ill-afford a repeat of that disaster. The whole future of the UN's peacekeeping role, not just in Africa but throughout the world, was hanging in the balance in Sierra Leone.

The rebel delegation which met them at Magburaka had a very different countenance. Arriving in a stolen ochre-painted UN jeep, there were just eight of them, with an average age of twenty-four. Barefoot, most wore dirty T-shirts and torn puffa jackets. Their leader, Issa Sesay, the RUF's young general, was an exception. Dressed in a white shirt and trousers, decked out with gold chains and rings, he had the look of an affluent West Coast rap star. In common with his boys, though, he never smiled once. The little group of rebel youth which met the UN's top representatives that day eyed the occasion with a hard, icy stare, and the disdainful awareness of the disproportionate power in their hands: that of simple, pure and absolute destruction.

Among them was a man whom I particularly wanted to meet, someone I believed could lead me to the killers of Kurt and Miguel. Jibrl Massequoi was a senior RUF member and just as hardline as the rest, but he also had the reputation, almost uniquely in the rebel army, of having an articulate intellect. A former RUF battalion commander and top aide to Sankoh, he had been present in the area during the fighting of the previous year and I had been advised by Corinne and others in Freetown that if anyone could give me a lead on the ambush, it would be him. So, during a break in the talks, I asked one of Sesay's raggaboy aides for an appointment with Massequoi. The kid came back a minute or so later and told me to go to his house in Makeni the next morning.

With time to kill, I spent the rest of the day hanging out with Lieutenant Tanku and the Nigerian battalion in Makeni. They were good hosts, taking me on a tour of their area and delivering a brief that was a potent mix of war stories, bush magic and politics. Tough, arrogant, proud, handsome, most of their troops bore traditional facial scarring, impressive slashes of symmetrical whiskers on either cheek, or mismatched stars and lines. I told Tanku what I was trying to do and he was frank and open in our conversations, though from a couple of remarks he made I suspect he thought I was an undercover war crimes investigator or British spook. Either way, it did not appear to affect his attitude towards me.

His battalion had to play with a very different set of rules up in Makeni's twilight world. There was no point in judging the situation there according to Western logic. It did not even come close. Even the Nigerian intelligence assessments slipped into the underworld. A few days before my arrival one internal report had drawn attention to the most recent Poro initiation ceremony held in the town. A group of boys had undergone the ritual, which in its most liberal form involved scarring and spells, but could in extremes have initiates cutting a beating heart from a sacrificial victim and eating it.

Normally the Nigerians would view Poro ceremonies as a sign of impending trouble, for the RUF often used them as part of a final induction before sending new recruits off to be blooded in action. Now, though, with the shaky six-month peace process ongoing, it was interpreted merely as a measure by the rebels to consolidate their numerical strength. The Nigerians' own counter-measures were similarly spiritual. Their commanding officer was a devout Christian who told me that he believed God had touched the wayward rebel hearts and peace was an unstoppable force. He was proselytising too, as was his Muslim Bangladeshi counterpart, another colonel up the road in

Magburaka, both men trying to pull rebel souls out of the darkness and into their respective houses of God.

Having fought the RUF many times over the course of the previous five years, the Nigerians' attitude to the rebels was a mixture of moral superiority, loathing and cautious respect. They had lost many soldiers to the RUF's aptitude for sudden raid and ambush. And they especially feared the infamous rebel Small Boy Units, the SBUs. Tanku told me stories of SBUs creeping up on Nigerian machine-gun posts in the night, invisible and unheard, devil children possessed by magic powers, who left the soldiers' bodies gutted like fish, 'chooked' as the rebels called it.

That very afternoon, travelling along a jungle track with a Nigerian captain in an open Land-Rover, we had suddenly noticed that there were two RUF boys sitting behind us in the vehicle. We did not know how long they had been there or where they had come from. We had not heard or seen them arrive, only knew for certain that they had not been there when we had started our journey. The captain stopped the Land-Rover and ordered them out of the back. Hissing and swearing, they left.

Further up the track, we had come across an SBU demobilisation centre. Some hundred children, the youngest six years old, had been gathered from the bush by a Catholic mission that was attempting to disarm and reintegrate them into society. By definition, each and every one of the children there had been trained to load, cock and fire a Kalashnikov, had been under command for at least six months, and had participated in combat missions. Devoid of the adult concept of mortal fear, with at best the haziest notion of right and wrong, by the time they had been seized from their families, trained by the RUF, put through Poro initiation, been given 'morale boostah' shots of drugs and alcohol, encouraged to carve up captives with machetes and axes, and undertaken strike force roles in attacks, their psychology was so far into the night that it was difficult to see how it could ever be brought back.

Wearing T-shirts bearing such logos as 'Trust No One' and 'Kick Butt First', bush hats, berets and talismans, their legs uniquely scarred by long jungle marches, and eyes bottomless vacuums without the slightest hint of any human reference point, few of the families from whom they had initially been abducted wanted them back. It was not hard to understand why. Though termed 'victim–perpetrators' by those trying to rehabilitate them, more than their catalogue of crimes and lost innocence they bore the aura of terrible wrongness. Stolen soul children, as a group their presence reeked of wickedness, a tainting shadow of wanton malice. Cute they were not.

That evening, Tanku ditched his uniform in favour of jeans and a T-shirt and got himself ready to go to an RUF party, an event he promised to be a once-in-a-lifetime, must-see occurrence.

It was 11 May, and the twentieth anniversary of Bob Marley's death. In Europe Marley is a partial preserve of the white middle classes, who can swing awkwardly to 'Jamming' or 'One Love' without ever understanding the black ghetto experience of poverty, violence and squalor which bred so much of his music. But to the RUF youth in Sierra Leone Marley was no simple good-time reggae artist but the figurehead of rebel culture, the voice of a dispossessed generation suckled on blood and thorns. So the anniversary of his death was quite an occasion for the rebels in Makeni.

Only a short time before, Tanku's presence at such an event would have been an impossibility but now, with the conflict in flux, he felt that he could get away with it. Like any good intelligence officer, he wanted to understand his enemy from as close as possible, and intended to use the chance to garner information. He invited me to come along. 'You've got to come. There's no way you can miss this,' he told me. Our needs were not so different that night, so, somewhat apprehensively, I agreed.

There were two decrepit nightclubs in the town celebrating the anniversary, scruffy affairs of warped wooden beams, palm leaves and corrugated iron, their sound systems run off generators in the absence of any grid supply. The club of Tanku's choice looked like a good place to get shot even as we arrived. There was already a fistfight ongoing at the gates between rebel security guards and a couple of youths who had presumably done something worse than break the dress code. Inside, the dance hall boasted a bar and realtime rebel DJ. The air was a deoxygenated fug of humidity, sweat, beer and marijuana as some two hundred rebel guys and dolls from the most heinous guerrilla army in West Africa bumped and ground on the floor to 'War' and 'Rebel Music' like they meant it and it meant them, their numbers swollen by a posse of hookers, Sierra Leone's notorious night-fighters, and the lovers of Nigerian officers who had moved up to Makeni to chance the ceasefire with their men. Neither group appeared mutually exclusive.

As the only white for many miles I felt very self-conscious, despite the dim light of the few token candles which batted weakly against the pervading gloom and the company of a slender, dreadlocked woman who had planted herself on my knee, announcing, 'Hey, whiteboy, cross me wrong and I hex you bad' as introduction. Even so, I knew that at some stage I would have to dance too, not because I felt obliged to do so, but because among these people could be members of the ambush group, or at least some of their acquaintances. And, in the spirit of the place I had come to, I felt that I should dance with my friends' killers. I needed the strength of that intimacy. So around midnight I took a blast on a joint someone offered me, sank a last long draw of warm beer, and gave it my best shot, doing the whiteboy's skank through and around the crowded floor as against my chest the brass vial thumped, and inside it Kurt's ashes gave a shake, rattle and shimmy of their own, while Bob and the I-Threes rhapsodised the victories of good over evil.

Staggering back to my lightless room in the officers' quarters at the Nigerian base late that night, I nearly fell over the still form of a naked young woman lying inexplicably asleep on a mat beside my bed, her arms flung above her head as if in sacrifice. I paused for a minute, trying to discern an omen in her slumbering, velveteen form. Whichever way I looked at her, as an augury, she seemed propitious.

CHAPTER 10

A group of child soldiers lazed in the sun outside Jibrl Massequoi's home, their eyes sliding lizard-like in my direction from beneath hooded lids, then away again in apparent disinterest. A tethered monkey hissed from the yard at the few passers-by, while under the shade of the wooden veranda two young women played with Massequoi's infant son, a pudgy, rambunctious brat dressed for life in a camouflage romper suit, watched by an RUF informer, fresh up from Freetown, who sat on the porch steps, waiting to be debriefed.

Alone, I sat down under a tree and waited, my mind sharp enough despite the sour aftertaste of the previous night's beer, and considered what I already knew of Kurt's death from past conversations with Mark and Yanis. On the day of his death, the three of them had moved up from Freetown towards Rogberi Junction in a blue Mercedes. Behind the wheel was their driver, a Freetowner named Abdul. Rogberi Junction, an hour and a half's drive north of the capital, marked the forward edge of the area controlled at the time by the government army and its allies, a renegade gang known as the Westside Boys.

Kurt went to Rogberi for two reasons. First, he was interested in the bodies of the UN soldiers found there by the army, men who had been executed after their position had been overrun by rebels. There was a rumour, unfounded as it happened, that the UN were to send a team of pathologists to the site that day to identify the dead. Kurt, having seen the corpses twenty-four hours earlier, intended to gather further information for his story from the pathologists at the scene. Second, the army commander at Rogberi, a Colonel Bangura, whom the three journalists had met several times before, had earlier notified them that he would be leading a fighting column from Rogberi towards the town of Lunsar, held by the rebels. Kurt wanted to accompany him.

But they were late for the rendezvous. They had stopped to buy some fish and whiskey for Bangura, and were further delayed when a tyre blew. When they finally arrived at Rogberi it was just after midday. By then, Miguel had made his own way there and was reading a book under a tree, waiting for the UN pathologists, his white Data jeep parked near by. Bangura and his men had set off up the road more than an hour earlier. In the distance, some miles away, gunfire crackled as his column, more than a hundred strong, made contact with the RUF. Kurt smiled at the sound. He, Mark and Yanis decided to go up the road to see the action. Miguel, somewhat more reluctant, elected to follow them in his jeep.

He was heavy with his own thoughts that day, having lost a close friend in Sierra Leone two years before. I had met Myles myself in Freetown during my ill-fated trip to the country in the nineties. He was the exact opposite of Miguel: blond, tattooed and broad-shouldered, he had the easy lip-curling smile of the libertine and the fast talk to accompany it. Legend had it that while covering a Democratic convention in the States soon after starting work for the Associated Press, security had found a bag of grass in his camera bag. The event was an otherwise boring affair, so the only photograph that ran on the wires was of Myles, a baseball cap reversed on his head with the AP logo prominent, handcuffed, being man-handled into a patrol car by two cops. Banished by the agency to Africa, a continent more suitable for maverick adventurers to win their spurs, he had gained a reputation for being a brave and talented operator. Here he met Miguel, who had himself relocated to Africa between the end of the Bosnian war and the start of the conflict in Kosovo, and their friendship was quickly cemented. But Myles was shot dead by the RUF in a Freetown street in 1998. Miguel was deeply affected by his death, and the desire to say goodbye to his dead friend had been one of the principal reasons behind his decision to return to Sierra Leone. Yet he had been troubled by the return, and seemed haunted by prescience. We had spoken about it on the phone several times in the days leading up to his own death.

'Listen to me, man, someone is going to die here soon,' he had said during a call a few days before the ambush, his tone tense and pained. 'It's incredibly dangerous but people don't realise it. The army don't know what they are doing or exactly where the rebels are. Some journalist is going to drive up a road and get killed soon. I know it.'

Yet, that day, Miguel had chosen to drive up the road behind Kurt and the others.

Abdul, Kurt's driver, refused to go beyond Rogberi, saying it was too dangerous. So, taking seven soldiers as escort, the reporters left him at the base. Two soldiers sat in the back of the Mercedes, with Yanis between them. Mark sat in the front passenger seat beside Kurt, who had taken the wheel. Another soldier rode on the bonnet. Following them in his jeep, Miguel had an SLA lieutenant sitting beside him. In the back were two more soldiers, while another, carrying an RPG, straddled the spare wheel mounted on the rear door.

The two vehicles moved east and passed through the abandoned village of Kontah, along a road flanked by thick jungle. Just beyond Kontah the route dipped, then began to climb again in a gentle incline, before reaching a bend with banks on either side. As the Mercedes drove through this cutting, small-arms fire erupted from the undergrowth to the left. Kurt slumped forward on the dashboard, blood running from his head. As he died, his foot pressed down on the accelerator and the Mercedes continued through and out of the killing zone, taking fire as it did so. In the back of the car, Yanis saw a group of rebels shooting at them from the bank as they passed at almost point-blank range. The vehicle then veered into a siding, some distance from the ambushers. Holding his injured hand, Mark leapt out of the car; as, eventually, did Yanis, although he had problems making his exit as one of the men beside him was dead and the other apparently catatonic with fear. Both journalists fled separately into the jungle. Neither saw what had happened to Miguel's jeep. Behind them, it had come to a halt right in the centre of the ambush.

Yanis hid in deep undergrowth. Mark, disorientated as he escaped, circled round and unwittingly reappeared by the roadside. From cover at the verge he observed a small group of rebels by the Mercedes. They were rifling through the car prior to torching it. Nearly an hour later, still in hiding, both men heard more firing. Bangura and his column had heard the ambush and were moving back down the road towards the scene, shooting as they did so to clear the roadside of rebels. As these troops drew level Mark shouted out to them. They stopped firing and called upon him to step forward. Emerging from the jungle, he saw beside the burning Mercedes the bodies of Kurt and the dead soldier. Both corpses had had their boots taken and their pockets turned out. Mark persuaded the troops to put Kurt's body aboard a truck that was accompanying the column. A heavy machine-gun was mounted on the back, and it began firing into the empty press of foliage as they approached the centre of the ambush position.

There lay Miguel's jeep, riddled with bullet holes and shards of shrapnel. A dead soldier lay beside it, along with Miguel, who had multiple gunshot wounds. Unlike Kurt, who had been killed by the first volley, no one was quite sure under what circumstances Miguel had died. Some of his friends later feared that he had initially been wounded, then executed.

The soldiers loaded these two bodies on to the truck, and the column set off for Rogberi. Once there, Mark tried to persuade Bangura to launch a patrol to find Yanis. As he argued his case, one of the soldiers shouted out in warning. A lone figure was walking down the road towards them: Yanis. He had moved from his hiding-place and walked several miles alone down the road to Rogberi with his hands raised.

Another truck then arrived at the Rogberi base, sent up from Freetown with a supply of rice, ammunition and machine-guns for the troops. As Westside Boys and soldiers began to argue among one another, jostling and screaming in a dispute over who was to be deployed where, Yanis and Mark loaded the bodies of their colleagues on to the new truck and waited for it to return to the capital. The rains at last erupted from the heavy skies, dropping in lancing sheets, and as the fighters raved and yelled around them, the water washed the two men's sweat into the dirt of the truck bed, where it mingled with the blood of their friends.

*

I did not disclose all these details to Massequoi once he had invited me into his house. I wanted to hear the uncorroborated version of what, if anything, he would tell me. If anyone could help me to find out what lay behind the rebel ambush, even take me to meet the fighters who had been there, it was him. I could not afford to blow it.

Massequoi was a radical even by rebel standards, a tough, uncompromising man. Perhaps no older than his late twenties, he had been abducted and forced into the RUF as a youth. Years of fighting in the jungle had removed whatever vestiges may have remained of the bewildered teenager seized from his family, replacing them with tight-skinned jaw, piercing one-dimensional eyes, and the passion, markedly unstable in its intensity, which fuelled his speech as he emphasised his arguments. If he did not have the same overt trip-switch psychology as his comrades, then his volatility was still apparent, a surging current beneath the veneer of restraint. Yet he was credited with initiative and fierce intelligence, and, as spokesman for the rebels and one of their chief negotiators with the UN, he understood how Western minds worked.

We spoke for a long time about the war before I let the question drop. 'You know how it is when a brother dies in action but you are not sure exactly how it happened?' I said. He nodded. 'And you know how you really want to find out what happened and how they died?' He nodded again. So I told him some of what I knew concerning Kurt's death, though not much of it, and asked if he could tell me more, adding that I did not want revenge, just to know the truth.

If I had expected a long pause to follow my question, or a blank denial of any knowledge of the event, then I was mistaken. Massequoi remembered it clearly. He could hardly fail to. For in its aftermath he had held a scorched television tripod in his hands as his returning men had told him they had just killed a couple of journalists. He was also smart enough to realise that though the shooting dead of two foreign reporters might not rank as a great feat of arms, under the circumstances of the day it appeared to be understandable.

Leaning towards me, his elbows resting on the table, he spoke without hesitancy, and his account largely dovetailed with what I

already knew. From his perspective that day, located at the RUF headquarters in nearby Lunsar, the army advance from Rogberi had pushed
his men from the village of Kontah, then become bogged down in
fighting in the next village, Kamrabai. Meanwhile, a rebel observation
team hidden behind the army lines reported that more troop reinforcements were moving up the road to join the action. Informed of this new
threat, the rebel commander in Kamrabai, Dennis Mingo, immediately
sent a group of fighters back through the jungle to set up an ambush to
hit the reinforcements on the road.

'He sent two squads, thirty men,' Massequoi told me. 'Meanwhile,
the army took Kamrabai but then were stopped by RUF reinforcements.
Two vehicles fell into our ambush, though, a Mercedes and a jeep. My
men saw the white skins inside but thought they may be British soldiers
who we heard were helping the army. So there was a shoot-out. Some
soldiers died. It was only when my men checked the bodies that they
realised they had killed two journalists.'

After looting the dead the ambushers had returned to their base in
Lunsar. Massequoi had met them there. Among other things, they had
showed him Mark's tripod, taken from the boot of the Mercedes.

He leaned back and looked at me. I had more to ask. I wanted to meet
the ambush group themselves, or at least their commander. I wanted to
know what kind of men they were, their backgrounds, and what they
were thinking the moment they killed my friends. I wanted to know how
Miguel died. But I was wary of pushing Massequoi too far in case I
spooked him and caused him to close down. Our meeting had been
relaxed, cordial even. The option was open for another. And in the
meantime I had a wealth of information to follow up.

I knew now that the ambush group had been based for a time in
Lunsar. It seemed likely that some would have been locals, indigenous
to the town. If a commander deploys an ambush group to intercept enemy reinforcements during ongoing action he needs them to get
to the right place fast, so among them would have been men already
familiar with the lie of the land: the location of the road, the best ambush
point, and the knowledge of how to access it through jungle trails. They
would probably have been led by a man of some seniority, too. Thirty

men sent on a snap ambush mission would have required some deft leadership.

And I now had Dennis Mingo's name. I had met Mingo, *nom de guerre* 'Superman', the last time I had been in Sierra Leone. He was a hero to the rebels, a short, burly man with a surprisingly cherubic face. Missing a thumb which he had lost in a gun battle, he was one of the rebels' principal field commanders and I assumed he would be easy to find.

I felt my timing could not have been better. If the war had still been raging at full throttle, I could never have reached most of these people, and would have found the rebels deeply hostile. But ceasefires and peace deals make fighters vulnerable to access for the interested party. They take the Kalashnikov from the man's hand, pull him from his bunker, separate him from his unit, open his mind to independent thought, sometimes involving feelings of guilt or confusion, then put him in a lonely field with a hoe.

Lunsar, I thought. Go next to Lunsar.

So I asked nothing more of Massequoi that day, other than his satellite-phone number for future communication. We stood up and I shook his hand. I felt neither animosity nor empathy towards him. He was an access point to information I needed, and I wanted to cultivate my relationship with him. Besides, so far, it appeared that Kurt had at least died by rules he would have understood.

Leaving Massequoi in Makeni, I hitched a ride with two brothers back towards Freetown, where I wanted to spend a day or two planning the next stage. The brothers described themselves simply as drivers, and I did not press for more, though suspected that no mere driver would risk plying his trade on the road between Makeni and Freetown even during a ceasefire. They played gospel music non-stop. The sound was soothing, an unlikely precursor to the experience that lay ahead. For our journey to Freetown would take me straight through the ambush site, on the very road on which Kurt and Miguel had died.

The road. It was a brown, barren slash through the encroaching green, an infected drip of psychic infection. Whether it was the single RUF checkpoint outside Makeni commanded by a rebel who introduced himself as 'Death'; the lifeless expanses of rutted tarmac; the abandoned, bullet-scarred villages which emerged then fled from my vision like pit-stops in a bad dream; or the wrecks of ambushed vehicles that decorated the verge-side foliage, it was never anything but all wrong.

At my request, we stopped in Kontah, a collection of tumbled earthen huts throttled by snaking creeper, where misspelled graffiti eulogising the prowess of a Colonel Blood peered through the leaves, and huge purple centipedes drowsed among the ruins. A small group of rebels loitered by a cooking pot at the road's edge, smoking grass. There were three of them: a boy in combat pants, his chest a constellation of Poro scarring; a tall figure named Mack who had an old bullet wound across his forehead; and their commander, a short man in a Manchester United T-shirt, a single dreadlock in his hair, his eyes a malarial yellow smear in which his irises seemed to be bleeding outwards.

'Hello,' I said, smiling and extending my hand. They each shook it unenthusiastically, without eye contact. 'Maybe you can help. I'm a journalist. I've got to do a story on the final days of the war last year. I know there was quite a lot of action here. Jibrl Massequoi has been telling me about it and helping me put the story together. He said there were a couple of foreigners killed near here. Maybe a German and an American. Or was it two Americans? It's in my notes somewhere. Whatever. They were with the army during a fight and got killed on the road. I know the RUF succeeded in pushing the army back that day. There was some tough fighting. Maybe you guys can help me understand it a little better. Were you around here at the time?'

Combine a little nurturing of a fighter's pride, devolve yourself from any suggestion of personal interest, incorporate the name of a senior commander into your spiel, make a couple of deliberate mistakes to encourage correction, and play the dumb Englishman abroad: it is a standard reporter's ploy for dealing with suspicious combatants. But it did not cut much ice with these men.

'No man has an identity in the time of war,' Commander Bad-eyes hissed at me. 'So I recognise no one from that time, and know nothing of what passed here.'

Yet they knew exactly where Kurt's Mercedes was. Seeing that I was not going to depart until they took me there, Mack finally agreed to get into the gospel brothers' car and guide me to the ambush site. Just before he climbed into our vehicle, though, the commander took his arm and whispered something to him. I noticed that the driver was close enough to have overheard.

The Mercedes lay where it had come to a halt seconds after the ambush, in long grass on the verge between Kontah and Kamrabai. It was burned out and rusting, and weeds thrust up into the wheel arches. Old bullet casings lay around the wreck. Glass from the windows crunched under my feet as I stood beside it. I stepped over the ground where Kurt's body had been found, then put both my hands on the steering wheel and tried to say a clumsy goodbye.

I waited in this way for a minute or two, my grip closed on the wheel's rusted metal, knowing that it was the last thing my dead friend had touched in life, and looked around me to the jungle, hoping for some sort of echo, or the glimpse of a figure standing there. But there was nothing save for the throbbing heat, the lurid green and the trill of insects.

I walked back to my car in silence. We dropped Mack back with his rebel comrades and headed off to Freetown. As they disappeared from view behind us, I asked the driver what he had overheard spoken between Mack and his commander.

'He said, "Be very careful what you say to this man,"' Gospel Boy answered. '"Say nothing of what happened here that time."'

I laughed, and the laughter kept rippling through me all the way back to Freetown. Everything seemed to be falling into place. I had the sense of having boarded a canoe and pushed myself into the flow of a wide river. It did not really matter what I did: the current was taking me to where I wanted to go. It was unstoppable. Some force was pulling me forward. There was no way back. All I had to do was go with it, and I would find what I needed. The feeling lasted for two days.

As soon as Allieu stamped on the mantis I knew we had crossed the Rubicon and would meet the curse. It was up there with hailing a cab on Bad Juju Avenue: you just don't do it. You never know who sits behind the wheel.

We had made it to Lunsar, the very town from which the men who had pulled the triggers on my friend a year before had originated. Kurt's killers were tantalisingly close. I had the name of their likely commander. My mind was completely locked on the moment when I would look into their eyes. The whole morning had throbbed with intense significance. Then Allieu crushed the mantis and it all went wrong.

A very thin man, with broken front teeth and a habit of stuttering when excited, I had first met Allieu in Freetown four years earlier when he had been working with Corinne. He was in his early thirties, a bright, resourceful Sierra Leonean whose abilities had elevated him from the position of fixer to being a journalist in his own right. However, something had changed him in the last few years: an aura of damage now hung around him. It could simply have been the war, or the early deaths of his parents and a sister to sickness. Whatever it was, he appeared isolated, somewhat forlorn and slightly out of control, a typical example of an intelligent young man who had seen too much blood, profited from it in a way, then subconsciously turned and daggered his own fortune. He had fallen out with his employers after a succession of arguments and lost his job. He had blown his marriage. He had started womanising and drinking heavily, burning up what little money he had in squalid night-time sessions in waterfront bars that left him penniless and almost incoherent by dawn. Broke, down on his luck, familiar with many dead friends, including Miguel and Myles, and an experienced field operator, to my mind all these qualities made Allieu an attractive choice as interpreter in my mission to track down the rebel ambush group in Lunsar. So on my return to Freetown from Makeni I hired him.

Everything seemed to go well during this brief turnaround in the capital, serendipity shining on my every move. Using the information given to me by Massequoi, I interviewed several government army officers as well as Nigerian troops with past experience of fighting the rebels in the area. The name Morris Kalon came up in every conversation. A colonel in the RUF, I was told that as the rebel commander in Lunsar he was likely to have been involved in the ambush at first hand, or at the very least would know the identities of those who were.

However, arriving in Lunsar one morning, energised by the thought of what lay ahead and the conviction that I was completing a task that Kurt wished me to fulfil, I ran into an unexpected obstacle. Stopping at a camp of Bangladeshi UN peacekeepers, for no other reason than to gain directions for Kalon's rebel headquarters, I became embroiled in an argument with their colonel and intelligence officer. Unwilling to give me a straight answer, and apparently unable to accept the simple story that I was just a journalist wishing to interview Kalon, they wanted instead to question me at length in a way that verged on interrogation. Next they insisted upon inviting Kalon to meet me in their base, a demand I fought due to the sensitivity of the issue. The last thing I wanted was to encounter him inside a UN camp, an alien environment outside his control that would make him defensive and doubly suspicious.

Seated around a table in the camp's guardroom, as I argued with the Bangladeshis, the mantis had fluttered in through the door, landing first on the colonel's leg. He brushed it off gently. Next it flew on to the intelligence officer. He too shooed the creature off his camouflage smock, the slow, hesitant flip of his hand almost deferential. The mantis batted its dark brown wings and landed on the floor, where it began marching towards Allieu. We all stared at it in sudden silence, the midday heat combining with this distraction to gel our disagreement into momentary torpor, my driver, the colonel, the major, Allieu and I. At a little under six inches long, the creature was large, even by tropical standards, and moved with implacable deliberation, its serrated claws held before it in quivering parody of supplication. We were transfixed by this perfect, beautiful agent of death.

Then Allieu stretched out his right foot and trod on it. The mantis crunched loudly beneath his tatty slip-on shoe. The sound broke our reverie. The major let out a little gasp of surprise. The colonel frowned. Allieu grinned awkwardly, as if suddenly embarrassed. I looked at the insect squashed on the ground. It still twitched and waved its claws, large globs of beige ooze leaking from its abdomen.

That, my friend, I thought, looking at Allieu, was a very bad mistake. And once more I fingered the vial around my neck, seeking relief from the creep of superstitious unease.

The situation unravelled even as the body of the mantis still writhed. Telling me to wait for a few minutes while they left the room to discuss the situation among themselves, outside of my presence and unknown to me the officers called Kalon to the camp by radio. Minutes later I was facing a worst-case scenario. Escorted by a soldier to another barrack room, I entered to find Kalon sitting behind a desk, with the colonel and the intelligence officer flanking him. To this day I can only guess at the Bangladeshis' agenda. Whatever it was, my chances of extracting anything of value from Kalon had been completely broadsided.

An emaciated, almost grey-skinned man, he thought I was an investigator for one of the special courts due to be set up in Sierra Leone to deal with war crimes. I could hardly blame him, for that was exactly what the situation looked like – a police interview. He barely caught my eye other than to shoot me looks of unadulterated hatred, and refused even to talk with me. Throughout the tense five minutes in which we shared the same room his hands moved constantly. They were very long and feminine. Even his wrists seemed stretched. They fluttered like wounded birds up and down the edge of the desk.

I exhausted every angle of approach I knew. I even rigged up my sat-phone through the window so that we could call Massequoi and have him reassure Kalon, only to find that Massequoi had disappeared from Makeni. Eventually Kalon simply stood up and walked out of the camp. The Bangladeshi colonel tried to apologise in a half-hearted fashion, attempting to distract my rage by talking about the humanitarian situation in Lunsar, while I fantasised about shooting him in the head at close range with a pistol. As soon as Kalon was out of sight they said I could go too, as if skewering the meeting had fulfilled their objectives for the day.

Back in Freetown that night, my anger ebbing, I sought to retrieve the situation and regain a little momentum. To have had such a key figure as Kalon sitting before me and then losing him because of some unseen agenda was a setback, but not a decisive one. Reasoning that if I tried to repair the mess with Kalon directly it would only make matters worse, I felt confident that if I could find Superman, or speak again with Massequoi, access to Kalon and the ambush group might open up once more.

So a day later I travelled back up the ambush road with Allieu, heading towards the diamond-rich Kono district, which borders Liberia. Word had it that Superman was in Kono, and I hoped that I could also find Massequoi en route.

As we began the long journey the dynamic in our jeep, a red four-wheel-drive Raider, was already uncomfortable. Our driver, Twin, was irritating, cocksure and clumsy. A Freetown roughneck in his early twenties, he came on hire with the vehicle. At first I tried to like him, and moreover thought he could be useful. His twin brother had been killed a few years before when fighting as a member of the army coup loyalists allied with the RUF. Twin's slum upbringing, lack of education and latent criminality suggesting ideal rebel fodder, he himself had been wounded in the neck and shoulder by an RPG while in action alongside the rebels. He knew the rebels, he knew the bush, he knew the roads, he knew blood: he knew the kind of things I liked a driver to know. And his twin brother was dead, which I hoped bestowed him with an energy that would serve us well. Unfortunately, he was totally useless . . . and a loquacious braggart and liar to boot.

Allieu was sitting in the back of the vehicle and I could sense that as the older, wiser man, he was waiting for the moment to assert himself over Twin, but until it arrived he had to defer to the scars on Twin's neck. Meantime, we drove. We travelled through civil militia lines, then through a government army area. We passed the new UN breakwater of Kenyan troops at Rogberi. We entered the rebel zone. Kurt's vehicle flashed beside us, a smear of rusted brown. A little later the self-named Death and his men waved us on our way from their checkpoint. A few miles before Makeni, the surface of the road improved and Twin put his foot down. The sun shone from a cloudless sky. We moved faster and faster. On either side patches of jungle gave way to small, badly tilled fields and farmland left desolate by war. Allieu leaned forward to put a new tape in the stereo. I leaned back and began to doze in the heat. The speed was hypnotic.

A report like a gunshot snapped me awake. As the jeep began to slew across the road my first thought was: Ambush. But there was no follow-up fire. A tyre had blown. Twin, in the latest of his many mistakes in life, jumped on the brakes and we spun like a Catherine wheel. As we lost the road our momentum was such that our first roll was from end to end, bonnet to boot. It ripped the entire roof off like a ring-pull on a Coke can, hurling the torn metal away into the sky. The smashing impact did nothing to slow us, and the vehicle continued to somersault across a wasteland of rocks and earth. It began to disintegrate. I had been in rolling cars twice before. Each occasion was by comparison an almost leisurely experience, with the sky and ground rotating slowly above me like slides in a lecture hall. This was altogether different, impossibly fast and furious, a series of momentous impacts as light, ground and metal whipped around me in strobe, a sensation suddenly terminated by absolute darkness.

CHAPTER 11

Consciousness reappeared in a single instant of burning urgency, carrying with it the immediate awareness that my eyes and nose were stinging with fuel. I was soaked in it. Upside down and wrapped in twisted metal, a state that took my brain some time to comprehend, getting out of the vehicle appeared a slow and complex challenge. After a few seconds' struggling in my cage, unable to accept that my head was where my feet should be, I noticed that below me glowed a small area of paler shade. I crawled towards it and fell upon the earth.

Wow, I thought, standing up and feeling my body for signs of damage, incredulous at my apparent ability to walk. That was close.

There was blood all over the ground and I stared at it dumbly for a moment, confused, until I realised that it was dribbling down from my wrists and misshapen head. From my left eyebrow up to my crown, the flesh was a swollen rubber lump, totally numb, roughened by bits of grit and stone chips dug into the skin. I turned back and saw Twin, unconscious and bleeding, still trapped in the driver's seat. It was difficult to make sense of the vehicle's mangled form. Belly up, roof gone, buckled doors splayed open, the steering wheel and dashboard muddled with the back seats, the ripped tyres hanging black rags against the sky; in a hallucinatory flash the wreck shifted shape, the tangle of crushed metal becoming the broken carapace of the mantis.

I shook Twin. He moaned and opened his eyes. One of his hands was hooked, penetrated almost right through by a jagged shard of metal. The spare jerry cans of fuel which we had been carrying in the back had broken open and drenched the wreck. Fearing that the whole thing would now ignite, I apologised vacantly, tore Twin's hand free and pulled him out of the vehicle. He shrieked in a succession of short piercing jabs, then lurched suddenly to his feet and ran off for some distance, a mad doll with arms swinging and jointed in all the wrong places. Stumbling, he fell to the ground and crawled towards a tree where he finally halted, panting and immobile.

Throughout all this I had seen no sign of Allieu. Locating him inside the vehicle seemed part of a mystifying test of logic in which I had to reconstruct the jeep from its new form into its original shape in order to work out where he might be. Very slowly, concentrating as deeply as I could, I concluded that his absence could mean only that he was elsewhere. Circling the wreck, I finally saw him, lying among the scrub on a patch of gravel. He was motionless, stretched out with his legs straight and arms by his sides. His T-shirt and frayed shorts were not even rucked. It seemed as if he had merely lain down for a sleep.

I began running towards him but the horizon began to wobble so I slowed to walk. There was a small boy calling somewhere – 'Allieu, Allieu' – full of concern and fear for a friend who has been hurt in an adventure that has suddenly spiralled out of control. 'Hey, come on, Allieu, we've got to get out of here.' The voice was mine. Allieu never moved. I bent over him. He had no pulse and was not breathing, though blood and froth were running from his lips. His eyes were wide open.

As soon as I knelt to resuscitate him the childhood vision disappeared. I was no longer looking at a friend but at a young West African male with a rapacious lifestyle who came from a city with a climbing HIV rate. His blood was bright scarlet. The moment lasted only a second before probability and necessity, the governing principles of life at base level, kicked in through the concussion to make the decision for me: I could hardly leave him to certain death for fear of possible infection. But as kisses go, I will not forget that one. Mouth-to-mouth resuscitation is not a simple or clean affair. It was exhausting and my mouth ended up slick with Allieu's blood.

As I worked on him between twenty and thirty people appeared from the bush and nearby fields, some of them armed with Kalashnikovs and pangas, others carrying hoes and rakes.

'Help us,' I mumbled.

Instead, they began to rob us, clustering around the upturned car carcass, running to and fro, sweeping up our scattered possessions: the food and supplies we had carried for the venture which now lay tumbled in a wide arc around the jeep. There were two exceptions. I do not recall their faces as I do not think I ever looked at them, but the hands of a man and a woman sometimes appeared in my peripheral vision to check Allieu's pulse.

Life clawed its way weakly back into Allieu's body, signified by the reappearance of a racing heartbeat and ragged breathing.

'Got you, you're back,' I heard myself say, triumphant, angry. 'You're not going to fucking die on me.'

But the signs never lasted more than a minute or so before fading again, a stuttering engine requiring continual restart. In a moment when he appeared to be breathing unaided I took a slow-motion stagger through the looters in search of my sat-phone, my brain still sluggish but extremely clear, trains of thought pooling with the slow definition of molten wax. The sky kept changing shade, as if being filmed through constantly shifting apertures. I knew that I had to get a call out quickly if there was to be any chance of saving Allieu. But the situation was deteriorating. The looters' preoccupation with our belongings was diminishing with the available spoils, and as they turned their attention to us I saw among them two men, both armed with machetes, who stood aside from the pack, sizing us up with cold, predatory appraisal as if considering finishing what the crash had not.

I found my rucksack, hidden by chance from the crowd under the jeep's severed roof. Almost everything inside it was smashed: my camera in pieces, even my supply of biros reduced to piles of shattered plastic by the crash impact. But somehow the sat-phone was still intact.

Between bouts of renewed resuscitation, spitting Allieu's blood and saliva out of my mouth, I rang the UN headquarters in Freetown, gave them my approximate position and requested assistance. Unconvinced that any aid would arrive in time from that quarter, I then called Jibrl Massequoi in Makeni, a short distance up the road. A voice I did not recognise took my call for help. Our brief conversation afforded a precious shield from the growing attention of the crowd.

'That was Massequoi,' I lied loudly, hoping that they might think twice about harming us now the rebel leadership was involved. 'RUF. He's coming. RUF. Understand?' The words checked them and they loitered in a sullen press, silent and staring as I continued tending to Allieu.

Minutes later, an RUF jeep arrived. Looking up at our unlikely saviours, seeing the rebels jumping down from the vehicle's sides and the driver's door open, I felt the dim burn of relief. Yet the thin figure that stepped out choked the breath in my throat. Radio in one hand, pistol in the other, aviator shades hiding his eyes from the world, the commander who walked up to me was the one I sought for my friends' deaths, not to save my own life: Colonel Morris Kalon.

After a show-stopping second we had a short burst of dialogue.

'Do the UN know you are here?' he asked, staring over my shoulder into the distance.

'Yes, I've called them,' I replied.

He barked a few words towards the crowd, who began to disperse, and then at his men, who bundled the three of us into the rear of their vehicle. Squashed in a tangle of bloody limbs, unsure if Allieu was even still alive, I continued with the resuscitation, my attention strangely distracted by the callused soles of a rebel's feet, hardened by a lifetime in the bush, which now rested casually on Allieu's shoulders. Lacking any apparent medical aid of their own or unwilling to get further involved, after a short ride the RUF disgorged us at the gates of the Nigerian base in Makeni, a procedure as simple as rolling us out of their jeep and spinning away as we lay in the dust.

A group of Nigerian soldiers carried us through the gates to an open earthen yard. They scarcely looked at Allieu before placing him to one side on a stretcher in a shaded, three-walled shack. I lurched over and started working on him once more, between railing and raging at the watching soldiers.

'Don't just stand there, get him a fucking doctor. Get him some oxygen. A drip. Anything. The guy's gonna die. Jesus Christ. Help me.'

There were five of them and they moved not an inch, but stood motionless in a row looking down upon me, their eyes blank, faces devoid of any discernible expression. What I saw in those placid brown pools was a listless over-familiarity with death and it enraged me. Fuck you all, I thought, gobbing more of Allieu's blood from my mouth in preparation for the next breath into him; fuck your awful continent where children's deaths are so commonplace as to be boring; fuck your mutilations and your mumbo-jumbo and your jungle and your disease and your poverty and your heat and your hunger. Fuck your endless reasons to die. Would that I could defy them all and save at least this one man's life.

Then one of them bent down wordlessly and stayed my arm. It was a profoundly human gesture, full of grace and compassion, and I stopped what I was doing and accepted its message, the madness leaving me in fleeing spirit. I closed Allieu's eyes and folded his hands across his chest. As one the soldiers sighed. 'Yes,' one murmured. I looked up. 'I am sorry,' each said quietly in turn.

I stood up. They put their hands on my shoulders and shook me, gently and persistently, with a soft incantation of a low, deep, repeated, 'Hey, hey, hey, hey,' a sound loaded with the deep understanding of sorrow, the echoed communication of the universal nature of death and loss. A huge wave of emotion gathered in my chest, forcing me to gulp. For a second I thought I was going to burst into tears. All I had wanted to do was say goodbye to my friends. Now another was dead. This cursed place was without mercy. The moment passed.

I leaned down and held one of Allieu's hands for a while, resting my other palm first on his chest, then on his forehead. His skin was just beginning to cool. He looked like a little boy again: a thin, brown wisp in his raggedy shorts and T-shirt. A dead African boy who had survived much and had just had what little he possessed taken from him by coming down the road with me for sixty dollars a day. 'Goodbye, Allieu,' I said, and walked away.

Soon the Nigerians were driving Twin and me up the road through the jungle to the Magburaka camp, where there were at least some medical facilities: iodine and suture kits. Once we arrived Lieutenant Tanku appeared among the gaggle of troops around us.

'There is some bad magic on that road,' he whispered. 'My men have gone to the vehicle and seen it. They cannot believe you could still be walking.'

Though it was not quite the moment to talk of any more magic, I was nevertheless grateful for his presence. I needed someone I knew. By contrast, Twin was a burden. He howled as the soldiers poured iodine into his lacerations and twisted so much as they tried to stitch his wounds that he had to be pinned down. Even given his bone breaks and the absence of anaesthetic, it seemed he had no pain threshold at all.

I called Corinne on the sat-phone. Allieu had a few extended family members left alive whom she knew, and I asked her to break the news to them. I recounted the abbreviated story of the crash, including the fact that I had given Allieu mouth-to-mouth.

'You what?' She sounded stunned. 'Oh my God, Anthony . . .'

It was not what I needed to hear. It was the first time that I had ever discerned fear in Corinne; and it was fear for me.

Eventually an officer explained that a UN helicopter was on its way to evacuate us to the capital, where the nearest fully equipped hospital was located. He gave me a cup of coffee and a biscuit, and I passed out untidily while throwing up in the soldiers' latrines. As the dirty ground swung up to smack me in the face the overwhelming sensation was one of release. There are times when the arms of oblivion are the sweetest going.

Covered in flies, blood and vomit, I awoke on a stretcher on the fuselage floor of a moving helicopter. The pressing weight against my shoulder turned out to be that of Allieu's body, which had been squashed in beside me. There was not a medic in sight, but someone had stuffed cotton wool in his mouth, ears and nose to prevent him leaking blood.

I did not know whether the cotton wool was standard procedure, but I was still thinking about the reasons behind it that night as I lay alone in a room in the UN-administered hospital in Freetown. Still in that emotionless shock zone, I had been X-rayed, had had my wrists dressed and had been doctored and cared for by the Jordanian UN medical staff, fussed over by Corinne and, under different circumstances, might have at least relaxed into surfing the survivor's wave. Instead, I was recalling the taste of Allieu's blood in my mouth. In the dim light and now in solitude, I was beset by both fear and extreme calm. I thought I would die of AIDS for sure, even though logic and probability were in my favour. My certainty came from acknowledging the power on that road. As I understood it that night, whatever cruel hunger in Sierra Leone had taken Myles, then Miguel and Kurt, and now Allieu, it was not going to let me escape with concussion, bruising and a few cuts. That I had initially survived the crash was incidental. That the crash had occurred in the first place, and that I had tried and failed to save Allieu, seemed too perverse a combination to suggest anything other than a grapple with a curse. My bloody kiss of life must now complete the cycle by becoming the embrace of my own death. I had been saved just so I could die. Indeed, the only way in which the story would not make sense was if I were to live.

It kills us all, I thought. Quickly or slowly, that road kills us all. It took a long time to get to sleep, staring at the roulette-wheel turn of the fan.

Waking from a fitful doze a couple of days later, I saw a beautiful Sierra Leonean nurse staring curiously down at me.

'You look like Mr Jesus,' she informed me, smiling, pleased to have matched the white skin and long blond hair on the puffy, bruised head before her with the illustrations in her Sunday school Bible.

Before I could think of an encouraging reply, Corinne breezed into the room behind her, an enthused expression on her face.

'Hey, you OK?' she asked. 'Look, I've got some good news. I told the Jordanian doctors about the scene on the road, with Allieu and everything, and they've done some tests on his body. It's clear. He's not HIV. You're OK. They say you should get another check when you get home but basically it seems you're gonna be OK.'

Life has few such moments, when you lie back, the concerns of the world expunged temporarily from the windows of your mind, allowing you to bathe in transient but absolute peace. This was one of them. It was all but perfect. Just one thing still niggled: I had less than forty-eight hours to get back up the road to the ambush site in time for the anniversary of Kurt's death.

I checked out of the hospital the next morning, just in time to see Allieu lowered into his narrow, irregular grave in a cramped cemetery at the edge of Freetown. In the absence of any immediate family, his funeral seemed a rushed affair, barren of even a single tear, and the gravediggers shovelled the earth back upon him quickly, as if trying to feed a greedy mouth. He did not even have a coffin, let alone a headstone. But his one-time glory days as a journalist years before had struck a chord within the city's local community of reporters. Freetown's *Unity Now* newspaper bore the front-page headline 'Another Worthy Son Bites the Dust' in tribute to him. I felt sure it would have appealed to his sense of irony.

As I watched the lumpy orange soil cover his face, the words seemed a little closer to the truth than was comfortable, though – empty of consolation, and I wondered to what extent his death lay on my ledger. Furthermore, I could not help but suppose, given the funeral's chicken-run nature, that the money I had given one of his friends to pay for the ceremony would instead be used to fund a protracted series of drinking and whoring sprees in the taverns of Man o' War Bay. Maybe Allieu would have wanted it that way.

Next morning, with dawn barely a glimmer over the wrinkled, wakening city, I got into a jeep and headed back to the jungle, towards Kontah. Three hundred and sixty-five days earlier, Kurt had just finished writing the introduction to his final story, and would have been pacing around impatiently, waiting for the others to wake up and get ready for the same journey.

Though my intuition discerned not a squeak of malice in the day ahead and I fancied that the runes once more read in my favour, just in case I had misread the signs I took along some heavyweight back-up: two Italian priests.

Kurt had always claimed godlessness. We had argued over the question frequently in the Drenica Valley. You can have quite a sharp theological discussion in the smoke of torched villages. One day we got into a particularly heated debate over the existence of the soul. On a losing wicket, I suggested that finding an upturned tortoise in the desert was the acid test to prove the spirit's presence. I had gleaned the concept from *Blade Runner*, in which it had been utilised as a test during interrogations to ascertain if individuals were human or advanced android replicants, and I was keen to use it on Kurt. In the film, if the subject elected to walk past the tortoise, it proved they were a replicant, fit for immediate liquidation. However, if they chose to stop and right the tortoise, giving it a chance to live, their response suggested they were human, governed by such illogical reactions as compassion. To my mind, that further implied the presence, with a stretch of the imagination, of a benevolent spirit.

Kurt scoffed loudly in response. 'If I found a tortoise in the desert, I would cut its head off, drink its blood and eat its guts to survive. And that's what most people in the world would do,' he raved, delighted to disprove the theory so easily.

Yet, at that precise moment, we rounded a bend and there in front of us in the middle of the road, a lugubrious manifestation of divine humour, was a tortoise. Kurt, driving like a maniac as usual, almost rolled the Land-Rover in trying to miss it. I nearly died laughing.

'It's God, Kurt. You've just seen God!' I spluttered, goading him.

He was so vexed he could barely speak. 'If God exists, you'd probably find he was an ant' was his eventual retort.

It was not for Kurt that I took the priests, though. I took them for Miguel . . . and for myself. My relationship with Kurt was the dominating influence which had driven me back to Sierra Leone, and it eclipsed my feelings concerning Miguel most, but not all, of the time. Yet I had been close to him, too, and when I thought of him I did so with great clarity and strength of sentiment. He was a devout Catholic, and I knew he would have wanted a priest at the ambush site. As it was, he got two.

As for myself, I have lived both with and without God. Faith and belief are as different seas as loyalty and conviction, and you can drown in either; just as you can die of thirst in a desert between. Yet I like hanging out with priests from time to time, so long as they are no strangers to the wrath of God and the malice of heaven. The search for the soul seems a voyage which, by its very nature, suggests the presence of an overarching force. If faith were an opinion, perhaps I could express it better. Moreover, that day, of all days, I did not wish merely to defy the malice of the ambush road by returning there to eulogise the lives of the friends it had stolen. I wanted to smash it. Short of calling in a massed napalm strike, bringing men of God to the scene seemed the best way to achieve that.

Fathers John Ceresoli and Graziano Rossato were good company. From the Order of Francis Xavier, between them they had been in Sierra Leone for a total of thirty-five years. They were tough men; they had to be. Corinne had found them for me. I had asked the British unit in Freetown if their padre could accompany me, but they would not go near the place. The Italians were a much better option anyway: in their time they had been prisoners of the RUF, they were familiar with danger and they had seen a lot of men die. Father Ceresoli had spent some years in Glasgow before coming to Africa, so spoke English, when he had a moment between cigarettes, with a Scottish–Italian accent, which somehow enhanced his credentials.

Father Rossato had known Miguel personally. During heavy fighting three years earlier the priest had sought sanctuary from the rebels in a church in Makeni. Nigerian forces were pushing the RUF out of Freetown and into the hinterland. As they advanced towards Makeni, causing the rebels to flee, Rossato had seen a tall, skinny figure approach the church surrounded by a clapping, singing crowd. It was Miguel: he had moved ahead of the advancing troops to film the action. He stayed in the church for four days with Rossato. They had taken mass together.

We arrived at the ambush site around midday and I showed the priests around. 'Jesus, Mary and Joseph,' Father Ceresoli exclaimed on seeing the scores of bullet casings which still littered the scene.

'Yeah,' I contributed.

As Miguel's jeep had long ago been towed away to be cannibalised for spares, we performed our small blessing by the charred Mercedes. The ambush had occurred around twelve-thirty, so we made sure we began before and finished afterwards. Somewhere in those minutes, as we stood there, time drew a perfect year-circle around the deaths of Kurt and Miguel. We were alone throughout, aside from one lopsided truck, piled with civilians and doubtless a few rebels, which clattered past. A man leaned out from his precarious perch clinging to the side and waved at us.

'Happy Christmas,' he shouted at the priests.

I smiled, and chose to believe that that was the exact moment when the shooting had started. It was the best I could do. For all I knew, the guy had been part of the ambush group.

Miguel died with 'God' as his last word. As the gunfire shattered his windscreen and began to sieve the jeep, knocking the RPG man dead off the back, his vehicle stopped, immobilised. Ahead he could see Kurt's Mercedes, repeatedly hit but still moving, and the first rebels emerging, shooting diagonally in front of him. An RPG round exploded near by. He opened his arms and slammed his hands down on the steering wheel and exclaimed, 'My God!' Beside him the SLA officer, Lieutenant Saquee, leapt out of the passenger door, ducking round to take cover at the back of the vehicle. Miguel never made it that far. He was hit by several rounds either as he got out or a second later. Before breaking for the bush, Saquee saw him go down. Peeping through foliage a minute later, Saquee saw a group of rebels clustered around the jeep, ransacking it, tearing at packets of food they had looted from the boot. Miguel lay dead and ignored beside the vehicle. Our fears were unjustified: he had not been wounded, then later killed. He had died within seconds of the ambush being initiated.

Saquee, by now a captain, was sitting in the officers' mess at Bengwema, a military camp just outside Freetown, as he told me of Miguel's last moments. He was concluding a training course run there by the British troops, who were revamping the government army as a back-up measure should the UN's peace process fail. Moving around Freetown and travelling back to bases in the jungle, in the days after the ceremony with the priests, I tracked down many of the soldiers involved in the fighting on the day of the ambush, and the same energy I had felt before Allieu stepped on the mantis returned. Kurt's driver Abdul; Captain Dumbaya; the soldier who had driven the journalists' bodies back from Rogberi Junction; the first man to see Mark step wounded from the bush. I found them all.

In Freetown, Colonel Bangura told me that a day after the ambush he had finally succeeded in advancing up the road as far as Lunsar. He held it for twenty-four hours before his men were pushed out. They fought their way back in a few days later and defended it for a week before infighting with the Westside Boys reduced their organisation to shreds. The RUF then rolled them all the way back south of Rogberi. A last subsequent advance then drove back the rebels, this time as far as Kontah, where the lines solidified with the ceasefire.

As for the UN, they were unwilling or unable to tell me the identities of the eight bodies whose discovery had first drawn Kurt to Rogberi that day, beyond confirming that they were indeed peacekeepers killed by the RUF. I was directed first to the UN press officer in Freetown, who introduced me to a UN investigations officer, who said he would help, but then referred me back to the press officer to get in touch with the UN senior administration officer for permission to ask the UN civilian police commissioner for advice, but he was not in. Privately, some officials told me that the UN, for all its bureaucracy, did not have accurate records of the precise numbers or identities of their soldiers in Sierra Leone. So those men who died at Rogberi Junction serving under the UN flag so far from their homes remain anonymous.

Of the rebels, Dennis Mingo, 'Superman', was missing in action, presumed dead. I checked with every source I knew: no one had seen him for three months, since he led a cross-border raid into Guinea. It was not the first time that he had been reported missing in action, but it seemed likely to be the last.

I never did manage to extract a confession from a member of the ambush group. It still preys on my mind, marked as unfinished business. Maybe I had danced among them in Makeni. Maybe scar-face Mack or Commander Bad-eyes at Kontah had pulled the triggers on my friends. Maybe Morris Kalon, my unlikely rescuer, had commanded the ambush group himself, as many suggested. Maybe I will go back some day and meet him again, and ask him a few more questions. It could be quite a wait. Kalon is currently in Pademba Jail on war crimes charges.

Maybe I failed in the task I set myself. Perhaps defeat was inevitable. The only victory that would have counted, indeed the one in many ways I had sought, was to turn back time and alter destiny, get Kurt to drive a little faster down the road, or a little slower, delay or warn or stop him, bring them both back alive, get the world back on its tracks again. And what if I had been there at Rogberi that day? Would I have tried to veto the plan? I will never know because I was not there. I never saw what they saw. It was their call.

But that is how Kurt died. He went up one part of the road to see if the UN were going to identify their dead. They did not then and still have not now. He went up the next part of the road to see some action, chasing his instinct in a moment of professional curiosity, passion and delight. Miguel followed him, troubled, thoughtful. They both took a chance; they were men who were uniquely gifted in taking chances and winning. But that day they were killed. It was not an otherwise significant day. It was a small, confused and bloody mêlée that was part of wider action. It was a moment in a war, a speck of dust among the shadows of history, a mite of spilled blood beneath the clouds of the dark continent and the void of the world's infinite noire. Nevertheless, it had taken our best.

I left Sierra Leone at the end of May. My new driver tried to rip me off at the landing strip for a last few dollars, and made himself just enough of a pain in the arse to get what he wanted.

'I'm going to brutalise you when I come back, Foday,' I told him, smiling, as I handed over the money.

'Yes, Mr Anthony, when you come back, you brutalise me,' he replied wisely, with eyes that said: 'You're talking of tomorrows but I live day to day and cash in hand now is better than the uncertainty of the future, so fuck you.'

It was raining as I walked towards the plane. As the heavy, meteoritic drops impacted on the dry ground with such force that they momentarily puffed up the dust, I thought back to when I had first met Kurt in Sarajevo. I thought of the countless adventures we had together. The memories were bright coals beneath the grey ash of the day. Despite everything, I felt unable truly to believe that he was dead. I could neither accept that I would never again share with him that quintessentially brilliant moment of driving up a silent dawn road into the unknown, nor acknowledge the abject imperfection proved by the world in its killing of him, nor comply with it. But even without my assent, the sense of loss was massive.

Yet, deep within me as I got on the plane, too far down and ethereal to sense with certainty but too persistent to ignore, clawed an awareness that somewhere out there in the jungle, between the crunch of the mantis, the bang of a tyre and the shout of 'Happy Christmas', just for a second my shriek into the infinite received a response. I guess that is as much of a goodbye as I will ever get.

CHAPTER 12

France, Summer 2001

For much of the summer that followed I withdrew into myself; rolling from the treadmill of war into contemplative recuperation. I had an ideal sanctuary: a small, three-room building in southern France, squat and unapologetic, with thick stone walls and tiled roof, it sat on the banks of a river, wide, deep and fish-filled. The French called it a *'maizet'*, but the term seemed a bit too grandiose. It was more of a converted stable. Once owned by my stepfather, the place had been an infrequent family haunt which I had more often visited alone. Life there was a gentle drift of siesta, eating, drinking and fishing, interrupted by the odd bout of writing on the rare occasions when the mood was upon me. It offered a stillness similar to the one I had known in the woods and fields around my mother's house. When my stepfather had put the cottage up for sale, around the time of his separation from my mother, I had bought it, quick to seize this outpost of peace before it fell into the hands of another.

Lying just beyond the furthest reach of the nearby village, by day it underwent a rude assault of heat, colour and noise. Shortly after each dawn the cicadas would start to tune up, their disparate zings and trills merging in minutes to create a polyphonic throb of sound that continued unabated until nightfall. Kingfishers blazed up and down the river in perpetual relay, azure stars above the limpid depths. The hatches of different insects, which so precisely marked each season, reached a high point in late summer, when the banks became a droning thoroughfare of winged things, pursued by damsel and dragonflies which scissor-slipped through the airspace in hunting cuts of electric blue and green.

Time itself became blurred beneath the sun, the knell to each hour ringing over a ten-minute period from contradictory church bell-towers along the valley, hammers stretching in the heat of high summer so that their peal became vibrato and tired, as if even they, the guardians of the passing hours, would rather have been sleeping.

As the sun dipped, its light becoming golden and warm, the cast of noisy creatures changed, the cicadas halting as one and handing over to the raucous croaks of frogs, blinking, well muscled and livid green, and, on occasion, the gentle melodies of nightingales. Some evenings the huge silhouette of an eagle owl swooped from the rocky outcrop behind the building in silent crepuscular hunt. The idleness of my days ended at this point, the creep of darkness signifying the moment for concentration and focus: it was time to fish. Checking the rod, line, bait and boat, I rowed out to moor on a flood-felled tree whose branches emerged from the waters in a spot haunted by huge wild carp. Wary of the sunshine and lazy in the heat, at night they would lose their caution and gain their appetite. They were true monsters, with some reaching over sixty pounds, the weight of small pigs. Long-flanked and broad-tailed, their enormous scales seemed to have been burnished by a celestial smith and in fight they carried the full power of the river.

They had every advantage over me. Though the river was expansive, and in places more than twenty feet deep, it was filled with weed beds, submerged timber and hidden snags, obstacles known in their finest detail to the fish, who had little trouble in repeatedly breaking my line. And they seemed to time the onset of their feeding hours to the moment when I had drunk the first half-bottle of wine, so that the sudden disappearance of my glowing float would catch me oil-necked, dreamy and unawares, the force of my late and extravagant strike spilling the glass and flipping me untidily into the back of the boat, on to the bait box and cigarettes as line, float and hook shot up from the water to wreath around my head. Untangling myself, ever surprised, I would cast again, often fishing through until dawn, escaping with the night and water, the prospect of just one victory each evening over those mighty fish enough for me to defy sleep.

In this place, indulging in the rare, short era of quiet introspection that followed my return from Sierra Leone, the usual build-up of angst that afflicted me in the absence of war assignments was temporarily but totally allayed. Gone too were the heroin cravings. The drug remained in place as a fall-back position; there had been no final farewell to it. So newly ashore, I was not about to scupper the ship. But after the intense and deliberate relapse I had put myself through in London with Jago, and all that had followed in Sierra Leone, it seemed as though I had walked out on the relationship for a time at least.

Kurt's killing had impacted heavily upon its lure in a fashion very different to that I would have anticipated. He seemed as generous a benefactor in death as he had been in life. I felt strong, an unwitting inheritor, aware of my fortune through my loss.

Core's past contributions in leading me to this state of breakout were impossible to dismiss. Its programme had achieved exactly what it had set out to do with me, untangling the mental patterns of my drug use and replacing them with enough mid-ground space in which to work out whether I wanted to continue life with or without a habit. Kurt's death seemed to have tipped the scales in favour of the latter.

Alternatively, perhaps a mighty whack on the head and a mouthful of African blood and dust were just what I had needed at the point when Core's subliminal ministrations had ended. Either way, I was not doing smack for the time being and regarded the future with wary neutrality, unsure when the habit fever might next run gibbering back in from the wings, but happy enough to enjoy the present.

So, between the occasional short Balkan assignment and visits from a girlfriend, I slept and fished, sinking into an enclosed and private bliss, the days drifting languid and indefinable from one to the next, on into early September, quite unaware that the world was about to judder on its axis.

The first tremor arrived for me a day earlier than it did for most people. On 10 September my phone rang. I was standing beside the door of the cottage, looking at the river, plotting the night's fishing. It was late morning and I stared sulkily ahead, frustrated by the unusual and unwanted interruption from the outside world, tempted to leave the call unanswered, finally reaching for it with perplexed irritation.

'Someone's blown up Masood,' the boss informed me. 'Reports say he's alive but badly injured. He could be dead, though. Can you write a quick profile on him?'

My resentment at having to write anything in France was overshadowed by immediate surprise. Masood hit? Maybe dead? Were it not for the fact of Kurt's death, I could scarcely have believed the news, for I had regarded Masood as another immortal. And the halcyon vision of water and reed before me blurred, replaced by a wilderness of desert sand and rock, the bumping movement of a jeep, and the nodding head of the warlord whose very name translated as 'Lucky'; a man destined to be flawed and thwarted by victory, magnificent and enduring in defeat.

A visit to Ahmed Shah Masood, a.k.a. the Lion of Panjshir, was an essential part of any reporter's itinerary in Afghanistan. No trip to the country could be thought complete without seeing him: he encapsulated the spirit of the Afghan people and their war like no other, and to ignore him would have been worse than visiting Cuba in '56 and turning down an interview with Che. Deeply charismatic, his pakul cap cocked jauntily to one side of his head, five perfectly symmetrical worry lines banded across his forehead, he carried about him the intangible, shining aura of an enlightened Brahman. As a guerrilla commander, his experience was probably unrivalled throughout the world: in nearly a quarter of a century of combat Masood had fought the Soviets, the Afghan army, rival mujahedin forces, Pakistani advisers, the Taliban and al Qaeda.

Born in the Panjshir Valley in north-eastern Afghanistan, he was the son of an army colonel, and for a time was educated at the French college in Kabul. The Afghan king was deposed and exiled while he was still a student, and two years later, in his first action, Masood had led a localised Islamic revolt against the new authorities. It had been bloodily crushed and Masood escaped to Pakistan with a bullet wound to the leg.

Returning to Afghanistan, he battled with the Soviets throughout their ten-year occupation of his country and gained the reputation for being the most sophisticated of any mujahedin commander. Studying Mao Tse-tung's guerrilla doctrines, he expanded his strategy through a series of phases, while surviving ten successive Soviet offensives against his valley bases. In the wake of the last, as the Russians again retreated, leaving their burning tanks and dead behind them, a Russian general labelled Masood 'unbeatable'.

Two years after the Soviet withdrawal, Masood led his forces into Kabul, far ahead of other mujahedin groups moving upon the city, overthrowing the communist President Najibullah. It was the high point of his career as a commander, but was short-lived. Appointed Minister of Defence, he spent the next four years outnumbered and outgunned, defending the city against a variety of hostile alliances, as the country he had fought to liberate consumed itself in civil war, its capital reduced to ruination. Whatever his personal charm, his men brought little to Kabul but fear, robbery and murder. Finally, in 1996, the bribed defection of mujahedin units holding a key pass allowed the Taliban to seize the city.

From then on Masood's fortunes began to slide further. Though remaining a superb guerrilla commander who inflicted massive casualties on the Taliban, repeated betrayals cost him dearly, and by 2001 his coalition force, the Northern Alliance, was hanging on to little more than 10 per cent of Afghanistan, forgotten heroes of the Cold War left to battle on alone against the numerically superior and better-equipped Talibs. Watching him wage war was akin to watching a chess master defend his king with only two knights and a bishop against a clumsy enemy with permanently replenished pieces: strategically limited, he was tactically brilliant.

However, Masood's assets in command were also his flaws. Wary of incompetence and treachery, he was reluctant to delegate tasks outside the small circle of his most trusted Panjshiri commanders, and so he assumed a huge burden of responsibility for the day-to-day running of the war, unnecessary details which both exhausted him and led to accusations of nepotism. I had seen examples first hand. Only a year before I had been staying as the guest of a warlord near the northern front when a mujahedin commander turned up, his face pale and dazzled with the legacy of leading the previous night's failed raid. Launched on his own initiative against a Taliban stronghold, without orders from above, it had been a minor but costly disaster. Sitting beside me in the opulent, carpet-strewn residence of my host, the commander fiddled despairingly with a faulty satellite-phone, steeling himself for the moment when he would make his report to Masood. Ornate pheasants strutted in the rose-filled garden outside, their vulgar pomp at odds with the commander's ashen skin and trembling fingers, and the sound of distant shellfire. Finally, he made a connection and stumbled through his account of the debacle. Masood, on the other end of the line, was clearly enraged. I could not help but grin sympathetically as his furious voice, almost comic in its wrath, reached scratchily into the room from the earpiece. The hapless commander looked completely crushed. That he was having to account to Masood for his actions, which however personally disastrous were no more than a tiny footnote to the war's bigger picture, said much about Masood's micromanagement of the battlefield.

Two days later I had taken a tour of the front with Masood himself, in what was to be the last of several meetings I had with him over the years. Though still as charismatic as ever, he appeared tired, enervated, and slipped in and out of sleep in the passenger seat as we drove, his lolling head threatening to crash into the door of the vehicle on numerous occasions as the vehicle bounced over the rough, arid terrain, but never quite doing so. During periods of consciousness he related snippets from his life at war, or talked about the future of the fighting ahead. By his own admission, he suffered from numerous demons.

'I have had so many "worst" moments in my life that I can't remember *the* worst,' he said bleakly. 'Also regrets. I have many regrets: regrets for things I have or have not done in the war; regrets that when I had Kabul I could not do better for the people; regrets that the system they lived under was so corrupt. Who would like to spend their whole life constantly fighting? I do so because I am without choice.'

There had been a thin ray of optimism during that day, though. The Taliban were already under limited sanctions for refusing to hand over Osama bin Laden, wanted at that point for the bombings of two American embassies in East Africa. And in the wake of the suicide attack on an American battleship off Yemen in another al Qaeda operation a month earlier, the CIA and Pentagon were considering rearming Masood to pressurise the Taliban. Masood realised that his fortunes may be about to reinflate as international opprobrium towards bin Laden and his Taliban hosts grew. All he had to do was hold out.

However, as the vehicle had continued to pitch and bounce over the trackless waste, I mentioned the failed raid of two nights earlier and Masood's mood plunged once more.

'He just went and attacked without even asking us at headquarters,' he erupted, still angry with his unfortunate junior commander, 'then called the next day to say he had been driven back and lost twelve men. Now his fighters have low morale and we have a problem.'

The question of cohesion was always his most sensitive issue. Masood's challenge in maintaining a unified force of diverse ethnicities was the same as that of a potter attempting to craft a tall vase from several different clays: it kept crumbling. Yet, without him, the Northern Alliance had no chance of survival. His inspiration and fighting abilities were unmatched. Should he die, then no obstacle would remain to halt the Taliban from securing the whole of Afghanistan, right up to the borders of Central Asia.

So now the news of his wounding in an assassination attempt, apparently conducted by two suicide attackers posing as journalists, carried with it an ominous implication. Even if Masood survived, his very absence from the field might lead the Northern Alliance to fall apart. Next day, as I mused on the future, the phone rang once more. This time it was my mother.

'Ant, they're saying on the radio that a plane has just crashed into the Twin Towers,' she told me, sounding a little uncertain.

'Huh? A plane? It's probably nothing, Mum: some businessman in a Cessna had a heart attack or something. I think it's happened before.'

A few minutes later she called back. 'Ant, another plane has crashed into the Twin Towers. They're not Cessnas. They're passenger jets. It's an attack.'

I did not rush back to England immediately. It was obvious that for some days, at least, all eyes would be on New York. A friend of mine, Shay, who coincidentally was also taking a break in France, pitched up at the cottage the next evening with his girlfriend to celebrate my birthday. A Dubliner in his early forties, whose tousled, corkscrew hair, stubbled jaw line and revolutionary specs suggested something of the bomb-maker, he was actually a photographer with whom I had worked on several Afghan jaunts, so we had much to talk about that evening. We invited some local friends over, lit a fire and had a barbecue. We drank our wine and were happy enough. The glowing flames sent sparks spinning into the starlit sky and from the river came the sound of the frogs and the splash of fish. But the scene was already losing its thrall, the colours draining, the noises becoming discordant. The itch was back, the hunger, my mind already moving away from France, heading to the peaks and valleys of Afghanistan, where so surely America's rage would fall.

CHAPTER 13

Afghanistan, September 2001

The blacks flags of mourning were still raised in Khwaja Bahauddin, stirring weakly in the hot, dust-filled breeze more than two weeks after Masood's death. Pictures of his face adorned every vehicle and an atmosphere of sullen anger lingered throughout the town. Turbaned, bearded warriors idled in the earthen streets, waiting for orders from their war captains, Kalashnikovs slung over their shoulders. The occasional helicopter sped overhead. Among the scabby bazaar stalls word of vengeance was traded along with merchants' wares. And in the far distance came the irregular murmur of shellfire. France was a very remote, two-week-old memory.

It was eventually revealed that Masood had been killed instantly by the suicide attack, but his death had been kept secret for a time by other Northern Alliance leaders, fearful that their demoralised soldiery would desert to the Taliban should word of his demise escape. The assassination had been carefully planned and conducted with chilling patience. Though the identity of his killers was still unknown, by the time Shay and I arrived in Khwaja Bahauddin, a frontier town on the banks of the Amudaraya in the far north of Afghanistan, site of both a Northern Alliance headquarters and Masood's killing, documents the killers had left behind lit a trail back to London. Both assassins were believed to be British residents of Moroccan origin who had travelled to Afghanistan on Belgian passports. Disguised as journalists from the start, they had flown from Britain to Pakistan in August, crossed the border and moved to Kabul on visas issued by the Taliban. In the capital they had picked up a television camera and battery pack with explosives hidden inside. Two weeks later they had crossed a stagnant stretch of the front line and moved to the Panjshir Valley, the area controlled by Masood's men. Missing the chance to interview him there, they had followed Masood north to Khwaja Bahauddin and again pressed for an interview. Masood finally agreed to meet the men over breakfast on 9 September, but cancelled the rendezvous at the last minute as he had been up for most of the night briefing commanders. However, as he left his headquarters for the front line later that morning the two waiting Arabs were again brought to his attention. He knew that they had been trying to see him for some time so impulsively granted them an interview. The meeting, conducted in a reception room inside the headquarters, began in credible fashion, up to the point when Masood was asked what he would do with Osama bin Laden if he were to capture all of Afghanistan. Before he could answer, the killers detonated their bomb. Masood, the cameraman and a Northern Alliance official died immediately in the blast. The second assassin initially survived, and as bodyguards rushed to the room in the belief that their headquarters had been hit by a Taliban air strike, he fled outside, bloody and blast-blackened, shouting, 'Allahu Akbar!' He was shot dead and his body thrown to the dogs.

The ruthless efficiency, technological competence and dedication of the assassins bore all the hallmarks of al Qaeda, and the Northern Alliance were certain that Masood's killing had been undertaken on bin Laden's orders as a gift and security measure to the Taliban ahead of the attacks upon America. With Masood removed from the equation, it would be only a matter of time until the Taliban swept aside the shattered remnants of the Northern Alliance, denying the United States any toehold in the country ahead of its inevitable retributive strikes. However, the chance delays the assassins had encountered in their journey to Masood had left too little time for the Taliban to capitalise on the killing before al Qaeda's hijacked jets rammed into their targets in Washington and New York, and when word of Masood's death did finally spread among his fighters their morale had already been buoyed by the awareness that they had a new, mighty and vengeful ally: Uncle Sam.

*

I had held Afghanistan close to my heart ever since my first visit to the country five years earlier. Its appeal was not instantly obvious. With war a mature, twenty-five-year-old strangler around the country's thin neck, life for most Afghans was a subsistence battle in a year-zero world. A third of its population were refugees living abroad. The remainder had one of the lowest life expectancies on the planet. A second generation of Afghan children had grown up without education. There were barely any roads left. No bridges, running water or electricity. Healthcare was all but non-existent. Bar the export of opium, emeralds and looted archaeological artefacts, there was no economy. Almost every machine in the land, other than those designed for waging war, had fallen into disrepair, so that whatever agriculture existed was reliant on the hoe, the plough and the ox. All major irrigation systems had been destroyed and much of the country was anyway stricken by drought. Hundreds of thousands of mines laced valley, village and city alike. As an entity, Afghanistan posed the bleakest and most absolute vision of failed statehood and collapsed infrastructure. Yet, in spite of it all, there existed not another place or people among whom I preferred to work.

Garrulous, secretive, proud, humble, ridiculously oversensitive and doggedly enduring, whatever the sheer jaw-dropping poverty of their country, each Afghan remained a millionaire in contradiction and spirit. They drew part of their courage from their faith: Islam was all pervasive, governing the smallest details of each day, from social and family interaction through to a community's structure of law; and it affected young and old alike. Wizened, illiterate elders in the hills could recite the Koran word for word, having learned it by rote. And in the country's few remaining hospitals even the tiniest children, their bodies wrecked by mines, cried out to Allah for strength rather than their mothers for sustenance when the time came for the excruciating pain of changed dressings. Afghans consigned their destiny to the will of God, and expected that will to be hard. Yet many were also deeply superstitious, forever wielding some or other charm to ward off the evil eye or the depredations of a malicious djinn, last-ditch defences in an otherwise perfect fatalism.

The country's war felt much older than a quarter-century, for across the monolithic, shark-toothed mountain ranges, to the highest peaks of the Hindu Kush and the lowliest swath of southern deserts, history shrieked in sedimentary layers of crumbled fortifications and the broken dreams of ancient invaders. The current cast of fighters included in their number the scions of Alexander the Great's Macedonian pikemen, Genghis Khan and the Persian Empire, and if they battled using the tanks, mines, helicopter gunships, long-range artillery and jet aircraft gifted them by the international politics of the twentieth century, then even that modernism, so rare in the country, had its throwbacks. For the shelf life of some weapons seemed curiously reversed: hundreds of Russian armoured vehicles lay rusting on roadsides for the want of spare parts; yet many Afghans still shot game for the pot, and sometimes each other, with British muskets lovingly maintained since their capture from dead redcoats by great-grandfathers a century and a half before.

My affection for the place, based on its ravaged beauty and the stoic complexity of its people, was widely shared by other foreigners who had visited Afghanistan, but it ended abruptly at the edge of that small circle. Until September 11th, the Afghan war was the runt in the market place, overlooked in favour of fatter fare by most of the Western media. It had not always been that way. At one time the country had been the ultimate coliseum of Cold War games as the West pumped vast quantities of arms to mujahedin opposing the Russian occupation, part of a policy to fight the Soviets 'to the last Afghan'. The strategy worked, but when the Russians eventually withdrew, so too did the international audience, leaving the theatre's stage heaped with over a million dead, a plethora of competing mujahedin factions, almost limitless arms supplies, and no peace in sight.

Having taken a circuitous route from London through Germany, Kazakhstan and Tajikistan, Shay and I had crossed the northern Afghan border and reached Khwaja Bahauddin in late September, each stop during the journey marked by a debauched revelry excused by the notion that we may have been on the threshold of World War Three, so that we finally arrived ready for war equipped with a weighty train of unnecessary baggage, fistfuls of bar receipts and stupefying hangovers.

A score or so of journalists had arrived in the town before us. Most of them appeared to have allowed themselves to be corralled into a walled compound by the Northern Alliance officials, where they lived scrunched up in tiny fly tents or cramped, dormitory-type rooms, sharing horrifying, dysentery-trap loos, fretting among themselves over how best to gain permission for access to report.

'Not my scene at all, man,' Kurt's words echoed in my mind.

We moved east to Faizabad, hired a clapped-out Red Army jeep and elected to take the long overland route south through the mountains to the distant Panjshir Valley, access point to the front line outside Kabul. We left a day later.

It seemed possible that at last Afghanistan, so racked, reduced and forgotten in war, may have its fate changed by the sudden light of so much new attention, and I gulped greedily at the chance to be there, the depredations of Sierra Leone pushed aside in my memory, other than fleeting moments when I sized up Shay with the eyes of a coffin-maker, noting his weight and height while wondering how easily I could extract his blanket-rolled corpse over the mountains if it all went wrong. Easily enough, I concluded, given a sturdy mule and a long, strong rope.

We stopped remarking on the beauty of the landscape a mere half an hour after leaving Faizabad. What had begun in the fresh light of morning as a leisurely adventure in which the full breadth of sky and mountain could be appreciated had quickly turned into something else entirely, and for physical discomfort the experience was unsurpassed. Crammed into our decrepit jeep with the ferret-eyed driver, his moronic mate who spat green phlegm on the floor twice a minute and a jinxed interpreter, Wahid, I fast lost sight of the aesthetic qualities of the route. Instead, we endured the single-lane track in a series of weakening 'ughs' and 'ooophs' as each new bump jolted our bodies. At times we passed through stretches of desert wasteland and the sand filled the car like a fumigating gas, so fine in texture that it permeated our clothing inside and out, and so abundant that it began to trickle undiluted from our noses and ears.

At other moments the track clung to the edges of plunging, vertiginous ravines. Hating heights and unnerved by one near fall the driver had already put us through, I spent those moments, if on the side of the car furthest from the chasm, half hanging out of the open door in the hope that I could bale out before the vehicle tipped to oblivion; if on the other side, I leaned acutely across the gear stick until I was nearly in the driver's lap.

The route was notorious for bandits so as dusk neared we stopped in a desolate valley village. Our welcome was not inspiring. Some twenty armed mujahedin, draped in bandoliers, eyed us from a bank, apparently ready to go somewhere bad and do something worse, and from the edge of the village someone fired a rocket which exploded on a nearby slope. The driver and his mate had the fear upon them, and suggested that we should move on as we were in the middle of a tribal dispute. But it was nearly dark, we had already been on the road for ten hours, and we trusted their advice no more than their driving skills. For his part, Wahid, foisted upon us by Northern Alliance officials in Khwaja Bahauddin, seemed to have lost all power of speech and was undergoing one of his mute phases. I swore that I would fire him as soon as we reached the Panjshir. Twenty-six years old and very dim, his last piece of official work had been to interpret over a three-day period for Masood's assassins. 'I thought they were strange when they asked me to join the jihad against Russia and said the Taliban were not all bad' was his canny assessment of the killers.

Shay and I approached the gunmen and, as imperiously as we could, demanded to see their leader. A bearded ruffian with amused blue eyes eventually appeared and, verbally throwing ourselves on our knees, we asked him for shelter. Traditionally no Afghan would abuse such a request from a stranger and indeed it worked immediately: we were quickly accommodated in a mud-walled barn-type building. Joined by the village men, Tajik mujahedin loyal to the Northern Alliance, we sat cross-legged around a mat, illuminated by a single flickering lamp as a veritable feast of goat meat, rice and nan bread was placed before us.

Isolated by snow for much of the winter, the mujahedin gave us a noisy résumé of their village society. Sharia law, as interpreted by their white-bearded elders, governed their codes and criminal judiciary. They existed on wheat and corn grown in their drought-denuded fields, and butchered their skinny livestock for meat. Sugar, salt and medicines arrived on a haphazard basis on mule trains from Pakistan, a ten-day journey away. Many malaria victims died for want of medicine and up to 40 per cent of the village had TB. In spite of their problems, they were talkative and friendly, as well as intrigued, as most Afghans are, by the presence of travelling foreigners.

However, without intending to, we nearly caused a major fracas. Wishing to give them something in return for their hospitality, we pulled two Western magazines from our rucksacks. Inside both were features on Afghanistan which included photographs of Masood. At first the mujahedin clustered eagerly around the lamplight to see the pictures of their slain supremo, but then, impatient as ever, they started flicking through the other pages. Conversation quickly faded as they noticed the models in the advertisements. Shay and I shot each other pained looks. Confronted by such *haram* imagery, the mujahedin reaction could have gone either way. Women at that time in Afghanistan, on whichever side of the line, appeared in public clad in nothing less than full burqa. So the plunging cleavages and odd peaking nipple so common in even conservative Western magazines could have caused any number of emotions – from delight to outrage.

Then one man noticed a picture advertising a double jacuzzi. It was tiny, barely postage-stamp size, but just about visible were a naked couple basking in the bubbles. Suddenly it felt as though we were watching pornography with our parents. In my head I begged the man to turn the page, but they were all entranced by the sight.

'Hmmm, life is good,' the chief suddenly announced, and the tension, to our minds at least, seemed about to subside. But next our thief-faced driver, literally trembling with ardour over the picture, grabbed the magazine for himself. The room went quiet. Shay told the driver to hand the magazine over to our hosts. Nothing happened. Shay repeated the demand. Eventually the magazine was passed across, with Shay receiving a murderous look from the driver. The silence broke.

I slept with the reverberations of sex, God and a major culture clash still ringing in my head. Shay slept worrying that the driver would cut his throat.

*

Two days later, sore-arsed, bone-battered and jelly-brained with the combination of the route's rigorous ascent, the jeep's spartan metal confines and the thin air of extreme altitude, we crossed over the mighty Anjuman Pass, already scabbed with snow and ice, and at last began to descend. I remember little of this stage of the journey. Whatever the magnificence of the views and wonders of nature on the roof of the Hindu Kush, as the jeep's bald tyres fishtailed one way and another on the icy hairpin bends, pitching us inches away from the next gaping void, I kept my eyes screwed tightly shut and reacted to Shay's repeated and perverse entreaties to share witness of the vista with an increasingly irritated 'I don't give a fuck. Just tell me when it's over.'

Whatever his good-humoured provocations, I knew that I was lucky to have Shay's company for the venture. Aside from Kurt, there was no one else with whom I could have so easily endured the discomforts and strains that the assignment so surely promised. We shared company by choice, for we were working for different employers. Though we had done a few assignments together since our first meeting, when coincidentally paired up by a magazine to go to Afghanistan five years before, more commonly we hung out in London bars. Free-spirited and worldly wise, in crossing the divide from my life abroad to my life in Britain he held a rare position. Most of my other friends belonged exclusively to one or the other area. Nor had he disappeared during the years of my drug use in London. Our friendship had endured over time, and his attitude to my addiction had been one of concerned laissez-faire.

Whingeing to him over a girlfriend's sudden departure one morning in a Golborne Road café a few years earlier, not having known each other long, he had replied: 'Well, Ant, what do you expect? You've been wearing the same clothes for a week, you take smack and live above a deli that smells of mouse food. You're not a great option at present.' For a few seconds I had puzzled over this straightforward observation with a furrowed brow, wondering whether I could accept such un-English frankness or if perhaps it marked the separating of our ways. The internal jury delivered a verdict of not guilty, and our relationship continued.

When we finally left the mountains behind, beginning the gentle roll down the floor of the Panjshir Valley, my composure and vision returned. Groves of dust-leaved mulberry and walnut trees, their trunks impossibly twisted, peered at us from behind drystone walls shored up with tank wheels as we drove parallel to the valley's fast flowing river. Between villages, old men rode on the backs of mules, their burqa-covered wives following as mute trains of porters; and ragged shepherd boys flicked switches at flocks of fat-bottomed sheep, cajoling them from our path aided by the snapping pursuit of huge, white-fanged dogs.

Resembling fresh battlefield corpses, our faces' every wrinkle smoothed by caked layers of grime, it was scarcely possible to recall the thrill with which we had begun the journey. With the chill of autumn already beginning to roll down the mountains in our wake, bringing with it the imminent promise of snow-choked passes, we knew that the only available way out of the country now lay in the dubious pleasure of a ride back over the Kush in a Northern Alliance helicopter, never an attractive option, or waiting for the recapture of Kabul to open lower-altitude routes eastwards to Pakistan. One way or another, it seemed we were here for the duration.

Passing westwards from the mouth of the Panjshir, the mountains fell suddenly from view, giving way to the wide, flat expanse of the Shamali Plain. Bisected by the shingle banks and curving flow of the river, in better times the area had been famous for its vineyards. However, for the previous three years the front line with the Taliban had cut directly across it. Twice the Talibs had swarmed from their positions to capture the entire plain as far as the entrance to the Panjshir Valley. Twice they had fallen back in disarray, outmanoeuvred by counter-attacks from Masood and the Shamalis, leaving the current front line entrenched almost halfway across the plain's dun environs in a series of bunkers and strongpoints, at its closest point only twenty miles from Kabul, with the vineyards lying black, ruined and abandoned, salted by the Taliban in vengeance. The tight grid of culverts used to irrigate the vines were dried by drought, shattered by war and seeded with mines. Among this ruined chessboard of burned-out tanks, bullet casings, mines and shell fragments sprawled the occasional village, earthen walls scarred by

203

shrapnel and tumbled by shellfire, the villagers eking out an existence in lead-ploughed fields, not a week passing without a man, woman or child stepping on a mine. It was to be our new home.

Keen to avoid the nannying bureaucracy of an official guesthouse policed by apparatchiks from the Northern Alliance's unseated foreign ministry, in Jebel Seraj, the bustling market town of traders and fighters which served as the mujahedin headquarters for the Shamali front, we found our own digs under an unlikely landlord. Engineer Ali was a senior Alliance intelligence chief. With tiny, father-twisted ears and a baby face, round and smooth and hard as a river pebble, he had the looks of a likeable rogue, an East End gangster who charms the gullible by day and pulls fingernails from the wise at night. In our introductory meeting he talked about gambling in Vegas, a city he had apparently once visited, and, having tolerated his reminiscences with patronising smiles, we discovered that we had somehow agreed to pay him an extortionate rent to live in a shed in a farmyard filled with household rubbish and donkey shit. The loo, latest but not last of a series of Afghan discomforts, consisted of a doorless longdrop in a nearby alley. There was neither running water nor electricity, obstacles surmounted with the purchase from the bazaar of a plastic bowser filled each day from a nearby spring, and a car battery and transformer to run the sat-phone, acquisitions that we made while consoling ourselves that at least we were devolved from official auspices. Not that this isolation prevented men from the ministry arriving in our shed each evening, like a repetitive bad dream or an old ska song, demanding money in broken English for unseen food, non-existent water and an absent generator. In this manner we waited for the war to move. The change came quickly enough.

The Taliban's refusal to hand over Osama bin Laden for trial in America was inevitable. As Pashtuns, their society was governed by the complex code of Pashtunwali, a social framework which precluded handing over a friend, or even an enemy seeking shelter, to a hostile force. Moreover, they owed Osama. Linked by family marriage to the Taliban leader Mullah Omar, bin Laden had been a valuable ally to Afghans in the fight against the Soviets; and since his return to the country in 1994 after exile in Sudan, a comeback ironically facilitated by the Northern Alliance, he had given the Taliban huge funding, military support and the death of Masood in return for safe haven and the use of camps to train al Qaeda recruits. But by protecting him now, the Taliban had harnessed the survival of their own regime to that of the al Qaeda chief, making Kabul a prime target for the recently formed, US-led coalition. The city had to fall.

How easily it could be captured was another matter. Though so close to the Shamali front, there was little appetite in the capital for an uprising. Kabulis are the bending reeds beneath Afghanistan's winds, pragmatic survivors, their relative sophistication delineating them as almost a separate people from the rest of the country. They had endured the eras of communist, mujahedin and Taliban rule with world-weary fatalism, and if resentful of their most recent overlords' joyless regime of civil restriction and ultra-fundamentalist Sharia law, they were in no hurry to replace it with the return of the mujahedin, regarded by most city dwellers as rural hicks whose last tenure of power in the capital was best remembered for its corruption, looting and lawlessness. Certainly the burqa, symbolic rallying cry to so many Western liberals in denouncing the Taliban's repression of all personal freedoms and women's rights in particular, was no less obligatory in territory held by the Northern Alliance than it was in Taliban zones. The mujahedin were fundamentalists, too, and if not as cohesive as the Taliban in their enforcement of Sharia, the differences were often merely semantic.

A mixture of bleak historical precedents, logistical difficulties and a revamped neo-conservative strategy precluded the deployment of a strong American ground force to fight in Afghanistan and recapture the city. Instead, the Americans placed their faith in small groups of special forces and airpower to back the Northern Alliance to do the job for them.

The mujahedin seemed confident that they were up to the task, in spite of Masood's death, aware as they were that the mercurial loyalties of their countrymen would lead many Taliban units to defect or flee when the offensive came. Most Afghan fighters regarded war as a boat, and what mattered most was staying on deck, not which direction it sailed. There was no shame in turning coat. All that counted was being on the winning side and, with the Americans now involved, the general perception was that the Taliban's power was in ebb.

So, in the initial absence of any tangible US presence, the Northern Alliance's preparations for the offensive began across the Shamali as an idiosyncratic mash of tribal shuras and ramshackle logistical moves, with stirring doses of polemic.

The mujahedin boasted that they had twenty thousand men under arms on the plain waiting to retake Kabul. However, few of these were actually present on the front, which was held by a comparatively small cadre of regular fighters. Under a feudal-style system, most of the total force were tribal reservists who continued to live in their local Panjshir and Shamali villages, their armed allegiance levied by tribal chiefs to the Northern Alliance warlords whenever it was required for the big push. Drinking tea, trading emeralds, selling sheep, buying firewood, smoking hash and waiting for the word for some seasonal killing and plunder: life had not changed much for the fighters on the plain since their ancestors had clashed with Alexander's army three hundred years before the birth of Christ.

What they lacked in modern heavy weaponry, they more than compensated for in the ingenious recycling of whatever was available to them. In the Panjshiri village of Parakh lay a major armaments workshop where mujahedin field engineers toiled among heaps of stacked tank treads, machine-gun barrels, tripods and rocket launchers to redesign or renovate weapons that had already seen three generations of war, including artillery pieces that had been transported from the snows of the Russian steppes, where they had bombarded the Germans in the Second World War, and into Afghanistan in 1979 to shell the mujahedin. Abandoned by the Soviets a decade later, they were now being repaired to blast away at the Taliban. Mending everything from jammed machine-guns to T-55 tank engines, the workshop sheds contained Russian-made lathes that the Northern Alliance had pulled from Kabul as they retreated from the Taliban, powered now by a single Soviet-era generator. Battlefield scrap was fed into the one solitary furnace, a dustbin-sized diesel affair fanned by motor-driven bellows, and melted down before being worked on the lathes to create spare parts and munitions. They were even designing new weapons, and were particularly proud of their mobile rocket system, a welded hybrid of cut-down rocket barrels, armoured vehicle turret and Russian jeep. Test firing any repaired or newly created weapon was an invidious task, however, a process which consisted of pointing the system at the nearest slope and pulling the trigger or pressing the button. If the payload hit the general target area without killing its operator, it was judged fit for front-line service.

Arraigned against the mujahedin, the Taliban held strong positions on high ground overlooking the Shamali Plain from its southern end. They were doughty enough combatants in their own way, providing they felt luck was with them. Prepared to accept monumental casualties, their offensive speciality was to send scores of pick-up trucks, each loaded with infantry, racing as fast as possible across the front, hoping that those who survived the minefields would be carried by speed and surprise to victory. Backed by Pakistani advisers and foreign al Qaeda units, they had trounced the mujahedin frequently enough.

Overarching this face-off between the two Afghan sides, the Pentagon bragged that its own smart technology would tip the balance and win the fight. Over the scratchy airwaves picked up by my small radio I listened to the BBC World Service as the usual queues of defence specialists, military pundits, spokesmen and retired generals reminded Western publics of satellites so powerful that they could read newspaper headlines from the heavens; of precision-guided bombs that could plop through a specific roof in a crowded city to explode on a designated floor; of unmanned predator drones controlled by an operator half a world away capable of whacking a Hellfire missile into a pick-up truck travelling through a remote valley pass. They usually neglected to mention that most satellite imagery becomes useless in the face of anything more than light cloud; that pilots get confused by speed, stress and ground fire; that operators in Atlanta often fail to distinguish between one group of bearded men and another. Privately, a few might have admitted that smart technology is only ever as clever as the man operating it. But they all appeared to have forgotten that, in war, man goes ape.

Every bit as childishly excited in my anticipation of the first air strikes as the mujahedin, when it finally happened a few days after our arrival in Jebel Seraj, the Americans' debut bombing run was more reminiscent of a teenage sexual encounter than Krakatoa: flash–wham–bam in the night sky and it was over, so fast that in a moment's distraction you might have missed it.

Up to the commencement of the air strike, the evening had passed like any other tired night of the old war: the familiar thump of shellfire, glow of rockets and sporadic chatter of machine-guns drifting to us across the Shamali front lines as Shay and I loitered in the company of some US television journalists who lived a farmyard away. They were altruistic comrades whose impressive supplies – including generators, lights, camp beds, booze and food – allowed them to indulge our poor-cousin status with a little charity. Then, suddenly, a new, heavier chord mixed in with the usual rhythm of the fighting – a distant thumping bass as jets made their inaugural attack run over the battlefield. Their arrival momentarily halted our conversation. Much to my relief, the hour was too late for the paper to require a story; besides which, there was little to write about save for the crashing anticlimax of it all. So, retiring to our shed, unrolling the sleeping bags and lighting a candle, we consoled ourselves with a joint and scaled new peaks of stoned buffoondom thanks to the mighty magic of Mazari charras.

Hash is an endemic part of Afghan society. Not everyone uses it, and it is principally a male preserve, but among the poor it provides a similar escape from life's harsh realities as gin once did in the early stages of Britain's industrial revolution. Varying in shade from black to pale brown and in consistency from malleable gum to crumbling slab, it is so cheap as to be almost free. Famous for the power of its stoning and the richness of its buzz, though other provinces compete closely for the title, the pollen-loaded residue from Mazari Sharif in the north holds the undisputed crown for being the best smoke around. Even the most timid of tokes trips the mind into the gentle eddies of a blissful river, quite unmarred by the remotest paranoia, whirling ever upwards as your thoughts bloom and wander along brilliantine trails to the first steps of wondrous revelation. Would that you could communicate its enlightenments to another. Unfortunately, though, any attempt at talking provokes a reverse labyrinth of instant amnesia, whereby each speaker forgets what they have said the moment they say it, and has to grapple cluelessly to respond to whatever reply comes their way, so that hours can be spent blundering around just trying to work out how the conversation even started.

'Hey, Shay, remember that thing the muj said?'

'The muj on the hill?'

'What muj?'

'Muj?'

Heeheehee. And so it would go on: backwards.

It was an innocent enough luxury with which to while away the long evenings, a take-it-or-leave-it pursuit that never rattled my addiction bars. My potential nemesis lay not in small time stoning, nor the land of war and the poppy, but in an empty London flat, a supermarket or shopping mall: the other world called peace.

Early next morning we drove off to Bagram airfield, centrepiece in the gallery of destruction on the Shamali front line, in an attempt to find out what had happened during the night's air strikes. Once one of Russia's principal military airfields in Afghanistan, now Bagram was a black hole to technological advance. One end held by the mujahedin, the other by the Taliban, the runway was a rutted beach of shrapnel and shell casings. Broken, rusting MiG fighters lay among reefs of war detritus; incinerated Soviet tanks slumbered half submerged among the rubble of hangars; and barrack rooms and outbuildings yawned as gaping, hollow shells, every inch of wire, tile and window frame long since looted or burned. Only the control tower remained standing in its entirety, though tattered and filthy, an Ozymandian edifice to the ancient memory of a long-dead progress. Whenever I saw it, leering stoically above the mess of wreckage, I could not help but remember the moment of post-apocalyptic realisation in the closing minutes of *Planet of the Apes* when Charlton Heston, pursued through the wilderness, sees the top half of the Statue of Liberty sticking up from the ground and realises that civilisation has been trounced not by the past but by the future.

'You maniacs!' I heard him shout. 'You blew it up!'

The mujahedin there seemed as unimpressed by the night strikes as we were. The older fighters could still recall the massive Soviet air strikes of the eighties, so, although they were happy enough to see the first proof of America's involvement, they were understandably peeved by this relatively feeble showing from the world's sole remaining superpower. We left sharing their disgruntlement.

On the way back from the front, with time on our hands, we saw an old man walking along a deserted mulberry-tree boulevard and asked him where he was going. He told us that he was on his way to a circumcision ceremony in a local village, and invited us to join him. Guided by the man through a maze of tracks, shortly we pulled up outside a garden courtyard where a group of mujahedin were sitting around getting stoned. The garden's roses were a deep scarlet and their fragrance filled the air. The Afghans love flowers, and even the shoddiest little earthen hutch usually presents a bright apron of blooms. Also present was a domesticated Taliban prisoner with one leg, apparently already an accepted member of local society and something of a mascot. Twenty years old, he had been captured three weeks earlier when his prosthesis fell off during a Taliban attack. He had originally lost the leg to a mine six months before on the same stretch of front line, but rather than learn his lesson and retire from combat, he had soldiered on. He said there was nothing else to do in his home city of Kandahar.

Minutes later, we were led into a wide ground-floor room, into which crammed the entire male population of the village: some fifty people, including boys as young as five. The white beards sat at one end, family members in the middle, and everyone else at the other. As guests, we were given central seating. No more than five feet in front of us, in the middle of the room, sat the seven-year-old boy who was about to get the cut. He was silent and stared slowly around him. Garlands of coloured foil had been placed around his neck and cruelly betrayed his fear: they shimmered and shook slightly, giving him the appearance of a stickleback shivering on a river bank.

The doctor arrived and in full sight of us all the boy was spread-eagled, pinioned gently by his uncle, and had his trousers pulled down. He cried, 'Allah!' three times as he received a local anaesthetic, then lay quietly as the doctor took a series of scalpels and forceps from his case. It was a gory operation. So close to it, at first I felt vaguely disgusted with myself for intruding on the intimacy of the moment, and did not know where to look. But as there was no way out, for to leave would have caused unimaginable offence, I realised that the greater shame would have been to try to ignore what was happening in front of me. So I sat through it and stared at the boy's calm eyes as the blood flowed across his loins and pooled on the matting of the floor beneath him. Around me the crowd leaned forward. There was neither silence nor much noise: some talked, others were quiet; it was a very relaxed atmosphere, except among the younger boys, who looked distinctly unnerved, wondering how they would handle the situation when their day came.

The operation suddenly over, the sound in the room erupted, everyone keen to have their say on the skills of the doctor and the courage of the lad, who was hoisted upon his father's shoulders and carried out from the room and around the village in exuberant procession, his initiation rite complete, a short and harsh childhood over, a life of war and hardship ahead of him.

CHAPTER 14

When there was action, going to the front with the mujahedin was always a ride on a ghost train: alternate laughs and hysteria. Afghans have a lightness to their spirit when going towards fighting: they grin and hoot and jeer and move with a spring in their step. It is not that they necessarily want to die, more that death is so familiar to them. In a country in which most adult males do not expect to live much longer than their mid-forties, and which has been warring for so long, getting killed in combat is an incidental prospect. War is in their blood. Or else they are at ease with all the death in their life. They are spiritual people, fatalistic in the extreme, regarding their individual destiny as ordained by God and their life as anyway no more than a fragile, transient stage.

Caucasians are usually much heavier in heart when going up the line, their gravitas stronger the further west their birthplace: the greater their country's affluence, the more secular their nation, the sharper honed their fear of death. Whether it was Bosnians, Croats or Serbs in the former Yugoslavia, or the Russians in Chechnya, the white infantry I had previously accompanied moved forward silently and brooding in their purpose, sometimes miserable and depressed, sentiments I felt more at home with on the front. Give me a moody Slav any day: at least I know we share the same unwillingness to tread so glibly down the dark corridor.

So, from past experience, I knew what was in store when we picked up a Northern Alliance commander, a Hazara named Jihad Yar, in Jebel Seraj and drove our jeep forward to a stretch of the line held by his men at the ruined village of Rabat. Jihad Yar brought his young son with him, a boy of seven at most, who had come along to see his father at work. Dismounting behind an earthen embankment at a secondary position, we left the reluctant child by a bunker and continued forward on foot. As we set off I turned around and saw the boy watching us, perched on a sandbag, a small cormorant in his dark shalwar-kameez, his unwavering stare pursuing our every step. Our new driver, Murzorahim, stayed with him, lighting a cigarette and waiting casually for our return with no more unease than if he had been doing the school run. A gnarled Panjshiri, he had seen it all before, having been shot in the legs during a gunfight with an enemy cavalry unit a few years earlier.

The afternoon's venture carried little more aim than to see the front line. Whatever personal challenges I sought there, it carried its own professional obligation beyond merely being a place in which to understand fear. War by its nature sets out to be the very negation of civilisation, an experience which, whatever the particular codes of the moment, has the quintessence of killing and destruction and is designed to extinguish the most sacrosanct of all human rights: life. The front line is thus both a precipice and an altar, and the details of those who live, fight and die there are vital knowledge for anyone wishing to get a glimpse of the caved beast lurking beneath society's thin topsoil.

The mujahedin at Rabat could not, of course, have cared less about the reasons for our presence that afternoon. For them, we were just a novel interruption in another day's boredom, and as we walked along the trench lines more and more of them left their posts to join us, giggling and pointing, wanting no more than to see what the two foreigners were up to. Their exuberance annoyed me. Intent on going as far forward as the final post, I needed at most an escort of one or two fighters, not a twenty-strong chattering cortège who were bound to attract trouble en route with their noise. And whatever their casual courage, they were not the kind of men to inspire much confidence in a gun battle. Most had already been wounded in past clashes, including one or two who were missing a leg.

Stopping at a forward position and peering over the trench ledge I could see no man's land as the usual jumble of brown, shattered village houses, weed-filled gardens, burned-out vehicles and broken culverts.

The mujahedin's fields of fire prevented the Taliban from cutting and salting the vineyards here as they had done elsewhere on the plain, and the vines lay unattended and tangled, corrupted by their abandoned growth, the stench of rotten grapes filling the air. Turning to the local commander, a mujahed named Sher Agah, I asked him to point out the Taliban positions, and was appalled when in answer he sprung over the lip of the trench and scuttled unstoppably into the rubble beyond, gesturing for me to follow. Emitting a grunted curse, I slithered out of the trench and skittered after him, trapped into the deal by a desire to save face more than anything else.

'Mines, mines,' he called out, pointing left and right through the wilderness, as I tried to keep up with him. One of the battlefield's most venomous presences, mines carry an endless list of threat. Tread on an anti-personnel mine and you will be lucky to lose only your foot. In over a third of cases, victims are made impotent by the blast or its accompanying shrapnel, or by the grotesque secondary impact of having part of their own foot blown into their groin. Following someone else through a mined area involves a balancing act whereby you need to stick close enough to step in their footprints, but far enough back that you are not scythed by shrapnel if they detonate a device. The process is further complicated by tripwires, double-pressure devices that are primed by the first footfall and initiated by the second, and by bouncing mines that spring to waist or shoulder height before exploding, in which case anyone in the vicinity will be hit, whether they tripped the thing or not. Double impacts are also common: in the shock and pain of a primary explosion, a wounded survivor frequently rolls on to a second mine.

Sher Agah entered a ruined house, nudging the door open carefully with the barrel of his Kalashnikov. The interior decor came courtesy of shot, shell and soldier: the window frames were splintered inward, the walls shredded and holed by gun- and tank-fire, and graffiti from both sides, surprisingly asexual, depicted only weapons and war.

The enemy were close. Peeking through a hole in the wall, Sher Agah silently gestured to the Taliban trenches as answer to my original, foolhardy question. Less than fifty feet away a machine-gun post was clearly visible, with a turbaned head crouched behind the weapon. A couple of other Talibs, fleeting shadows, scurried between fallen earthen walls ahead of us. Sotto voce, Sher Agah boasted that three weeks earlier, during the last big Taliban raid, more than a dozen of their men had come to grief on his mines. But five days ago, in the same house as we now stood, it had been one of his own men, Faizhuddin, who had tripped a mine and lost his leg.

Suitably briefed and remembering never again to ask an Afghan to show me the enemy positions, I was happy when we tumbled back into the trench line unscathed. A group of Hazara reinforcements were waiting for us, men who had come to bolster the lines against possible Taliban night attack. As the light faded, we moved along the front with them, Sher Agah designating smaller groups to various strongpoints on the way. Their faces Asiatic and incongruous beside the Northern Alliance's Tajik fighters, the Hazaras were descendants of the Golden Horde, their name derived from the Persian word for a 'thousand', which as legend had it was the strength of each garrison left behind by Genghis Khan. Afghanistan's most downtrodden ethnic group, they nevertheless carried their ancestors' reputation for being fierce and unforgiving combatants.

Having sacked the simple-minded Wahid a day or two before, our new interpreter, a tortoise-faced doctor totally lacking in his country-men's fighting ardour, slipped suddenly into a passive funk and without so much as a word sat down to have a cup of tea in a bunker. Refusing to shift, he resembled an overloaded donkey pushed too far up a mountain. Possessing negligible linguistic skills, his English learned in bed with a German tourist in Kabul in the early seventies, I tried not to shout at him – he was in his fifties and had family stuck in Kabul, so had good reason to avoid the battlefield – but I could see that his term of employment was going to be limited.

As ever on the front line, my senses were heightened, making the world a brighter, more colourful place, filled with sharper sounds and clearer scents. Moreover, there seemed little to fear at that moment: the front snored on with little more than the odd cough, scratch and belch to suggest wakening. So, leaving the translator behind us, we pressed on with the fighters. Somewhere in the lengthening shadows, a Taliban fighter noticed the movement and next a PK machine-gun opened up on the Hazara band, sending orange tracers hurtling overhead. There was some jabbering on a radio, a little ducking and running to the cover of two fortified farmhouses, then the fire fight picked up: three rounds of incoming mortar fire exploded around us; the Hazaras blasted back with their RPGs; and through the swirling dust came the inimitable rattle of Kalashnikovs and the distinctive crack of passing bullets. Despite a few seconds of bedlam, with people running and shouting and shooting as some mujahedin tried to grab us to lead us further forward while others attempted to restrain us, it was a manageable enough scrap. There was plenty of cover around and we would have been unlucky to be hit. Laughing, his arms spread wide and palms open in the pose of a master of ceremonies, Jihad Yar stood in the middle of the trench shouting out in English, 'It's easy, not difficult.'

The fire fight withered away of its own volition as darkness closed upon us and the night came, bringing with it the peculiar lights of the front: bouncing headlights from Taliban Toyotas as they ferried their own reinforcements from Kabul to the line; and the flat streaks of an anti-aircraft gun that strafed the Northern Alliance lines in red spurts of fire. The sound of shooting was consoling, for night on a front line holds its own special fears, allowing imagination to take over from where vision ends: far worse than the noise of a fire fight is the silence that can squeeze out a man's courage.

The Hazaras had divided their lines into sectors, each held by sixty fighters, who in turn were divided into ten-man satellite positions among the ruined houses, reached from the main trench line by waist-high crawl lanes. Between these strongpoints stretched the black emptiness of the vineyards and culverts. When attacked at night there was no retreat: the men simply fought out their tiny individual battles as best they could and prayed for the dawn. Sher Agah told us that his own headquarters post had been overrun twice at night that year.

Yet, huddled inside a bunker, when the talk of killing the enemy with US air strikes, mines, rockets, tanks, artillery, machine-guns and rifles finished, when the Hazaras ceased damning the luck of the likes of Faizhuddin and his lost leg, and Muhammed, killed by a mortar a few days before, a peculiar equanimity emerged. The Taliban commander whose men they fought was known personally to the Hazaras. He was originally one of their own, and had been part of the Northern Alliance force in this very same sector of the plain until he had defected with eleven hundred men. Between cursing him and his fighters, the Hazaras seemed curiously ambivalent towards their familiar enemy.

'Usually before a really big Taliban attack one of them warns us on the radio,' Sher Agah revealed. 'This front is difficult for us and difficult for them. Sometimes we fight and fight hard. Recently we've often asked the commander if he and his men want to come over to our side. He has said he will not move at the moment because his men have all been paid well, probably by the Arabs, and have good positions. But if he wants to come and join us then there is no problem. We would be happy to have them back.'

Trudging back to the jeep a short while later, we found Jihad Yar's son waiting by the bunker where we had left him, still seated on a sandbag, still staring towards the front line. He was thrilled to have seen and heard the fire fight from this vantage point, smiling in rapture, and as Jihad Yar swept him proudly upwards into his arms, again repeating, 'Not difficult, it's easy,' in affirmative mantra, the starry-eyed boy continued to gaze over his father's shoulder, across the wretched landscape of broken houses, fortifications and ruined vines, illuminated modestly by the light of a clouded moon.

Later that night, back in our shed, stretched out on my bedroll, tired but too fired up to sleep, thoughts of the Afghans' careless attitude to death closed in upon my mind, and before I could distract them elsewhere, they had waltzed me back through Sierra Leone and into the murky press of my own squeezing fears.

If I was repelled by the mujahedin's apparent cold-blooded acceptance of death, then I also saw its attractions. To drive down the empty road or not? It was a question I had faced on countless occasions in war. Sometimes, as Kurt had done in Sierra Leone, I took the chance with a smile that was as heartfelt as any of the leers I had seen on the mujahedin's faces that day. At other times I turned back, usually pursued by doubt and self-irritation, sensing I had baulked at the joust.

Was death so unwelcome? In this regard, at least, there was a cross-over between the one-time exemption offered by heroin and the escape of war, an attitude shared to some or other degree by drug addicts, smokers, mountaineers, test pilots, racing drivers, almost every war correspondent I had ever met, along with anyone else who gambled unnecessarily with their life. We did not choose death but neither did we fully accept life. The space between was its own world and definition, and I mustered there with like-minded comrades under the banner of a mortal procrastination, abjuring verdict and choice. Death looked too final, life too painful for the requirement of either to be acceptable. Both were unavoidable: but as outsiders in another country's war the terms on offer seemed easier to dictate. It was a standpoint that endowed us with ideal qualities for the job we performed, but was also one that ensured that neither surrender nor victory were ever options.

Some very simple and pragmatic reasons had taken me from the Gulf War to Sarajevo and on down the road to the Shamali Plain. Among these were the facts that reporting was an alluring job that paid the bills, and one that I could perform with the increasing benefits of experience. But it was also a vocation which involved repeatedly spinning around on the edge of the chasm into which so many other people had fallen, and accepting, even embracing, the chance that I might similarily slip, while at the same time scrabbling to avoid it.

The pursuit of courage was an essential part of this doubt-filled state and its many fears, in whose heart lay an abject terror of loss. What disturbed me most in war was neither the prospect of my own anihilation, nor the ease with which humans killed one another. Killing comes quickly enough and most people can do it when certain influences are either removed or exerted. Instead, it was the sight of the bereaved which chilled my core. I had seen them in every war I had visited, thousands of people who had to deal with a sudden shell, bomb or sniper's bullet that in an instant had torn from them one or several of their greatest loves. And they had managed to absorb that pain and carry on. How did they do it? Such cruel, gratuitous suffering seemed to be much more of a mystery than death itself, far harder a sentence to bear than merely dying.

While in no great hurry to die, I was in even less of a rush to face more grief. I had had enough of bereavement, which I regarded as a pinnacle of pain, and could not face losing any more of the few remaining people who were close to me. Coming from such a small family, the deaths of my grandparents and aunt had left deep shadows in my childhood. Though I had not really known my father, and recollections of him were tainted by the bitter memories of our disputes, his death had added its own specific imprint to my fears. We had not spoken for a couple of years before it came. One morning in Bosnia, I was informed in a letter that he was sick with cancer. A few weeks later, he was dead. Far from getting the chance for any farewell, or a last-minute rapprochement, the heat of anger followed us all the way to the coffin. He had not wanted to see me before he died. Instead of a goodbye, I received a letter of damnation, dictated in his last days, which produced a death-clinch rage that held me in its grip for years.

As legacy, farewell had become a matter of dread, made worse by later events. Allieu had ended up dead during my efforts to say goodbye to Kurt and Miguel, who himself had been killed, in part, when trying to say goodbye to Myles. Unsurprisingly, by now I had grown to hate goodbyes of any sort, and saw death peep through even the most casual adieu.

I had once asked Kurt what made him weep, supposing perhaps that his self-possession would have held him back from such release. He said that he had cried when his mother died. Then again in Hong Kong in 1997, a year and a half after the end of the Bosnian war, when he witnessed the British handover of the colony to the Chinese. Kurt's hotel room there afforded an outstanding view of the harbour. Sitting down, he watched the evening departure of the British ships simultaneously on television and through his window, a moment accompanied by sombre ceremony, lowered flags, fireworks and a torrential downpour. Suddenly he found himself crying. I was amazed at the admission. How could this man, who jumped from second-floor windows into snow drifts to test their depth, who was more likely to take off his flak jacket under fire and hand it to the nearest woman than take cover, who could smile under bombardment and hitch his thumbs in his belt, weep at another nation's farewell to mere territory?

'Because it was a goodbye and in this game you don't often see any goodbyes,' he explained, still slightly vexed by the emotional ambush. 'War isn't about goodbye. It's about unnatural and sudden severance. It's about people being there one minute and gone the next, leaving their family with just a pool of blood and a cold body to deal with . . . if they're lucky. All those years I had spent in Sarajevo, those hundreds of times I saw for myself people who had no time to say any goodbye, who were just signed away in a splatter, they came back to me when I saw it being done as a ceremony with such perfection.'

Yet loss had often rewarded me with some surprise and unexpected gift. Lying there that night, staring up at the flickering shadows thrown by the candles upon the rat chewed wattle and dobe ceiling of our shed, I realised that whatever else I had found in Sierra Leone, my attempt there to say goodbye to Kurt was an experience that had broken my own father's curse upon me. I had returned from the jungle no longer a damned and disinherited son. Yet this revelation was itself accompanied by the imposition of another layer of fear. In facing up to the fact that the world wasted even its best without compunction or second thought, I had been forced to realise that anyone else I deeply cared for was just as likely to be seized by a similar lightning strike. Who next would leave me behind? The question did not bear thinking about. My sister? Why not? Her youth and health would not necessarily save her from the cruelties of fate. My mother, the central figure in what was left of my family? It was my greatest dread. What would be left of us without her? What else but appalling solitude could follow the removal of such great love? She had lost her own parents and sister while relatively young. Wouldn't this offer her some form of dispensation? She was a nurse, adored by her patients. Was that a caveat? She was strong and healthy. How long would that give her? Ten years? Twenty?

There was no escape, for any of us. Peace and age kill just as surely as war. But in war existed the fantasy of a surprise, sudden and instantly fatal bullet on a job one day – nothing too protracted, for I was unsure how well I could face the moment. One shot to clear the tray marked 'pending pain'. The thought was a powerful tranquilliser, anaesthetising the reality of so many fears, preserving my suspension in a place between worlds. No more goodbyes.

The sense of a gradual surrender to an inevitable force shrivelled the last of the leaves on the few trees not felled for firewood, casting a drab brown uniform across the plain and mountain slopes, whose peaks now glittered with snow in the rays of the morning sun. There was a sudden crispness to the air and in the lowlands villagers hurried stocks of kindling and logs into their yards for what lay ahead. Autumn in Afghanistan. It is the shortest season of the year, and like Auden's roll of thunder during a summer picnic, the first bite of October chill signifies a change that will not be long in coming.

As the month progressed so too did the Americans' air operations over the Shamali Plain. No longer the coy hit-and-run affairs of night, now attack jets and bombers appeared by day, in flagrant and riveting spectacle that had the locals gathering in audience on their flat rooftops. As F-16s performed their graceful ballet of bomb runs upon the Taliban and Arab positions between Rabat and the contested Bagram airbase, the ground beneath them soared skywards in geysers of brown dirt. Cluster bombs flashed in a broader scatter of orange among the blast haze and sometimes a pilot, perhaps riding a moment of irresistible impulse, strafed the area with the rolling belch of cannon fire. Even the hopeless pom-pom-pom of Taliban anti-aircraft fire had a theatrical ring to it, and when the jets released their payload, the bombs, clearly visible, looked no more than the slivers of a mirror drifting slowly downwards. Death seemed far away, hidden beneath the smog of rising dust over the Taliban positions.

Only on rare occasions, if an ammunition dump was hit or the Americans dropped a daisy-cutter – a huge, terrifying bomb that cut through everything existing an inch above ground level over a radius of several hundred yards and sucked up the vaporised soil to form a mushroom cloud of mini-nuclear proportions – did I get a sense of real destruction taking place. In humble exception to the rule, one afternoon a warplane's smart bomb drifted miles off its target, killing a young seamstress at work in her Shamali village far from the front line. Pulling her remains from the rubble, most of the dead woman's neighbours appeared philosophical rather than angry over her bad fortune, and seemed convinced that civilian casualties were fewer than they had expected not as a result of technological advance, a concept which they could not imagine, but because the Americans were using women pilots who were more sensitive in their choice of targets. It was an unfounded bazaar rumour that had gained credence merely because it was attractive and intriguing.

Yet, behind the high-profile rendition of the bombing campaign, with its big public bangs and little private killings, the key to unlocking the war's stagnation lay not with the pilots, the special forces troops or even their Pentagon commanders, but in the callused hands of secret envoys, men who throughout the centuries had hurried down the darkened passes by night, representatives of Afghanistan's oldest and most potent weapon: treachery.

Loyalty, allegiance, even fear and hate had become almost abstract concepts in Afghanistan's war. Sometimes, should I have ignored the evidence of foreign collusion in the conflict, it seemed that the struggle was fuelled by little more than its own malignant momentum, devoid of any ideological clash: fought by Muslims against Muslims, each of whom foremost considered themselves to be Afghan, whatever their ethnic variations. Above the foundation of their shared cultural and religious tenets, the whole edifice of the war swayed to the rhythm of shifting alliance. Sher Agah's open-handed regard for his enemy and one-time friend on the front at Rabat was so commonplace throughout the country as to be almost unremarkable. Listless through war fatigue, poverty and hunger, differences in tribal and ethnic allegiance were often easily expedited by Afghans for the requirements of survival or cash.

And seldom had deceit been so well utilised a phenomenon as during the ascent of the Taliban. The Talibs had seldom displayed any great military prowess. Instead they had gained most of their territory and major cities after the defection of mujahedin units. With the war now entering a new phase, erstwhile turncoats across the land were reconsidering their loyalties. But, like surrender, the moment of betrayal had to be carefully chosen: make the call too early, and you were slain by your own side; too late, and you died at the enemy's hand. The mechanism of success was like a complicated courtship ritual, and lay with a few individuals, those men chosen to cross the lines as representatives of the would-be changelings to conduct their clandestine business on enemy soil.

By the autumn, the Northern Alliance on the Shamali Plain had their own reasons to achieve victory through defection rather than force of arms. Fortunately, I had a friend who could explain the microcosmic details of a trade that was so central to the development of the Afghan war. Going by the name of Sharif, he was a Hazara rapscallion in his late forties, and a natural survivor. A handsome, broad-faced man, his slanted eyes and dyed beard suggested both Hemingway and an eighteenth-century corsair. Trained as a bona fide engineer, unlike most Afghans who claim the qualification if they can spin a wingnut, he had once been a civil servant for the communist regime and had visited Russia and East Germany, experiences which had gifted him an insight into the world beyond his country, another rarity among Afghans. Metamorphosing effortlessly after the demise of the communists, he had worked for the mujahedin, becoming for a time the governor of a medium-sized northern town. Labouring under the notion, accurate in its way, that he was a pearl in mud, he was a terrible snob, regarding himself as a fallen aristocrat whose God-given right to a life of indolent luxury was being temporarily frustrated by the circumstances of the moment.

When I had first chanced upon him, looking for an interpreter during a previous Afghan assignment, he had been a refugee, having fled the Taliban advance upon his governorship. Nevertheless, he had quickly shamed me. Telling him one evening to prepare himself for several days' work on a cold mountain front line, I had been angered to find him the next morning dressed in no more than sandals, his shalwar-kameez, a waistcoat and a thin patou cloak.

'Sharif, I told you to bring things to keep you warm,' I had snapped irritably.

He had opened his arms expansively, dignified but offended, stared me hard in the eyes and said simply: 'This is everything I own.'

Incorrigible, hedonistic, witty and vainglorious, he possessed a Shakespearean sense of drama and vernacular, often delivering his lines with a rolling, thespian flourish. 'May we find great fortune and wondrous reward in our venture, that we emerge triumphant. Herrumph. Yes. That will be good,' he would inform me as we set off to work. I had once given him a tattered English phrasebook to help him brush up on more practical aspects of the language and after several hours' sulking at the perceived insult, he had waited until we were hiding in a bunker under a Taliban artillery barrage for his revenge, flicking open the book with contrived disdain, clearing his throat and reading as an announcement with slow, deliberate sarcasm: 'Hmmm . . . "John has diarrhoea. Is there a lavatory here?" Yes, this book is most useful.'

On another occasion I had borrowed a horse from a commander to ease the tiring passage of slope, sand and rock. By the end of the journey, Sharif was astride the animal, an Afghan Admirable Crichton, giving the royal wave to passing mujahedin while I limped along on foot cursing, leading the beast as no more than his mutinous vassal. If I had believed that he was merely my sometime employee and interpreter, Sharif had seen himself as nothing less than muse, guide and mentor who indulged me with his company out of a sense of patronage and *noblesse oblige*. Our friendship had cemented itself across the unmoving battle lines of these separate convictions.

Sharif was now working in Jebel Seraj, where he had reinvented himself as the aide to a senior Northern Alliance commander and fellow-Hazara, General Sahid Hussein Anwari. Reviving our friendship provided a refreshing break from the daily toil of loitering around the front line. Our meetings, haphazard but frequent, always involved food, and between scooping globs of Kabuli pilau into our mouths with our fingers we joked affably over life's ironies, complained about the lack of sentient pleasures, and discussed the fighting. He was discreet enough, never giving away too much of the Alliance's plans, but while talking with him one afternoon after my sojourn on the front line with the

Hazara fighters, puzzling over Sher Agah's empathy with the enemy, as a favour he suggested I accompany him to one of General Anwari's war councils.

A day later I found myself sitting at the back of a room beside Sharif, watching a gathering very different in nature to anything seen in Western defence ministries. Before me, some thirty Afghan subordinate commanders and tribal chieftains sat cross-legged around Anwari on the cushioned floor, prayer beads clicking in their roughened hands. Shrewd and intelligent, Anwari was heavyset, black-bearded and renowned for his foresight and sophistication. An old-school mujahed who had fought the Russians, he was now the respected leader of one of the Northern Alliance's principal factions, commanding units across the Shamali front, and had called the shura to issue orders to his men for the planned recapture of Kabul.

He spoke eloquently, surmising succinctly the current state of military and political planning, telling his commanders to prepare their men for action as soon as possible. But then each and every one of them requested extra food, ammunition, clothes and fuel. It appeared that their troops were ill-equipped to advance anywhere at that moment. Anwari listened to their pleas patiently. To most, he issued a signed chit allowing the men to draw supplies from the Alliance's logistical depots hidden in the Panjshir. Next an aide appeared and presented him with a black briefcase. Opening it, Anwari handed out two thousand American dollars to pay for the requested fuel. Yet, even with these logistical preparations in motion, an obvious shortfall in supplies remained. Of special concern was a Taliban-held district on the western flank of the Shamali Plain, Ghowr Band.

'We need the Taliban's equipment there,' Anwari explained of the area. 'They have many trucks, radios and munitions. If we can take the district without unnecessary killing then all the better.' He then instructed one of his commanders, Ahmad Gulkhan, to make contact with the Talibs in Ghowr Band to encourage them to defect.

The meeting broke up soon afterwards, and, intrigued by Gulkhan's mission of subterfuge, I asked Anwari if he would allow me to track its developments.

A week later I was again invited to visit his headquarters. Seated in an otherwise empty room, with Gulkhan beside him, was a Taliban envoy.

Over the course of just three years, Shah Mahmud had graduated from mujahedin fighter, to deserter abandoning his unit, to defector joining the Taliban, and now to go-between returning to his original comrades-in-arms with a message of submission. He bore not the slightest shame in explaining to a foreigner the mechanics of betrayal, and once I had listened to his story I understood why, for within the context of Afghan life there was no dishonour attached to it: loyalty was not a concept they saw as necessarily linked to courage. His prosthetic leg detached and placed before him like a symbol of amnesty, Mahmud told me that he had originally been an Alliance fighter commanded by Gulkhan, and had carried a gun since the age of twelve. Retreating down the Shamali Plain towards the Panjshir Valley during a Taliban offensive three years earlier, he had become separated from his unit: his right leg had been blown off by a mine a few years before and the ill-fitting prosthesis had slowed him.

As he lagged behind, his thoughts turned to his wife and four children, who lived on his farm in Ghowr Band, which had simultaneously been overrun by the Taliban.

'I was becoming exhausted trying to keep up with my group,' he remembered. 'I was thinking of my family and wondering what would become of them. Who would support them with me gone?'

In the confusion he had abandoned his rifle and taken refuge in an empty building. Bypassed by the advancing Taliban, two days later he had begun the trek home. On his return he had found that the Taliban occupying his village looked upon him without malice. One-legged men have a status of some respect in Afghanistan. Besides, dozens of his mujahedin comrades from the valley had also drifted home, and simply transferred their allegiance to the valley's new masters.

As I listened to Mahmud speak, I noticed Gulkhan nodding in agreement. There was no animosity between the two men. Instead, the older man seemed to judge his fighter's original desertion as something of a relief. Of nearly five hundred fighters in his force at the time, barely half had survived the retreat as far as the Panjshir Valley. Some had been killed, some wounded, some captured. A few had wandered up the passes to Pakistan to live as refugees. The majority of the absentees had gone over to the Taliban. Gulkhan was not unduly disturbed that they had done so.

'We just didn't have the logistics to support all the men or their families,' he told me. 'In the Panjshir we were short of food, munitions, housing, equipment and money. I could not have sustained all my force there even if I had wished to. So, many chose to return to their homes to survive. And, of course, most of those joined the Taliban. Some chose to, most had to.'

Mahmud had been given a choice, although not much of one: join the Taliban for the Afghani equivalent of six dollars a month wages, or pay them a levy of eighty dollars each year for military exemption. He was poor, he needed the money to feed his family, so he joined the Taliban.

There were other distinct advantages. With open-road links to their Pakistani patrons, the economy in Taliban territory was more stable than that in Northern Alliance zones. A kilogram of rice was significantly cheaper in Ghowr Band than in the Panjshir; and fuel, salt and sugar, rare commodities elsewhere, were readily available. Furthermore, as the Taliban were subsidised by powerful Saudi donors, including Osama bin Laden, they paid their troops regularly, and their men were better equipped, clothed, armed and fed than their Northern Alliance counterparts.

Heavy fighting along the Shamali Plain had begun again at the close of 1998 as Masood's fighters swept out of the Panjshir, pushing the Taliban halfway back across the plain and to the fringes of Ghowr Band District. Suddenly, the men who had defected were facing their former comrades, still commanded by Gulkhan, across the mountainous front line. At times, the fire fights left men from the same family dead on either side of the line.

In other societies this may have led to irreparable social schisms. But in Afghanistan feuds are usually short-lived and changing, and its current generation is so inured to war that the transient divisions formed by combat can be of little more consequence than individual eddies in a whirlpool.

'Many times I have known a soldier to leave one side, kill a brother or cousin fighting on the other, change sides again, kill again, then desert once more,' Gulkhan explained in a matter-of-fact fashion. 'Habitually, it has been like that in the years of our war. Conflict is not the deciding factor in the way we judge each other. If we have a purpose for it, then we fight. If we don't, then we can greet our enemy as brothers.'

Two further years passed, with Mahmud continuing as a farmer and a Taliban fighter, alternating the gun and the hoe according to shift and season. Then the September 11th attacks occurred and the valley's economy changed in an instant, causing an immediate shift in the local atmosphere. The local Taliban fighters grew suspicious of their Kandahari overlords from the south of the country. The Kandaharis began to rob the locals of their wood stocks to help themselves survive what looked like being a long winter. Conscription was raised from one man per household to two. Fuel became scarce. Food prices rose. Every advantage that there had been in living on the Taliban side of the line began to fade. Furthermore, people were frightened. They knew that in lying on the western flank of the Shamali Plain, the central axis of approach to Kabul, Ghowr Band was a necessary acquisition in the Northern Alliance's plan to return to the capital. Its people feared air strikes would destroy their homes, and that a ground offensive by the Northern Alliance would finish them.

So, once more, the time was right for defection.

It was at this point that Gulkhan had been sent by Anwari to meet secretly with a group of local Taliban commanders. It was a night-time rendezvous in no man's land, ten thousand feet up in the Hindu Kush, and the seven-man Taliban delegation were all personally known to Gulkhan. They had grown up together as children in Ghowr Band and fought the Russians in the same unit as young men. They told Gulkhan that while they may be prepared to defect with their fighters, they were concerned about the difficulties posed by feeding and housing their families in Alliance territory should they come across. In response, Gulkhan instructed them to remain where they were, explaining that they were needed to turn on their Kandahari and Arab allies at the given moment. The meeting broke up before dawn without firm agreement.

But only a couple of days later, as American air strikes intensified and the economic situation worsened in Ghowr Band, the would-be defectors summoned Shah Mahmud to their headquarters in the valley. Explaining that secret front-line liaisons with the Northern Alliance were becoming increasingly difficult due to the suspicions of the Kandaharis, they ordered Mahmud to deliver a less ambiguous message across the lines to Jebel Seraj.

'I have come with an offer of submission,' Mahmud revealed. 'My commanders are frightened by the air strikes in Ghowr Band, and angered by the behaviour of the Kandaharis there. They do not want our people, our houses and our farms destroyed. They are ready to submit to the coalition.'

Treated with the respect of an old friend, Mahmud was accommo-dated and fed as his words were relayed to the Northern Alliance's top commanders on the Shamali Plain. Two more envoys from Ghowr Band would follow him to Jebel Seraj in the three days after his arrival. They carried further details, including the specific identities of those Taliban commanders in the district wishing to defect.

Then the waiting game began, with both those who had asked for submission and those who offered it assessing when the time was most ripe for turning.

Though the story shone with exotic details of midnight subterfuge, double-cross and secret agendas, there was really very little romance or glory about it. More than anything, it was a crushing example of how eroded and overwhelmed by war the country had become, to the point at which fealty and allegiance were bartered like bazaar baubles for the sake of survival. The Afghan poor could no longer afford to fight for ideology, belief or conviction. Instead, they killed and died for whichever side offered the best chance of a more secure life, and the definition of that decision was ever-changing, and formed by pressures over which they had not the slightest control.

On hearing Mahmud's tale, my own understanding of the importance of courage in a man suddenly seemed like a privileged plaything, a quite irrelevant acrobatic display when placed beside this simple, raw necessity for survival. Until I met him, I had been obsessed with the coming battle for Kabul. Now I realised that though the September 11th attacks may ultimately prove to be the death knell of the Taliban in the city, it was unlikely that there would be a glorious march, battle and victory in the fight for the capital. Rather, the impoverished and ill-educated armies of both sides seemed set to trudge into combat through the mire of defection, sacrificing whoever had not managed to jump ship in time, along with a few hardliners and any interlopers who did not understand these uniquely Afghan rules of war. And with that victory Shah Mahmud, his task completed, would simply hobble back to his scrape of land and scratch out his existence as best he could, worrying about water and the weather, until the course of the war one day turned and it was time to defect again.

CHAPTER 15

In Golbahar I waited for the man. As the twisting helix of defectors, air strikes and front-line clashes wove around the plain, loading each day with buzzing intensity, I found that the evening step-offs into stoned oblivion were a little too steep a pressure drop to endure. Requiring a more flexible form of relief, the thought of vodka had suddenly gained allure. Unfortunately, it was nearly impossible to find, but a grape-based moonshine proved slightly easier to come by.

A small, lively bazaar town just outside the mouth of the Panjshir Valley, Golbahar was the hub of trade entering and leaving the Shamali Plain, and its crowded streets were busy thoroughfares to horse traders, gun runners, emerald dealers, medicine quacks and caravaneers. Away from the firing line and out of reach to all but the most powerful artillery, it was also a good backseat listening post from which to hear the war's other voices, with the streets' rippling currents carrying the latest word from the hills or Kabul, and the teahouses and kebab stalls natural stopping points for the travellers, refugees, envoys and the occasional exchanged prisoner who had crossed the front at more porous points than the tense, mine-sown arena in the centre of the plain.

Fundamentalism had accelerated to such a degree over the previous five years that on the Shamali Plain, as elsewhere, alcohol was an illicit luxury. Yet, among Golbahar's pharmacists – their premises sweet-shop paradises where dusty counters fronted shelves stacked with multi-coloured glass jars, tempting chalices full of rainbows of gobstopping Pakistani qualudes, Mandrax and Valium – existed an underground network of bootleg stills. The pharmacists needed alcohol to make their medicines, and a few of them had diversified. Shay and I had already sampled their wares. Neat, the clear liquid tasted like a wince-inducing form of grappa. Mixing it with fruit juice imported over the passes on mule and camel trains from Pakistan and Iran, though, and the result was not too bad; although the joy of our first test-run was soiled by fears of imminent blindness. To work out the quality, you poured a drop on wood and tried to light it. If it ignited with a blue flame, you were in luck; if not, the grog had been cut with meat fat and you had been ripped off.

Now we loitered once more in the bazaar as a contact disappeared with half a million Afghanis, about twelve dollars, to go and score the liquor. He took ages and eventually we drifted off to the town's CB station to blunt our impatience. Set up by two brothers, Golbahar's radio room – 'Shaker', as it was known on the air – was a commercial enterprise located inside a sun-buckled wooden hut. Arab fighters, Tajik generals, refugees, car mechanics, bazaar traders, the angry, sad and hungry: all the voices of Afghanistan's war crackled over the receiver in the confines of the blue-painted walls within. The technology was minimal: one small radio set and mike, two car batteries to power it, and an antenna rigged to the roof. A pair of headphones hung on the wall so that more coy customers could at least hear, if not speak, in private. For a country without telephones or a postal system, whose roads were barely existent and whose bridges had been blown, Shaker and stations like it were the only means by which most Afghans could communicate over any sort of distance.

'Six thousand dead in America? Thanks be to God! We are so happy! They were unbelievers,' shrieked the voice of an ill-informed Taliban commander on a nearby front as we entered. It was such a familiar refrain from the Taliban hardcore that it was almost a platitude by then, so until the commander disappeared with a squawk of static, his disembodied, ranting voice caused barely an eyebrow to be raised among the seated queue of Tajiks awaiting their turn to speak.

'Tell that donkey Daud he better get a new crankshaft brought down here from Faizabad and stop lying to me or I'll send someone big around to really get his attention,' a furious driver demanded of a voice two hundred miles to the north as he took his turn to squat by the handset.

Calls were charged at a fixed rate for a maximum five-minute duration. Beneath a Dari sign that read: 'Quiet Please . . . Try Not To Talk About Politics', as each new customer hunched before the radio one or other of the brothers searched for the appropriate band, tuned in and called up the station in whatever town was required. The set could reach anywhere in Afghanistan, as well as frontier areas in Pakistan. Most callers simply gave the operator's voice on the other end an address, told them to find it and fetch the relevant individual, and informed them that they would call again in an hour's time.

Few conversations were personal. Afghans never gave away much sentiment in public, and their subsistence economy did not allow them to spend money discussing their feelings. Instead, they called each other to arrange the movement of necessities across the mountain passes, usually wood, fuel and vehicle parts. Almost every conversation seemed to snag on the issue of money, a moment always marked by a pause, that tilting second of challenged pride or grace, before the speaker either asked for a loan or agreed to give one.

Radio traffic from the front lines also entered the room, sometimes in hissing snatches, sometimes as entire conversations between battlefield commanders.

'When there was a lot of fighting on the Shamali Plain we often heard Arab voices on the front,' Mohammed, the younger brother, told me. 'The voice I remember most, though, was Ahmed Shah Masood's. We heard him many, many times giving orders to his units. He always spoke using code words and names but his voice was unmistakeable and his commands were perfect in their precision. Hearing him conduct battles was something I'll never forget.'

The Afghan net had been broken badly over the previous month, however. CB stations in Taliban-held areas had always been illegal, but existed underground and were widely used by families who had been separated by the fighting. Until the terrorist attacks upon America, Shaker had usually contacted Kabul's secret station every couple of hours or so. But after September 11th communication had become less frequent. Mohammed had known the Kabul operator, codenamed

'Kabuli', by voice alone for more than six months, and understood that he was minimising his airtime to avoid capture by the authorities.

But just a week before, Kabuli had gone off the air for good. Repeated transmissions to him did not elicit any response but the hiss of static. The man's fate would have remained a mystery were it not for a refugee from Kabul who had crossed the lines to Golbahar and arrived at the radio station with bleak news. He said that the Taliban had found Kabuli, destroyed his station and taken him away. It was a serious charge: torture and imprisonment were certain, execution possible. In ironic epitaph, during the refugee's story Mohammed discovered Kabuli's real name for the first time: it was Zulmay.

Walking back into the sunlight amid the bustle and dust, the growling camels and the knee-high chorus of 'hello mister, hello mister' from the bands of ragged urchins who pursued every foreigner on Afghan roads, we discovered our booze contact waiting for us. He ushered Shay furtively to one side and slipped the goods into his camera bag. The whole palaver seemed faintly ridiculous for the simple pleasure of a drink that evening, but it was as much entertainment as we would get on an otherwise quiet afternoon.

Back in our jeep, though, as we bumped home to Jebel Seraj, Shay inspected the goods, then began swearing furiously. 'The bastard's given it to us in a goldfish bag,' he exploded, 'and it's leaking bloody everywhere.'

Urging Murzorahim to speed up, on arriving home we rushed into our hut to check the damage. Sure enough, we had been given half a pint of spirit in a dribbling fairground bag. Outraged, we quickly decanted what was left into a glass jar, and when the dusk settled over the plain we sat down for a drink. As the alcohol spread its glow through my stomach, I relaxed in contented reflection. Our roughshod living arrangements, once the source of both novelty and complaint, had over the past weeks become acceptable, even enjoyable. Like dogs rolling in fox shit to disguise their scent to their quarry, our adaptation to the war's environment was now all but complete, the dirt, darkness and squalor familiar and inconsequential. Bearded, grubby, foul-breathed, inured to the rancid smell of our own sweat, we had made efforts to transform our shed into a place that was at least habitable. Our furniture, bought in the bazaar, was rudimentary but no more so than that which most Afghans had in their homes. We had a wide plastic mat and mattresses for sleeping upon; an old ammunition crate as a seat; a Russian candelabrum; a padlocked tin chest to keep any valuables we could not carry with us safe by day; our small bowser for spring water; and a petrol lamp to supplement the candles.

Murzorahim slept in another room, leaving his jeep parked in the yard, and collected our interpreter, the days-numbered doctor, each morning from his nearby home for work. By juggling car batteries – one in the shed and the other in the jeep and therefore on charge – our power supply remained constant. My transformer was a special source of wonder. Made originally in Kabul, it comprised a walnut box about eight inches square, fronted by a single red bulb and plug socket. In order to write, I clipped it to a battery, plugged in my laptop and lit a couple of candles to see the keys. The box allowed me five hours of power and hummed as it did so, red light pulsating, like a prop from a fifties sci-fi set.

We ate the same food as the Afghans in the bazaars – goat meat, mutton and rice – but dropped iodine into our drinking water, a precaution that had so far prevented either of us from falling sick. And the air strikes and travails of the envoys had added a sense of progression to the war, lightening my heart with suggestions that the long-awaited push for Kabul was imminent. Home felt a universe away. I felt quite at one with the world.

Then the Americans arrived.

The spoor of American special forces had been faint on the ground across the plain, though rumours of their arrival bubbled through the bazaars, fuelled by the mysterious nocturnal passage of unseen helicopters beating overhead. However, the night life of our mysterious host Engineer Ali began to change. On several consecutive evenings, across our yard the doors to his inner sanctum opened to allow inside cloaked, armed figures with an accompanying squelch and hiss of radios.

Then, one night, a team of Afghan bodyguards appeared and sealed off the whole compound. Peering from our shed, we saw a succession of porters going through the central doors, bearing plates heaped with food in preparation for a feast. A couple of hours later, to a roar of engines, the front gates were flung open and three jeeps lurched inside. Shadowy silhouettes emerged, large and moving with the clumsy gait of Westerners, rifles in hand. Rising above the welcoming murmur of Dari came an American voice. 'I guess no one here speaks English,' it boomed jovially, hopeful for contradiction. There was more muttering and a second American spoke, less distinctively. The voices receded as they stepped into the central quarters, and were cut off completely as the doors closed. The guests had gone by dawn, but their visit drew to a close our stay in Engineer Ali's shed. No longer willing to tolerate the continued tenancy of a couple of journalists now that the Americans had begun to drop by with their plans and maps and secrets, we were gracelessly ejected from our home.

Piling up the jeep with our furniture and other belongings, protesting loudly at our eviction, we clattered southward across the plain in search of new lodgings, as scruffy and insolent as any diddycoys on the move. Our search ended in Charikar, the last town before the front, on the invitation of a three-war friendship spanning several years.

Peter was a former paratrooper with a knowledge of Afghanistan unrivalled by any foreign reporter. Very British, square-jawed, blue-eyed and with raffish moustache, his behaviour, speech and looks were those of a Victorian political officer on a special mission to outwit tsarist agents beyond the Khyber Pass. He had worked as a cameraman in the country throughout the Russian occupation, crossing the mountains of the Pakistani–Afghan border with infiltrating mujahedin on countless assignments that involved weeks of marching before filming could even begin. Covering the subsequent civil war and ascent of the Taliban, over the years he had become a close friend to many Afghan commanders, including a number of Taliban leaders. Between assignments, he would often return to Afghanistan on his own, just to be there. Phlegmatic, tough and unsentimental in his regard for the land that so attracted him, Peter would neatly summarise any situation with one of two phrases: 'tic-tac' or 'rather annoying'. The former covered everything from day-to-day normality to total delight; the latter was reserved for situations of traumatic stress that most people would label 'catastrophic disaster'. If he ever said 'bloody hell', it was time to shoot yourself.

Ensconced now in the abandoned and gutted carcass of a communist-era apartment block in Charikar, he had been hired, on account of his expertise, to work for the grandee British television correspondent known privately to myself and Shay as Big Sim. There were rooms to spare and, sympathetic to our plight, Peter suggested we should take one.

No more than three miles from the front, the bare concrete shell of our new second-floor abode came complete with a balcony, giving us an outstanding battlefield view of jets hitting the Taliban. Peter dropped by to see how we were settling in and as we mused on the possible timescale of Kabul's recapture he unconsciously entertained us with the reasons behind his own need for a quick liberation of the city.

'I've got two dead Russians stored in a cellar in Kabul,' he informed us, as dry and abstract as ever, as if they were bottles of vintage wine saved for a special occasion. 'They are locked in boxes. The caretaker is very nosy and has the keys. I'm sure he's looked inside and wonder what he'll say when I arrive. Probably nothing. Basically, some friends of mine killed them years ago and I dug them up.'

There quickly emerged two drawbacks to our new home. First, it had no loo. While we were quite used to the absence of electricity and running water, this lack of even a 'short horror' perplexed us. In their separate wing of the block, Big Sim and his boys had had a commode specially installed. But though we got on well enough, I would no more have asked Big Sim to use his loo than I would attempt to kiss the Queen. Second, our new landlord was a mujahedin commander whose financial acumen was the same as Rachman's, outshining even Engineer Ali for its naked avarice.

Haji Bari lived in a pink-painted emporium at one end of our filth-ridden corridor. Occasionally chauffeured to the front in a grey Volga with tinted windows and a picture of Saddam Hussein mounted on the back windscreen, he was about forty, wore charcoal mascara, controlled a mini-army on a stretch of the line and carried the nickname 'Haji

Dollar'. After an exhausting battle, we were bamboozled by him into paying 250 dollars a week for our room. Under normal circumstances I would not have kennelled a dog in it: until shortly before our arrival, Haji Dollar's men had used it as a latrine, and in spite of numerous attempts at cleaning the floor, the room still reeked. We hired a carpenter to tack some polythene across the glassless windows and mend the half-door, and tried breathing out as much as possible.

At first, Haji Dollar included one gunman as escort and a personally signed daily pass to the front in the rent. Then, realising this tiny loophole of generosity, he installed his own checkpoint on the road outside the building and demanded thirty dollars every day before he would let us cross it.

His goon squad of teenage mujahedin loitered permanently in the corridor outside our room. Most of the time they were quiet enough, but sometimes after dusk they lost their minds to an unknown narcotic and the place became an ape-house as they ran, roared and gibbered down the dark passageway, leaping in and out of the wrecked rooms in pursuit of one another. From his pink palace, Haji Dollar roared back. And, increasingly, Shay and I hooted and howled in return.

Our behaviour fast succumbed to a kind of cultural osmosis on other levels, too. By night, we pissed off the balcony; by day, we filled a slop bucket and emptied it out of the window, where it joined our rubbish in the street below. Further solution to the loo problem was found by crapping in the Charikar Cinema, a truly Grand Guignol experience. Situated some hundred yards from Haji Dollar's apartments, it had been wrecked when the Taliban, who regarded film as *haram*, had first captured the town five years earlier. Abandoned, dark and silent, it made for an ideal loo. After a labyrinthine wander through the empty stalls, up the winding staircase, through the barren cloakroom, up more turning stairs, along a dust-filled corridor, lay, illuminated by a single shell-hole in the roof, the projection room. Dropping my trousers before the smashed projector, I squatted happily in this secluded silent place, running strips of mangled Russian films through my fingers, pondering the cycles of war and civilisation as well as more prosaic matters, such as whether there would be any packets of Seven Stars cigarettes in the bazaar that day. A dollar for twenty, they were the best local tobacco available, their acrid, woody smoke affording great sense of luxury.

But one morning shortly after our arrival in Charikar, I found no joy in the cinema's privacy. A violent fever had left my sleeping bag sweat-soaked during the night, and it continued still, shaking my body with mechanical power. Trousers down, my experience in the projection room seemed more dramatic and bloody than any American air strike I had witnessed. I was too drained by the sickness to worry at first, but as the day progressed and my trips to the cinema accelerated into staggering sprints and increased bleeding, I realised dimly that I had contracted some form of dysentery.

The fever departed that evening, but the stomach cramps intensified and I became more listless and enfeebled by the hour. Returning from a 3 a.m. fall from grace in the cinema stalls, I stumbled on to the balcony of our room. In the darkness below an unseen figure shouted hoarsely into the night – Charikar's watchkeeper, charged with calling out to the town's watchmen to keep them from falling asleep. Across the Shamali Plain, a series of huge bombs erupted for an instant in red explosions on the Taliban lines.

Normally, I would have appreciated this moment, as lone witness beneath the moon. Yet, feeling almost too drained to walk, the view instead seemed rather miserable and suffocating, and I wondered with the fretful sensation of falling how much weaker the sickness would make me.

I returned to my bedroll fighting off sleep, worried that its release would lead me to crap in my sleeping bag. As I lay there, staring at the ceiling, trying to chart the progression of my spasming stomach, I mused petulantly whether this concern was part of being 'honoured to bear witness', or just an unlikely component of the job's assumed glamour.

His bladed stare a mixture of glittering fury and blank despair, in a land where almost everyone was keen to tell their tale, Karimullah stood out as one Afghan who had no desire to relate his own war story. Maimed and alone, I found him standing in the narrow midday shadows at the edge of a courtyard in Golbahar. Run by the Red Cross, the site housed a clinic which specialised in making prosthetic limbs. Yet, among so many men whose legs and feet had been torn from them by mines, Karimullah's injuries appeared as unique as his reticence. Mines can remove both legs and both arms, the limbs of one side but not the other, or, more often, a single leg or foot. But a blast seldom cuts in a surgical diagonal.

Fistfuls of Iranian antibiotics purchased in the bazaar had put the brakes on my dysentery. Though the side-effects made by head feel as if it were clamped in a vice and a listless depression dogged their course, they had induced a slow, measured recovery. Lying on my mat a day earlier, the thump of war sounds from the front heightening the boredom of convalescence, Shay had returned to our room from a speculative venture on the plain to tell me that he had encountered an angry Afghan who was missing a foot and a hand. Staff at the prosthetic clinic had mentioned to Shay that the man had a story to tell, were only he inclined to do so.

When I met him, at first it seemed that Karimullah's rage had entirely robbed him of speech, and he greeted my tentative introduction by turning away his head. A thin, almost emaciated Tajik, his face sunken and pale, with great reluctance and periods of lengthy silence, moments in which he trembled with the effort of some huge internal wrestle, he eventually squeezed forth his burden, talking a little more in each fit of conversation, while my own questions diminished until finally I could say nothing at all.

Using a single crutch, he had hobbled across a quiet sector of the front a few days earlier, minus his left foot and right hand. Now twenty-six, the eldest child of Tajik parents, he had fled his home in Kabul when the Taliban first seized the city, though his parents and siblings chose to remain. Moving to a village on the Shamali Plain with his wife and two young children, he found work as a farmer on a vineyard. He stayed for two years until he became a refugee after fleeing a subsequent Taliban advance, whence he picked up a gun and joined the mujahedin. A year later a tank shell hit his post on the Shamali Plain, killing four of his six comrades outright. A Taliban raiding party sprayed the survivors with gunfire. Wounded in his thigh, Karimullah escaped and found refuge in a Pashtun village on the front. The next day the villagers handed him over to a Taliban patrol. Tried by a military tribunal in Kabul, after torture he was sentenced to imprisonment in Kabul's infamous Pulecharki Jail for having served with the Northern Alliance. Twelve weeks later three Taliban guards entered the cell that he shared with nine other mujahedin prisoners. They called out Karimullah's name and told him he was to be released. Baffled but relieved, Karimullah was led out of the prison with the three escorts to a Datsun pick-up. It was a Friday afternoon in winter, and the vehicle wove through streets blurred with fog. After a while Karimullah noticed Kabul's Ghazi Stadium looming ahead. Unnerved, he asked his captors why they were taking him there. They told him to be patient, that he would soon be freed.

The pick-up drove into the centre of the stadium. From the stands, thousands of silent spectators stared at the vehicle through the mist, while a group of adjudicating mullahs sat on a line of chairs in the middle of the field. Karimullah was pulled out of the Datsun and pinioned, spread-eagled, face upwards, on the ground. The mullahs, breaking from the usual form of public punishment, neither asked his name nor addressed the crowd. Seven doctors walked on to the pitch. They were dressed in grey uniforms and wore surgical masks and gloves. Karimullah noticed that one was crying. They injected him and his body lost all feeling, but he remained fully conscious. Surgical clamps were put on his ankle and wrist. The doctors sawed off his hand and foot simultaneously. Karimullah felt no pain, but was transfixed by the sight of his foot being removed. Five minutes later the operation was over and a sigh and murmur rippled through the watching crowd. The Taliban guards bundled Karimullah back into the pick-up. They did not speak, though one of them was also in tears. The vehicle drove to the city's Wazir Akbar Khan Hospital and Karimullah spent over a week in bed there. Eight of his former Taliban prison guards came to visit him. They brought a bag full of apples and 600,000 Afghanis as consolation, apologised, and insisted that they had not known of his fate in advance. Karimullah hurled the fruit and money back in their faces.

Early in the morning of his tenth day in hospital he was discharged. A taxi took him to his parents' home in the Kote Sangi quarter of the city.

His parents had no idea that their son had even been captured, let alone that he had been mutilated by his captors. Karimullah's eight-year-old sister Razia answered the taxi driver's knock on the door and burst into tears when she saw her brother sprawled in the back of the cab. Worse was to follow. Masherin, his mother, though only in her forties, had been ill for some time with a cardiac condition. She collapsed the moment she saw her son. Briefly regaining consciousness, a few hours later, she had a heart attack and died.

Karimullah became a beggar on the city streets, his mutilation carrying with it the stigma and shame of the thief. Eventually a cousin, a mujahedin commander in Jebel Seraj, passed a message through the lines offering assistance. Borrowing a spare prosthetic leg from a mine victim in Kabul, Karimullah limped northwards in a journey lasting several days, crossing the front with other refugees and reaching Golbahar just two days before I met him.

The Red Cross were now in the process of fixing him with a new prosthetic lower leg. But scars run deeper than skin.

'I am finished,' he spat in conclusion. 'I have no future. I cannot work. I am the eldest son of my family but cannot even support my wife and children. I have had everything taken from me by the Taliban. Before they came to Kabul I was a student in the tenth grade, an educated man with some chances before me. I still don't know why they amputated me. Someone told me a rich Pashtun had committed a crime, been caught, and paid the corrupt mullahs to use a prisoner of war for public amputation instead of himself. I don't know if it's true. But I hate them. I dream only of having my hand again so I could carry a gun and go to the front line and kill and kill. I'd kill them all, every Talib and every mullah.'

So his story ended. There was nothing for me to say, so I left him where I had found him, standing in the courtyard's sharpened shadows, and drove back to Charikar. Yes, I was appalled. The weight and range of injustice in his tragedy were terrible, and as the landscape of dust, rock and men with guns swept past the vehicle's windows I muttered 'Jesus Christ' once or twice, sincerely enough. But his tale was good currency for a journalist. The best war reporter is just the skilled conduit of other people's pain, an effective intruder upon their most extreme moments of vulnerability. I had done part of what was considered a good job, coaxing a reluctant and traumatised man into revisiting in full detail the horror, the absolute horror, of his experience. Now, to complete the task successfully, I had to convey that experience to others. So, after a few more 'Jesus Christ's I began to construct the story in my head while still on the road, working out how best to impact it into a reader's mind. How many adjectives had he used? Did the story even need adjectives? For the full shock of his fate to come across on the page should I mask the fact that he had lost his hand and foot until near the end of the piece, or flag it up baldly at the start? Where to drop in his mother's death? I would have to place her fate well, lest its weight become lost in the other details. There were so many things to think about.

Later that day, having written the story and beamed it over the sat-phone to London, I visited Charikar's hamam, an excursion of guaranteed ecstasy. A gloomy subterranean passage of heat and steam, it was the only available means to bathe. Led by an expressionless attendant to one of some twenty stone cells, I stood naked beneath the narrow ray of sunlight which shone through a single, small aperture high in the domed ceiling above me, so thin and perfect in its delineation from the darkness of the chamber that it hit my skin like a white spear. Somewhere in the catacomb-like complex the Afghans had rigged up an unseen water tank, from which pipes travelled over a fire and then into the cells. I turned the blackened tap, filled a bucket with hot water and tipped it over my head, then repeated the process time and again. It was the most sensual experience I had had since arriving in Afghanistan so many weeks before, and with water such a rare and luxurious commodity in my day-to-day life, it verged on the auto-erotic.

Rubbing every inch of my skin and hair with a brick of soap, I paused for a second, spluttering bubbles, happy as a baby, then swashed it all away with new draughts of water until my whole being tingled, stung and shone with the sensation of cleanliness.

'Hmmm, good story,' I muttered to myself, reborn and rejuvenated, as I thought again of Karimullah. 'Good story.'

And through an invisible drain cover in the shadows beneath my feet it all swirled out of sight: the grey lather, sweat, dirt, grime and almost all of the awareness of a betrayal.

As the autumn slipped into its sudden November retreat so too did my patience. The offensive to recapture Kabul, so long heralded, remained a chimera. My tolerance of goat meat, dust and beards was finite, and harnessed to a sense of the war's movement. Though the mujahedin war captains were down from the hills, congregating on the plain in a series of daily meetings, and small teams of American special forces, no longer the hidden entities of the night, could often be seen along the front directing the daytime air strikes, the Taliban defence lines appeared fixed and unshaken. Were it not for the backstage scurrying of envoys laying the groundwork for defection, on the battlefield the Taliban seemed bolstered rather than intimidated by the bombing. One morning on the front I had seen three of them praying among the rubble across no man's land, quite unperturbed, as behind them American jets pounded their lines.

And listening in to the mujahedin bicker with the Taliban over their radios – traditional front-line sport for fighters sharing the same frequencies and language – a Taliban commander had goaded his enemies with telling irony: 'We shall have a long wait to be martyrs at the hands of the American bombs.'

With war as familiar to them as the seasons and the harvest, few of the mujahedin soldiery displayed any particular zeal for a speedy push, regarding the possibility with a Zen-like, laissez faire attitude, suggesting the event would occur more of its own volition than due to a schedule. It was a perspective that was at odds with the time-obsessed Western mindset. To them, knowing no peace, their war was anyway not so much defined by the single incidents recorded by history, but more by its continual grind and eventless presence, an essence which made specific happenings incidental, even trivial.

They would still fight fiercely enough, but often for very different reasons from those anticipated in the Pentagon's operations rooms. Taking a drive early one morning out to a mujahedin unit on the front line east of Bagram, I found the fighters there in good spirits in the wake of a raid into no man's land that had just concluded. Proud as ever, high on adrenalin from the fighting, they told me about it with typical frankness. The operation had been a spur-of-the-moment affair which had ended in a desperate fight, not for greater gain or glory, but for a more practical, cold-fleshed reward.

The dawn had started with howling wind and racing leaden skies, finding the mujahedin shivering in their trenches against the first snarl of early winter. The luckier ones wore surplus combat smocks, trousers and boots. Most had little more than the de rigueur, all-season dress of pakul cap, desmal scarf, shalwar-kameez and jerkin. Then, in the group's headquarters, a wrecked Soviet building at the furthest reaches of the former airbase, a radio crackled into life. The mujahedin commander took the call. A few hundred yards away two of his men in a forward post told him they could see a group of five Taliban digging a new position in no man's land. The commander ordered the pair forward in ambush.

The Taliban were taking advantage of the half light of the early hour and bad weather. A windstorm ripped across the battlefield and rolling clouds obscured the sunrise. Situated among long-abandoned runway workshops, far from Bagram's ravaged control terminal, the elements transformed the scene into a desolate vision of dust, rubble and sleet: rags and shredded plastic skidded through the wrecks of the jets, rusted APCs, bombed hangars and bullet-riddled fuel tanks.

The two mujahedin fighters crawled forward from their post. Mayel Agah carried a Kalashnikov; his immediate superior, Hadayatullah, had a PK machine-gun. They scuttled into no man's land and crept along an old trench towards the Talibs. Dressed for death, the Taliban were wearing white, Islam's purest colour and the shade of choice for those anticipating martyrdom. Sneaking to within forty yards of the oblivious men, Mayel Agah and Hadayatullah found a good position, then leapt up and raked the Talibs with bursts of fire. One white-clad figure dropped dead, another was hit and rolled away; three others ran behind a low earthen wall.

The hit complete, the element of surprise now lost, and still outnumbered, many fighters would have quit while ahead. But not the mujahedin. They wanted the Taliban corpse, so they fought on for it.

The trade of bodies was a well-established ritual on the Shamali front line. A dead local Talib could be exchanged for one live mujahedin prisoner; a dead Arab or Punjabi for up to five. The corpse of an important Taliban commander upped the rate even further. When the Taliban had first advanced on Bagram, the body of Mullah Boimohammed, the son of a senior Taliban official in Kabul, was exchanged for fifty Alliance prisoners held in the capital. In common with Muslim fighters the world over, the Afghans attached huge importance to speedy burial and ceremony for the dead. The thought of a slain combatant being given a hasty burial in enemy lines or, worse still, rotting in no man's land was anathema to them, so the retrieval of the dead was accorded as much importance as the return of the living. The Taliban had the upper hand in the bartering, because over the previous three years, whenever they had entered Tajik, Hazara or Uzbek territory, they had incarcerated hundreds of men, regardless of civilian or military status, so now had large reserve stocks of prisoners to offer in exchange.

The market had produced mini-economies in several sectors of the front. Few local commanders on the Alliance side were willing to hand over their captured assets, dead or alive, to headquarters, preferring instead to keep them in villages near the front line until they could be used to effect the return of their own missing kin. If the family of a prisoner held by the Taliban knew that their local warlord had no corpse or captives to trade for their man's release, they could go to a neighbouring commander and buy one in order to set up a private deal for his return.

Knowing that this stretch of the front was manned on the enemy side by Pakistani and al Qaeda fighters, Mayel Agah and Hadayatullah were optimistic that the man they had just killed would have a high value. Only six weeks before, their unit had fought for four days in an attempt to recover the body of Mullah Majid, another high-ranking Taliban they had slain in no man's land. So, even as the three surviving Taliban soldiers began to return fire at the two men, Mayel squirmed forward. He was tantalisingly close to the blood-soaked body but could also hear the crack and whip of the bullets around him. Cut by a flying fragment, he was already bleeding from an arm. Meantime, Hadayatullah was giving him covering fire with his machine-gun, but himself was targeted by rocket-propelled grenades and automatic fire.

Then a Taliban tank, one of the few to have survived the American air strikes, joined the fracas, sending detonations blasting around the two mujahedin fighters. Deciding that discretion was the better part of business, Mayel crawled back to Hadayatullah in the trench and apologised for his failure to secure the goods. They waited until the Taliban fire died down, then made their way back to their own line. Hours later, the body had gone, retrieved by the Taliban.

As we sat together drinking tea and smoking in the ruins of a hangar, peering across no man's land in the hope of sighting another Taliban work party, the skies cleared and the air strikes began again. The crews of the B-52s were dealing death the American way, packaged in thousand-pound bombs dropped from an invulnerable altitude, totally unaware of the exchange-rate intricacies of the Afghan system beneath them.

Shay and I dined that evening in an expansive Afghan home in Ghulam Ali, a small Shamali town just to the rear of the front. As ever in Afghanistan, the presence of women in the building was discernible only through the occasional slither of distant giggle, or the banging of cooking utensils in another room. Our host was Fahrid Ahmad Shafaq, a clan leader commanding the sector of the line which had seen the morning's action. An intelligent, educated man of twenty-eight, we had first met him at the circumcision ceremony a few weeks earlier, an event that now seemed much further in the past than it really was: Afghanistan's warclock had begun to warp our awareness of time. Born to a powerful Shamali family, Shafaq was the eldest son of a martyred commander who was killed fighting the Russians. By trade he was a businessman, dealing in construction and carpets. No small-time merchant shunting around the odd kilim, he was a big employer who owned large premises in Kabul that had imported and exported carpets throughout Central Asia. However, the Taliban's seizure of the capital cost him his business and forced him back to his Shamali home, where he commanded his clansmen on levy to the Northern Alliance.

After admiring the three herons wandering through his garden – as well as flowers, ornamental birds are a source of endless fascination to Afghans – we sat on the baked-mud floor to enjoy a lengthy feast of chicken, rice and watermelon and debated the war in lively exchange. Shafaq was keen to stress that Islamic fundamentalism was not the all-encompassing trait of Afghan society that I perceived it to be. Like any Westerner looking in, to me the rules and rituals of Sharia law seemed a generalised blanket, with the variations in its observation throughout the country small and unremarkable. I saw the conflict as a series of ethnic, tribal and opportunistic grapples for power that slid unfettered across the nation's imploded infrastructure, fuelled by outside interference. The Taliban's rise to power had been largely ignored for years, but now their extremism was being used as a primary justification for the US-led attack on Afghanistan, even though the West's allies, the Northern Alliance, espoused essentially the same tenets of Islamic ultra-conservatism.

Yet beyond the issues of ethnic power dominance, men like Shafaq had serious beef with the Taliban. On one hand, he was a local Tajik warlord, a man of the gun, a devout and pious Muslim living his life according to the rules of the Koran. On the other, he was also an astute businessman with an awareness of both the world outside and the possibility of progress in Afghanistan itself. He knew that there was more to education than learning the Koran by rote; that there was more to life than a valley cut off by broken bridges, blown roads and minefields; that children did not have to die of malaria; and that the appalling death rate of women during childbirth could be reduced if more women trained as doctors. And, like most Afghans, he had a well-developed concept of freedom and fun, albeit not in the Western sense of material possession and liberty. Rather, he relished the many choices and pleasures afforded by the Koran and his country's varied cultures. But in areas under Taliban control men were thrown in jail if their beard was deemed too short. Girls were banned from attending school. Children were forbidden from flying kites. Even kaftar bazi, the treasured Afghan sport of jousting with rival flocks of pigeons, was illegal. Television, music and video were all no-nos, along with any replication of natural image: in the city of Herat, the Taliban had cut the heads off four bronze horses decorating the central fountain because they considered them un-Islamic.

I had met the Taliban on many occasions while travelling in Afghanistan in the late nineties, had seen them fight, and had experienced Kabul under their jurisdiction. Topped in magnificent black or white turbans, many with their eyelashes adorned with charcoal, dark-skinned and robed, they were nothing if not ornate. Even the name – 'Taliban' – sounded like a glam-rock band. To my eyes, they looked cool. But they were a crushing disappointment, so limited and narrow in vision that dialogue with them was all but impossible.

They advertised themselves as purist, peacekeeping law-enforcers, but beneath this projection lay one of the most ethnically intolerant prejudices of any faction. Predominantly Pashtun, the Taliban had killed thousands of Hazaras, Uzbeks and Tajiks in massacres during the course of the war. And though they had brought a degree of stability to trade routes, freeing them of endemic banditry, and stifled the lawless whims of rogue mujahedin groups, their popularity was never very strong outside their southern heartland. As time passed, their tenure began to display some of the same traits of corruption, division and confusion that the mujahedin's once had.

More than being mere ethnic rivals, Shafaq saw the Lalaland authority of the Taliban, moulded by ultra-fundamentalist madrassa preachers in Pakistan and the Pashtun south, as a cage to the country's future and development, a humourless desert of rules that nailed the Afghan spirit into a medieval wasteland. It was an imposition he felt he had to fight. And he suggested that my belief that the Northern Alliance and the Taliban were essentially cut from the same cloth was a clumsy and disingenuous generalisation.

It remained true that most Afghans, especially the urban communities, felt trapped in the middle of the conflict, the issue of liberty overridden by both sides. In some respects their suffering cut to the heart of the great philosophical debate over whether freedom must be limited to be obtained. A year before, far up in the north of the country, I had encountered a young intellectual from Kabul who had spent months being tortured in a Taliban prison. Released by a family bribe, when I met him he had crossed the lines and was recovering from his injuries in the house of his uncle, an Uzbek warlord. Yet, rather than exalting in his liberty, he had been critical of the mujahedin, including his own family, comparing their criminality with the relative stability of Taliban areas. 'Until I was put in prison at least I had peace in the Taliban zone,' he had said. 'You are not free. You are very restricted. But you are not robbed. In the mujahedin areas you feel free but insecure, free but frightened, free without much to lose.'

I had then asked him which way of life he preferred, peace with limitation or war with freedom.

He had looked at me as if I were a child, and laughed good humouredly. 'You never find this answer; not in your country, not in ours. Life is the condition of the search between.'

Now I recited the conversation to Shafaq, and he too laughed, opening his arms wide, unfazed.

'The answer is the question,' he replied, 'but the options don't have to be so restricted. There is a place beyond war or tyranny for Afghanistan.'

The discussion meandered elsewhere as his aides cleared the remnants of our supper from the floor. Then an ancient black-and-white Russian television set was pulled from behind a curtain, clipped to a car battery, and attached to a home-made satellite dish on the roof. There in the room, before myself and Shay, Shafaq and a dozen mujahedin, appeared the face of Osama. They had picked up BBC World and the planet's most wanted terrorist was having his latest video aired by the service. Bin Laden was warning Muslims against collaboration with America in what he termed 'the war against Islam'.

Beside us, the mujahedin watched impassively, but, later in the night, as our conversation seemed ready to wind down and the room's occupants prepared for sleep, a new question was suddenly put to us by Shafaq: 'Do you believe that America's war is a war against Islam?' he asked, leaning forward, suddenly intense and concerned.

I responded as honestly as I could, telling him that I thought the war was not a religious conflict, but one fought against an aggressive, militant organisation. He nodded as the other mujahedin murmured their agreement, but there was uncertainty in their eyes. Silence followed, until one by one the mujahedin stood to shake hands and say farewell, leaving us to sleep. Pulling a patou over my shoulders, I lay back on a floormat, the sense of the men's doubt lingering in the room even after their departure. Whatever the vagaries of Afghan loyalty, at that point in time they did not question the legitimacy of their fight against the Taliban and al Qaeda. They understood that they needed American military support to ensure victory, but they were obviously deeply worried that America might so mishandle the conflict that it would one day become perceived as a Western war against their Muslim faith, leaving them on very much the wrong side.

Eventually I drifted off. On the wall beside me, Shafaq's father dressed in full mujahedin regalia, stared down from a photograph, hawk-faced and certain, long dead in a fight with another foreign power that had once advertised itself as the guardian of progress until its cack-handed management of war brought the roof down on Afghanistan's head in jihadist conflagration.

CHAPTER 16

Battle finally came to the Shamali Plain with the tardy, unapologetic demeanour of a long-awaited camel caravaneer arriving for business in a bazaar, quite oblivious to the frayed patience of his customers, aware of no timescale save for the one set by the single-speed, supercilious tread of his beasts; confident, arrogant, certain of a sale. Defying the pressures of American advisers, even H-Hour – the moment when thousands of mujahedin fighters swarmed forward in attack – came six hours late.

This leisurely final build-up befitted a poor man's army. For two days beforehand, mujahedin reinforcing units either tramped across the plain to their holding positions on foot or huddled in groups by the tracksides waiting for lifts to the front from passing vehicles, hunched silhouettes with ragged shalwar-kameezes and patous blowing in the wind, whiling away the hours playing karambol, an Afghan version of chequer billiards, smoking hash, wrestling with one another and laughing, apparently unconcerned with the fight ahead. Tankers, dented kickabout cans on wheels, lumbered around the rear lines, filling the mujahedin's few T-55s and APCs with much-needed fuel; and last-minute supplies, RPG warheads, hand grenades and belted chains of machine-gun ammunition were distributed among the men. As this readiness for war progressed with the same flagrant labour of a medieval siege, word spilled through the trenches of a victory in the far north of the country, where the city of Mazari Sharif had fallen to the mujahedin, injecting optimism into the Shamali fighters.

And just in case anyone should have been dull-witted enough not to realise the imminence of the push for Kabul, the general charged with leading the operation came and told us about it in person. Gul Haider was a famed mujahedin raider who had known Peter for several years. Though missing a leg, he possessed the burning energy often found in fighting-column commanders. Appearing one evening at Haji Dollar's block, he stomped up through the darkness of the stairwell and into the glow of our candles and storm lamps, a powerful, thickset figure in olive combat dress, a black-and-white dogtooth desmal wrapped around his head, Blackbeard on the eve of a freebooters' voyage, with a Makarov for a cutlass. Sitting down on the floor beside Peter, he announced unceremoniously that the battle for Kabul would begin the next day, unrolled a map and talked us through the plan, stabbing at the contour lines with thick fingers as he did so.

The concept was simple enough. An armoured vanguard of fifty Afghan tanks and APCs would storm across no man's land accompanied by assault teams, followed by two columns of mujahedin, each purportedly ten thousand strong. One column would advance along the Old Road to Kabul, the other up the New Road. Among the force, a couple of thousand men were tasked with mop-up operations in villages bypassed by the advance, and another three thousand would comprise a mobile reserve.

There were three lines of Taliban defences to break through, including strongpoints held by al Qaeda and Pakistani volunteers. Yet, with many Taliban units now ready to defect, Gul Haider seemed certain that these would not prove too difficult to overcome. Neither the Afghans nor the Americans were keen to allow the fighting to spill into Kabul's streets, so the plan was to break through the front, advance twenty miles to take the high ground of Khair Khana in the city's northern outskirts, and hope that the Taliban, their southern supply lines to the city already under pressure from air strikes, would then retreat from the capital of their own accord.

The idea seemed plausible, but would it work? Could the mujahedin penetrate the minefields of no man's land? Would the tanks, most of them rusting Soviet-era hulks that for years had been denied proper maintenance and upkeep, keep moving long enough to open the front?

How many of the anticipated defectors would really change sides? There were any number of imponderables. Time and time again throughout history, the seemingly flawless plans of an attacking force have been thwarted by some isolated group of men, fighting on to hold a key point with unexpected ferocity, affecting an entire battle's outcome; or by the sudden death of a charismatic commander causing an advance to falter, momentum to be lost, the men to become demoralised, their disciplined drive snarling up into the reefs of disarray.

I did not voice these questions because I knew there were no answers. And as Gul Haider left us, hobbling off on his pegleg to gather his war captains about him, he gave us the sign-off used each day by every Afghan in acknowledgement of destiny's caprice: 'Inshallah', God willing.

The confirmation of the impending fight left me excited and energised. The potential recapture of Kabul from the Taliban, so long anticipated, was the focus of all my work on the Shamali Plain over the previous weeks, and there could be no richer fulfilment of that effort than to accompany a mujahedin force as it struck southwards across the front to fight for the capital. But only a fool laughs on the eve of battle. So, as Shay fiddled with his lenses and cameras, the favourite pastime of any photographer, and I packed and repacked a small rucksack with sat-phone, water, bandages and patou, checked my body armour and knocked back a couple more tablets to quash the vestiges of dysentery, we spoke little. Our stock of moonshine and hashish lay ignored that night. There is no guide in a fire fight other than your own senses and judgement, so you straighten up, get serious and generate a little fear: it may be all that keeps you alive when the metal starts to fly.

Knowing war's random handouts well enough, Kurt's death still heavy on my mind, I was calm but introspective as I settled into my sleeping bag. I looked long at the bare details of the room and then at the stars burning coldly through the window in the winter sky; smelled deep the ambient scent of the Shamali – concrete and crap and woodsmoke; tasted the oaky burn of the evening's final cigarette; listened to the murmur of the mujahedin in the corridor and the tick-tick-tick of my wristwatch by my ear. And I savoured them all, holding the impression of each sense close. Because you can never be sure in war. You can never be bloody sure.

Battle, by its nature, is designed to impose profound shock and extreme stress on the human system; so much so that whatever the conclusion; few return from the experience of its intense violence quite the same as when they started. Subliminal or overt, there is always a change as the psyche, thrown up and shaken around, settles back upon itself when the gunfire and explosions fade – same shape but different pattern.

Set-piece battles are comparatively rare entities, the high tides of conflicts whose day-to-day front-line flow usually consists of fire fight, raid, ambush and localised attack. I had known only a few in all the wars I had seen since first travelling to Bosnia. There had been the long, drawn-out siege of Sarajevo, but that was more a protracted strangulation than a battle. Closer to the standard definition had been the rolling offensive by Bosnian government troops across the west of the state in the closing weeks of the war, a fast-moving series of fights across a wide front. And then there was the slam-dunk, word-robbing horror show of the Russians' first capture of the Chechen capital Grozny, a battle experience from which even the most hard-bitten of my war correspondent friends had staggered homeward gape-mouthed in mute disbelief, considering new careers in horticulture and social work.

As an outsider going into action with foreign troops, whether during major offensive or small-time skirmish, it is best to have at least one of your own kind as company to share some of the pressure, multiply the assets borne of your combined war wisdom, and provide back-up if one of you gets wounded. Conversely, you should avoid a large group and preserve as much unilateral integrity as possible. During fighting, any crowd of non-combatants tends to be afflicted by the paralysis and fears of herd instinct, their best attributes becoming negated by the passivity of the weakest member.

So, as the early morning sun shone across the rubble of the front on the Shamali Plain and the last assault groups of mujahedin formed up in readiness for the attack, sporadic artillery duels thumping across the lines in warm-up for the push, I felt in good company. Our jeep parked in cover to our rear, Shay sat on a bunker beside me, still dusting his lenses, while Peter and Big Sim promenaded on a track before us, their pace slow and deliberate, seemingly as satisfied as spring visitors to Kew Gardens. Their measured tread was familiar. Gearing up for action, Kurt had always abandoned his usual short, restless pacing for a similar beat-cop walk.

Not even the overhead whistle of an incoming round disturbed their patient perambulation, though it had me slide sideways to roll into a shellscrape quickly enough: there is no glory in dying before H-Hour. Besides, I had never managed to hold my nerve under shelling with much aplomb, unable to escape the memories of the revolting mutilation shrapnel inflicts on the human body. Having grubbed shamelessly along trench floors in various wars at the start of even the most inaccurate barrage, by now I had become rather proud of my acrobatic ducks, dives and rolls. Not that it prevented me from appreciating the guileless sang-froid of braver men. I always give them a mental thumbs-up and make a note to attend their funerals. Someone has to survive to tell the tale.

Dusting myself off, returning to my seat and lighting a cigarette, the skies above us began to reverberate with the sound of engines: F-18 attack jets and inbound B-52s, come to bomb the Taliban lines. Performing strike after strike, in a magnitude unseen before over the Shamali, they were guided to their targets by spotting teams of American special forces scattered along the front. One team – their buzz-cuts, blond beards and wide-shouldered physiques highlighting them among a surrounding gaggle of mujahedin despite their efforts to don local dress – stood brazenly on a nearby rooftop, gallery ducks to any half-competent Taliban marksman. It was as well for them that the close-range sprays of Kalashnikov culture had long ago eroded the infamous skills of Kipling's jezail-wielding Afghan sharpshooters.

Before us, as the air strikes intensified across the battlefield, adorning the alluvial expanse in wreaths of smoke, the final straggling files of mujahedin jogged through the earthen alleyways of the ruined front-line villages and into their places, their late arrival causing the scheduled H-Hour to roll back. It was an inauspicious start. In some areas their form-up was already under shellfire from the Taliban artillery; and, despite the smothering air strikes, the enemy's fire increased throughout the morning, so that by midday a lively artillery exchange was in progress, surface-to-surface missiles and shells detonating on opposing positions either side of no man's land. One small, panic-stricken group of mujahedin fell back from their trenches, running past us, shouting that a Taliban tank had broken through the line. We could hear its approaching rumble clear enough ourselves, and eyed each other nervously, for there is nothing like a rogue tank to sow chaos among the infantry. However, it was audible to the American spotters, too. There was a flurry of activity around their radio and minutes later the grinding of tank treads was given final punctuation by the air-sucking blast and thump of an F-18 payload.

Switching position, we joined Gul Haider on the thickened walls of a fortified farmhouse overlooking the Old Road. He was in his element, seated on the lip of the wall, pegleg stuck out before him towards the Taliban lines in accusation, binoculars to his eyes, half a dozen aides around him carrying radios linked to the various sectors of the front. From time to time he would grab one to bawl an order to his fighters in the trenches.

Up to that point it had all been good theatre, no more than the opening stages of the fight as the various units jockeyed to reach their jump-off positions and the opposing artillery wrestled for dominance. But at one o'clock in the afternoon, as the Taliban fire began to slacken in subjugation, the mujahedin armour surged forward into no man's land and files of vanguard troops ran behind them to force the breach: H-Hour had arrived.

On the farm's high walls everyone craned forward, trying to discern through the smoke and hammering gunfire the outcome of this moment, so crucial to all that followed. Then, over a radio crackled a desperate, panting voice from the assault commander at the breach: 'I need another fifty mujahedin here now . . .'

And Gul Haider swung around to his entourage of commanders, eyes ablaze, yelling in triumph: 'The lines are breaking! They're fleeing! Don't let them escape! Go, go go!'

Below the walls, scores of waiting mujahedin screamed in jubilation, rifles and fists raised high, their hour at hand, and rushed pell-mell forward to cross the trench lines in a speeding rampage. In a crunch of gears and a blast of black exhaust smoke, a T-55 took the lead, pitching forward into no man's land, rolling like a ship, the mujahedin racing behind its track lines in column to avoid mines, using the tank's armoured bulk as protection against return fire.

Charging from the farmhouse, we ran with them.

Utter pandemonium, gunfire, whistling bullets and exploding shells; RPGs and mortars rending the air near by; hoarse shouts and the chatter of radios; the roaring of tank engines and crash of air strikes; the hard sounds of war rolling along the Shamali front line, dust and smoke all around. Unable to run any faster than the man in front of me – a clod-hopping, RPG-laden dolt who seemed to be jogging on the spot – unwilling to step aside from the tank tracks and chance a mine, no man's land, perhaps only fifty yards wide, unfolded around me with the limitless threat of an ocean. How fast my thoughts raced. How slow my movements seemed. How far, far away the cover of the broken Taliban positions appeared.

At last, after several mental odysseys venturing through the labyrinths of chance, probability, wound-to-kill ratios, the effects of different weapon systems on the human body, and the usual abused promises to God, I made it, scrambling over a sand berm wall and dropping down into a Taliban trench. A dead, bullet-riddled defender was sprawled in the dust at my feet, mujahedin already clustered around him looting the body. Gunfire crackled. More shouts. More mujahedin piling into cover, wild-eyed, revved up, faces contorted, fervorous. Just ahead, over the lip of the berm three fighters ran through a vineyard. Mujahedin? Taliban? For seconds their fate hung in the balance as a commander tried to halt the smattering of fire they had attracted from his men. 'Don't shoot, their ours,' he screamed, as the trio ducked, jinked, ran, bullets puffing up the dust around them.

But then they turned and fired upon the mujahedin, and the killing cry went up: 'Taliban! They're Taliban. Fire, fire, fire . . .'

An RPG exploded to one side of the fugitives, knocking them down momentarily, before they rose once more from the dust, stunned now and no longer in flight, and twenty mujahedin leapt straight over the lip of the berm after them, regardless of the whipping bullets. For a tantalising second, as the first men reached the Taliban fighters, it seemed as if they may be taken captive, but then the mob of soldiery overwhelmed them, tearing their weapons from their hands, and they were gone, no quarter given, a chatter of Kalashnikov fire sending their brains rolling into their unravelling turbans as close-range retribution ended their lives, ID cards and small wads of money spilling into the dust as the hasty looting of the dead began.

More mujahedin jumped into the captured trenches around us, while other groups took on Taliban strongpoints to our left and right, the sound of grenades and machine-gun fire dulled behind the walls as the occupants were killed. They carried the fight and before them the Taliban defences melted. Most ran, some surrendered and survived, others tried to but died, some fought on and were killed amid the wilted vines of the abandoned farms. The first line was taken.

As the mujahedin consolidated their breach, thousands more troops followed in through the gap to push ahead to the next objective. They moved by whatever means they could: hanging from tanks, trucks and jeeps; running in exultant columns, stirring up clouds of dust which joined the smoke from bomb strikes and fires to grey the sun, forging ahead into a battlefield already tilled by five years of fighting. It was a landscape of shattered trees and gutted villages; barren, drought-bleached and desolate, pock-marked with the fresh lunar craters of aerial bombardment.

The marauding mass of vehicles and men poured unstoppably forward in a riot of sounds and images, but isolated details spun out to lodge in my mind: a gut-shot mujahed kneeling immobile in the dirt as his friends left him, a spreading scarlet stain seeping through his fingers as he clutched his belly, eyes staring with surprise at an unseen horizon; Taliban dead being pulled at, mauled and robbed; prisoners being slapped and abused; two soldiers praying in the ruins of a newly captured village; and a one-legged mujahed, his prosthesis lost, hopping desperately through the smoking wasteland to keep up with his comrades, gun in one hand, crutch in another, trying in vain to grab hold of the side of a passing lorry, frantic not to be left behind, the maimed and mad emblem to the afternoon's heaving, hot breath.

The advance halted at nightfall, a few miles short of its objective at Khair Khana. By then, it was obvious that the edifice of Taliban resistance had all but collapsed, their staunchly constructed cabin, its outward impression of strength undermined by the termites of defection and weakening resolve, crashing down in the face of applied pressure. By the standards of most wars, it had not been a ferocious battle: the Taliban had fought using a diehard blocking force while pulling the bulk of their men back to Kabul. But as I hunched over my laptop back in Charikar that night, stained head to foot in ash and grime, dehydrated and exhausted, wanting nothing more than to go to bed and knowing that another day of it might lie ahead, I struggled to write even a single word to send to the paper. The more intense an embrace with a moment in war, the harder it is to explain to an outsider, and far from being a pinnacle of reportage, the culminating *schwerpunkt* moment of the assignment left me vacant and empty, as confounded and failing in my role of messenger as the dreamer who upon awakening attempts to explain the essence of his night's visions to another.

For every war is a secret war, known only to those who were there. Whatever you say, however you say it, you can never explain that despite the fire, the fear, the smoke, the chaos, the killing, the madness and the loss, there exists something far beyond the trite accounting of collective risk and mortality: the best-kept secret of battle – the shared and terrible love of it all.

A single Talib stared up from the tarmac into the bruised dawn sky. Robbed of his Kalashnikov and turban, he lay on his back, arms flung wide, knees slightly bent. A rivulet of blood poured from his groin, streaming down the road's slight incline to form a pool more than ten feet away. His body was otherwise unmarked and his pale blue shalwar-kameez was clean and quite unsullied by the fight. He appeared to have been killed by the simple act of castration.

Around him was only emptiness. There was not a living soul in sight and the landscape of yellow earth and dead vineyards was all but devoid of feature. The wind was cold and the sun had not yet risen above the distant mountains. Shay and I stared at him for a minute or two, then stepped back into the jeep and drove southwards, leaving the body where it lay, lone sentinel to the sunrise on Kabul's liberation day.

Unfurling our sleep-stiffened limbs in the darkness of early morning, an hour earlier we had loaded our Charikar belongings into the jeep and sped across the empty battlefield to catch the mujahedin advance units before Khair Khana, certain we should reach Kabul that day. Its access opened by the offensive, the Old Road at first allowed us fast movement and in the wake of the mujahedin push the debris of battle passed beside us in a blur of torn metal and the occasional twisted limb as we raced over the plain before entering the featureless expanse of uncontested desert.

Barely a mile after seeing the emasculated soldier, as dawn shed its first weak pink rays over the landscape, we found death again waiting for us on the pitted tarmac. Five more bodies lay in the middle of the road. Taliban, killed only minutes earlier, gore-spattered and bullet-holed, their blood was still bright and flowing. Two were entwined in an embrace. We stopped beside them, curious to know whether they had been executed or killed in action.

As I stepped among them one moved. Then he sat up. There was blood gurgling from his mouth and his torso was riddled with wounds. A waxen dullness had spread over his face. Life would leave him soon. I photographed him, preserving his face as he slid away. The act was unnatural, diminishing, even sociopathic, and it bothered me slightly. But it was a strong image and I was not being paid to adhere to social norms. Belatedly it occurred to me that he might have something to say, so I asked him where he was from. My interpreter was a chubby young chemist from Golbahar whom I had employed after finally sacking the doctor a few days earlier. An educated man with good English, he was, however, passive to the point of laziness, given to daydreaming and lassitude, and had the annoying habit of sucking sweets throughout any conversation. Now he stared at me fixedly, apparently appalled by my indifference towards the dying fighter, and a couple of reluctant seconds passed before he translated my question.

Croaking and spluttering, at first the fighter claimed he was a wounded mujahed. There was another momentary, judgemental pause as the chemist digested the answer, before he was transformed with a sudden bolt of rage. 'You're lying! You're a Talib,' he spat at the man. Now it was my turn to stare at him, amazed at his vindictiveness.

Lolling, then falling on an elbow, and finally lying down to die, the man admitted that he was a Talib from Kalakhan. Trapped by the speed of the mujahedin advance, he and his men had attempted to escape in a Datsun pick-up. Only moments earlier they had run into a mujahedin unit and surrendered. The mujahedin had gunned them down, taken their vehicle and driven off, believing them all to be dead.

There was not much else to say and nothing more to do. There was no place to take the man for assistance. The mujahedin would only finish him off if they saw him in my jeep. We had no medicine and I needed to preserve my stock of dressings in case one of us was hit. He was all but through anyway. So we left him to die and moved forward towards Kabul.

At the pass above Khair Khana, the gateway to the city, we found hundreds of Northern Alliance fighters crowded together in a wide defile, as tanks and APCs, laden with more infantry, moved to flanking positions on the high ground. They were cheering and jubilant at the speed with which they had routed the Taliban, who, having been pitched from their positions on the plain the previous day, had fled that morning with barely a fight. In a quieter moment a group of them robbed some passing Kochi nomads, Pashtuns, kicking and punching them while ripping their brightly coloured belongings from the backs of pack-ponies, fighting over the clothes and grain in the dust.

The way ahead was blocked to all by two APCs and a cordon of troops, as mujahedin commanders waited for orders as to whether to enter the city, cupped in the lowland below us, its nearest suburb no more than a few hundred yards away. A senior mujahedin commander forbade us from progressing any further, explaining that it was unclear if the Taliban were still in Kabul.

I waited for a while in frustration as a column of several thousand Kabuli citizens walked out of the city to greet the victorious fighters. They seemed genuinely elated by the arrival of the Northern Alliance, handing the men sugar cakes, shaking their hands and embracing them. Their mood softened the attitude of the cordon.

The sun rose and it became hotter. I again approached the mujahedin commander and implored him to let us through. The conversation blustered around inconclusively for a few minutes. He never acquiesced directly but eventually merely stepped aside and walked away. Interpreting this as permission, we drove through the cordon. One of its men fired two warning shots over the jeep and yelled a bit.

'The general said it was OK,' I offered hopefully. It seemed to suffice, and with a dismissive wave of his hand the guard gestured us down the road to Kabul. It was ten o'clock.

I felt neither brave nor particularly euphoric. Though all the signs, the silence of the streets and the word of passing civilians, suggested that the Taliban had withdrawn from the capital, I knew that entering a newly fallen city, whatever the ostensible absence of defenders, is a formulaic way for a journalist to die. In some respects a battle is a safer place to be. Senses on overdrive, parameters defined by the noise of fighting, there are usually clear signals governing movement. To enter a city whose defenders have capitulated in surrender is one thing, but to move into the limbo between a retreating army and an advancing one is quite another. The boundaries are blurred and confused, and all it takes to be killed is a chance encounter with the wrong group of looters, who traditionally swarm into a vacuum faster than anyone else in wartime; a rearguard force; a sniper; or the enraged tail end of the fleeing army.

And I felt ill. A recurrent bout of dysentery was back and cramping my stomach. A week-long diet of Pakistani biscuits and boiled eggs had not done much for my energy level, and I had enjoyed little over four hours' sleep in the previous two nights. So, drained, bad tempered and in need of a loo, I entered Kabul, increasingly suspicious that the scene with the dying Taliban fighter may have tainted my fortune for the day.

As we drove into the first bazaar a crowd of about a thousand people surrounded our vehicle, leaping on the bonnet, applauding what I think they believed to be two American soldiers. There were no mujahedin or Talibs to be seen in the city, and the appearance of our white faces and camouflaged jeep sent out entirely the wrong impression to people hungry for any sort of reality on which to project their delight. A man wrenched open the jeep doors and threw glitter all over me. I cringed with embarrassment.

'Er, are there any Talibs around?' I asked him with a stiff smile.

'Taliban far, far away,' he replied, 'they go last night in a big caravan.'

The day improved a little after that. An hour or two later the mujahedin arrived in marching columns, and Alliance tanks distracted the attention of the crowds as they rumbled through the streets. There was little looting and Kabul seemed happy, if not overjoyed, by the new turn of events.

Many hours later, as dusk descended, having checked into the Hotel Intercontinental, a shoddy, veteran building of mouldy walls, broken windows and dirty carpets, host to various travellers throughout the many eras of Afghanistan's war, I met a fellow-journalist and we started talking. Cold anticlimax was upon me and I had already forgotten the novelty of the first flushing loo and electricity I had experienced in two months.

'Did you see those five dead Talibs on the road before Khair Khana?' the man asked, keen to relive the scenes of the advance.

'Yeah,' I replied, and left it at that.

A day after liberation, in the first symbolic step of bidding farewell to Afghanistan and reintegrating with the half-forgotten world outside, I had my beard shaved off.

'Were you open for business yesterday?' I asked as I settled into the barber's chair, taking a last loving look at the fine black and red growth in the mirror before me.

'We would have been but we were worried about the looting,' the barber replied calmly, flicking out a cut-throat razor and laying it on the shelf beside him. 'And then five Arabs were found in the park. They fought with the soldiers for over an hour and killed two of them. Eventually they gave up and were shot. Their bodies were left in the park and we decided it would perhaps be better for business to wait until today. Now, this may hurt a little, I'm afraid. Until today, it's been five years since I've done a clean shave.'

It was not the most encouraging start to a barber's shop conversation between customer and proprietor, but the razormen in Kabul had endured a strange existence since the Taliban had seized the city five years earlier. Hair had become one of the most contentious targets amid a host of repressive laws enforced in the capital by the ultra-fundamentalists' Ministry for the Propagation of Virtue and Suppression of Vice. According to the Taliban interpretation of Islamic law, beards were compulsory and must be long enough to show through a clenched fist. Violators were imprisoned until their beards grew to acceptable lengths. By contrast, long hair on the head was punished by a full cranial shave.

Now, as Kabul basked in its first day of relative freedom and its citizens realised that they no longer had to worry about the whip-wielding vice squads on the streets, the beards were beginning to fall, at least partially. In a seated queue behind me a dozen men awaited their turn in the barber's stall beside the Shahr-i-Naw Park, grinning broadly, stroking their beards and insulting each other.

'Hey, Ahmad, with a face like yours, I wouldn't bother . . .'

'You can talk. The zoo hasn't had a baboon in it for years. Get into a cage and save yourself some money.'

'I must have trimmed nearly a hundred beards today, and you are my tenth clean shave,' the Afghan Sweeney Todd informed me blithely, with scarcely an 'oops' as the first trickle of blood rolled down my chin.

Afghans are notoriously vain and individualistic, so it was little surprise to learn that even in the Taliban era many men had rejected the Sharia look of long beard and cropped hair. To cope with the demands of these fashion rebels, the barber had had to keep his one shop as an official front for the Taliban cuts and open a second 'speakeasy' venue in secret.

'It wasn't easy,' he told me. 'Many barbers were thrown in jail for deviating in their work. Fifty of my friends throughout the city ended up in Pulecharki Jail for illegally trimming beards. And it was even worse during the *Titanic* phase.'

This era, one of Kabul's sorrier cultural nadirs, came when the traumatised population became fixated by the film, relating to its depiction of tragedy and the watery fate of its star, Leonardo DiCaprio. Fuzzy pirate videos smuggled in from Pakistan were shown in cellars across the city night after night in another grave breach of Taliban authority. 'Titanic' became a clothes brand and, more disturbingly, the 'DiCaprio' haircut became a rallying point for Afghan youth. Hundreds were incarcerated as a result, and hundreds more preferred to hide their short-sides/bouffant-top look beneath turbans and admire themselves in private at night.

Yet, for all the jocularity in the barber's shop that day, fear lingered. None of the three barbers at work wanted their name used or their shop identified.

'People here are not sure that the Taliban will not return,' one remarked as I got down from the chair and paid, naked face burning in the aftershock of a blitzkrieg of local aftershave. 'That's why most customers only want a trim rather than a clean shave. The Taliban have gone for the moment but the political situation is very unstable and who knows when they may come back?'

Their doubt was reflected in the minds of people throughout the capital. Liberation may have passed without any of the looting or disorder so feared by its population, yet their reaction to it remained low key, even disinterested. Music, banned under the Taliban, was already being played in public, but with the low-volume conservatism of a grandmother's radio. A few kites flew. Women were walking on the streets unaccompanied by their husbands, fathers or brothers, another violation of Taliban edicts, but they remained in burqas. There was no flagrant release of tension in the capital, no street party or public celebration, and people viewed the future with a mood somewhere between cautious hope and subdued scepticism.

Sprawled across a sandy plain beneath a wide encirclement of mountains, Kabul was testament to both the ravages of war and the resilience of its people. Though little damaged by American air strikes, the destruction of the civil war had reduced it to a skeletal urban wreckage, a few islands of comparatively untouched residential areas existing among the shredded wastelands of former front lines, fought over between rival mujahedin forces prior to the Taliban's ascent, when entire city quarters were so battered and blasted as to resemble ancient archaeological sites.

'Kabul', wrote Nancy Dupree in a 1977 edition of *An Historical Guide to Afghanistan*, essential reading matter for Afghan aficionados, 'is a fast growing city where tall modern buildings nuzzle against bustling bazaars and wide avenues fill with brilliant flowing turbans, gaily striped chapans, mini-skirted school girls, a multitude of handsome faces and streams of whizzing traffic . . .'

Twenty-four years later, the city she wrote of was no more recognisable than the photograph of a beautiful woman taken before the acid attack of a jealous husband. Absolute poverty now consumed its citizenry, who eked their survival among the thinly stocked bazaars; the city's wide avenues were full of rubbish and faeces, beggars, cripples and mullahs; there was not a mini-skirt in sight. Only the traffic remained, lurching around the pot-holed streets from one jam to another, throwing a smog into the sky which was held in the windless atmosphere to sit over the streets each dawn like a brown umbrella.

In the poorer ghettos beneath the ruins of British hill forts, thousands of survivors, displaced and dispossessed by the years of fighting, crammed together at night upon blankets in any room suggesting a semblance of shelter, with children running in packs through the wreckage on new walkways of collapsed floors and teetering masonry.

Amid the sadness, the wistfulness for the distant past and the daily toil of survival, however, Kabulis remained humorous, stoic and friendly; even magnificent in their reduced state. Whenever the capital's name cropped up in conversations between war reporters, irrespective of our current circumstance or location in the world, it always provoked a wry smile, laugh and sense of engendered affection similar to that of an absent accomplice held close despite the wayward complexities of their character.

Though happy to encounter the city once again, and relieved that the development of events may have given it a chance to regenerate, I was deeply tired. The months spent on the Shamali Plain and the energy required to follow the story to the point of the city's recapture had left me void, suddenly empty of motivation and unable to devote myself to the further progression of the war.

Meanwhile, the fighting continued on new battlefields far from Kabul. In the distant south of Afghanistan several mujahedin groups moved towards the city of Kandahar, the Taliban's traditional stronghold and the home of their leader Mullah Omar. And in the east mujahedin units pushed from across the Pakistani border into Jalalabad, giving lacklustre chase up the Tora Bora Valley to Bin Laden and a column of al Qaeda fighters. Inevitably, the mists of Afghan fealty and the widespread defection that had caused such speedy collapse among the Taliban also served the fugitives well. Though the same tribal chiefs who had supported the Taliban now turned against them, in many instances they did so while remembering their past allegiance. There was killing enough, but most of the Taliban and al Qaeda leadership escaped safely into the mountains, allowed either free passage or the time to flee by pursuing mujahedin forces as the Americans scratched their heads, unable to comprehend how their reliance on air strikes and indigenous fighters had confounded their plans to capture Omar and bin Laden.

These distant events brought their own bitter conclusion to my brief time in the capital. Forging ahead of a group of journalists moving from Jalalabad through the foreboding passes towards Kabul, along a road notorious for banditry, a vehicle was halted by armed men and its four occupants, all reporters, murdered. Among the dead was a friend of mine. Maria Grazia was a brave, charming and attractive Italian correspondent with whom I had once travelled on assignment in Central Asia. Aware that she had been in Pakistan, I had been looking forward to seeing her again in Kabul. Now she lay dead among the roadside rocks, killed on the whim of a feral gunman.

Word of her killing reached me hours later. It was of news value, so the paper asked me to write about it. My memories of the time we had once shared together concluded with the tapping reduction of a keyboard in my hotel room, a few soulless lines, hard news, no adjectives, writing as if I had never known her, turning her into just another war death. I hoped no one had photographed her body.

Sitting on a shingle bank beside a footbridge over the Panjshir River three days later, I could not wait to get out, home, somewhere, anywhere. With the northern passes blocked by snow and the bandits not yet removed from the road east, a ride by helicopter over the Hindu Kush to a point near the Tajik border was the only means out. However, forty-eight hours after Shay and I had first appeared at the small landing strip deep in the valley, our morale was in steep decline, our hopes of a speedy exit diminishing by the moment. The Northern Alliance's small helicopter force of battered Hip transporters was overloaded by commitments of its own, and the few touch-downs and take-offs we had seen allowed space for nothing but ammunition and mujahedin.

In order to lift our spirits we began to laugh at the labours of a few mujahedin across the river. They were clustered around an abandoned Hip, a machine of drooping rotors and bullet-riddled fuselage that was obviously so lacking in airworthiness as to be ignored by even the most death-charged pilot. The toil of these men progressed throughout the morning in a series of hammering and screeches, as they performed their tasks with what appeared to be no more than a few mallets and screwdrivers. At first I presumed they were scrap merchants stripping down the helicopter for money, but after midday two crewmen walked into the vessel.

'I don't believe it,' Shay snorted. 'They're actually going to try to fly it!'

Roaring with laughter, we took cover behind the bridge's concrete foundations and peered out as the engines fired up and the blades began to turn, certain that we were about to witness a crash. Nothing in the first minutes of the machine's reawakening suggested otherwise. With a rattling, discordant throb, it shot suddenly skyward, dropped stone-like to hover barely six feet from the ground, then veered backwards and sideways as ground debris, smoke and dust flew in every direction.

Landing with a hefty thump, the engines began to wind down as we heaved sighs of relief and continued to rock with mirth.

'Jesus, guess they worked out that one's a no-no.'

Ten minutes later, the pilot walked over the bridge and approached us. 'If you want a ride, then that's the machine,' he informed us. 'We leave as soon as everyone is on board.'

So I crossed the Hindu Kush as I had arrived, with my eyes screwed shut, but with the added delight of my clothes being coated in aviation fuel from a leaking pipeline, sure that the crate's every grind and plunge would be its last.

CHAPTER 17

Iraq, March 2003

After my days at Core, and so long at war, I thought when it came to compulsions that I had heard it all before, but Burkhan Ismail craved a fix so peculiar that it made the Curry Kid sound like a figure of anodyne banality. It was a lethal itch that scratched out his eyes in two-way tears of fear and wonder. But, of course, it never got him to where he wanted to be. Small surprise that in the dog days of sputtering conflict that marked the start of the war in northern Iraq his words held a special personal significance.

He was addicted to clearing mines. And it terrified him.

I met him on a small roadway beside one of the heavily mined positions abandoned by Iraqi troops a few days earlier as they fell back towards Kirkuk. In a landscape of ravine and defile, the afternoon heat was turgid and the sun high. Iraqi artillery had just finished a sporadic bombardment on nearby peshmerga posts. There was a minefield on either side of the rutted tarmac, one of a multitude in the area, and the flat grey caps of Italian-made anti-tank VS-2.2s and Iraqi PMN anti-personnel mines could be seen, just, lying flush with the broken ground.

Then a jeep filled with peshmerga pulled up and Burkhan leapt out. Tall and skinny, he strode straight into the middle of the minefield with speed-freak alacrity and began stabbing at the ground with a bayonet, his movements as sharp, fast and angular as a secretary bird attacking a snake. Black PMN mines flipped out of the ground left and right. The PMN is a model of capricious lethality which professional mine-clearing organisations destroy on site rather than attempt to clear, such is its

sensitivity. Yet Burkhan's party piece, having lifted a loose handful of
PMNs out of the soil in no more than a minute, was to place one on the
road, unscrew the fuse cap, and stamp on it. Without the retaining cap to
activate it, the fuse shot out of the side without exploding. Yet all it took,
I realised as I hunched behind the engine block of our jeep, was for one
grain of sand to have wedged inside the fuse tube and at best Burkhan
would be joining the queue for a prosthesis or two. He tossed me the
deactivated PMN body and I caught it, flinching. Light, the weight of a
dead blackbird, it would nevertheless have been powerful enough to
take off a leg at the knee.

A group of Kurdish merchants appeared in a second vehicle and
waited for Burkhan to finish fooling around so that they could buy the
mines. Once extracted from the devices, TNT was a good commodity in
the bazaars. Business complete, a few notes richer, Burkhan turned to
speak to me for a while. Far from puffing out his chest with braggadocio,
he was shaking in the backwash of what he had just done. He told me
that he had been clearing mines since he became a peshmerga at fifteen,
thirteen years earlier, and had worked in so many minefields that he had
lost count of the thousands of devices he had dug up and disarmed.
Operating as a freelancer, he cleared mines for both the peshmerga and
merchants. More often, though, he worked just for himself, locked into
his own terminal chance-and-probability trip.

'I like fishing,' he said blankly at first. 'I don't use a rod. I dig up some
anti-personnel mines, attach wire to the fuses, lob them in the river and
detonate them. I always get loads that way.'

After a while he unwound a little and confessed more. The art of his
survival lay in understanding the configurations in which most mines
are planted within their field. Iraqi troops favoured the figure-four
pattern. Once Burkhan had found the first mine, the location of the
others became part of a known variability that decreased with every
subsequent discovery. Working with no more than a bayonet and
apparent intuition, he knew well enough that eventually a booby-
trapped device or rogue mine in a patterned field would kill him.

'One day I will miss one and then . . . But it's like a challenge I can't
get rid of.'

He said that his feelings when he was among mines were an obsessive pendulum swing of anticipatory fear, adrenalin high, post-clearance calm and subsequent regret. Trying not to laugh, I took a few notes and left him to it, driving off in my own circle as he returned to jabbing the desert with his knife and bomb crush, just another troubadour who loved in the wrong way.

I had crossed the Iranian border into northern Iraq a few weeks before. The road wound down from the mountains and heavy February rain splattered across the taxi's windscreen, blurring an undulating landscape of green meadows and low foothills. I had been confident in my choice of destination as a jumping-off point for the war. Mindful of my experiences in Priština, I felt certain that journalists based in Baghdad would be thrown out of the country as soon as the fighting began and the Ba'ath regime felt their fortunes declining. The alternative, to head to Kuwait and report as an embedded journalist with the coalition forces, was too appalling to consider for much more than a minute. Though military press officers can sometimes be decent, even forthright, in their dealings with journalists, they are usually tightly chaperoned by government press officials, suited pukes with a political agenda intent on keeping the message on track. Any useful information these politicised civil servants impart usually travels first through the prism of lies, twisting, obfuscation and distortion, the very skills in which they are trained, long before being relayed to a reporter. I assumed that in Kuwait they would be shadowing the embedded journalists' every move, directly or otherwise. Truth is as much a weapon as a casualty in war, and however dull-witted and unimaginative the suits can seem, when it comes to bullshit they could sell Dunkirk as a divisional beach party. I wanted to avoid their influence at all costs.

The area of mountains and pasture in the north of the country, populated and self-governed by four million Kurds, thus seemed an obvious place to begin the assignment. As well as offering an insight into the realities of chemical warfare, an ease of travel and an absence of official minders, the territory sat on the main axis route for the planned thrust of the American 4th Infantry Division from Turkey southwards, into the heart of Iraq. These troops had not yet even landed in Turkey, though, and as the coalition's war preparations in Kuwait were still far from complete, I felt sure that I would have a few weeks to travel around and familiarise myself with the region before slipping easily alongside the American vanguard, sweeping up the laurels so inaccessible to my thwarted, morale-shattered colleagues elsewhere, so that I could leave Iraq having covered the fall of Baghdad while the late arrivals followed up the rear to work on reconstruction stories. There was even a semi-decent hotel, complete with a bar, in the city of Sulaimaniyah, where I planned to stay. No desert hardships or army rations for me – at least not until the big push began.

Twelve years before, as we had cleared the last group of Iraqi prisoners from their position at the conclusion of the war to retake Kuwait, my company commander, a man afflicted by a sense of anticlimax similar to my own, had asked me if I thought anyone would have noticed if we had not turned up. The question still haunted me. However, now it seemed clear that as long as I did not get shot or blown up, fate was conspiring to bring me full circle, back to the location of my first war, to reap the rewards denied me earlier. Baghdad was almost in my grasp. The plan was so watertight I think I was even smiling as Sulaimaniyah rose into view from the mists ahead.

Still trying to make time and war fit into some sort of pattern in spite of all the senselessness and chaos I had witnessed, as the car approached the city I felt that I was heading towards a point of genesis in my life. Kurt was dead; my addiction was missing, presumed dead; too many wars; too much hatred and blood; too much destruction. This latest war must surely, I thought, involve some culminating revelation, a shaft of light that would strike through the receding storm to leave me wiser at last. There was just one small trace of lingering doubt to interrupt this comforting vision. Exactly how long would the war go on?

Flying out from London to Tehran a few days earlier for the initial leg of the journey, public support for the impending conflict was very different to that I had enjoyed as a soldier when deploying to retake Kuwait, and begged some pointed questions. As I was boarding the aeroplane a million people were taking to the streets of London to protest against the war. My sister and mother were among them. Every husband, every father and every grandfather of those two women had at one time served their country in uniform. Rather than being benign pacifists, they came from a militarised segment of British society that regarded soldiering as a profession of honour, and intervention, even pre-emptive attack, as sometimes necessary for moral objective or national interest. But even they did not support the coming war. They shared the widely held sense of having been lied to by their government and that of the Americans. They did not believe that Saddam Hussein still posed a serious regional, let alone international, threat. And, crucially, they feared that the blowback of invading Iraq to disarm the Ba'ath regime would undermine their country's ability to fight a more complex conflict that *was* both legitimate and unavoidable: that against terrorist networks.

While sharing these views in part, I presumed that the war, even if embarked upon for the wrong reasons, would probably have a positive conclusion. Military victory seemed guaranteed and in its wake the Iraqis would perhaps be moderately grateful, quickly purging their society of Ba'athist elements and regenerating their country on peaceful and pro-Western lines. An emerging Iraqi democracy would leave Britain safer and the Iraqi people better off. The whole affair must be over by spring, I reasoned. Saddam was all but history and the powers that be must surely have a detailed plan of how to reconstruct Iraq in the wake of his demise.

Nevertheless, doubts flickered through my mind. The coalition's war in Afghanistan had been far easier to justify than this latest venture. I had spent much of the previous year in return visits to the country and had seen nothing to contradict that belief. Lacking any obvious link to the September 11th attacks, Iraq was a very different proposition. As it loomed, I found myself missing Kurt more than ever, and not just as a friend and accomplice. Among the multitude of journalists, he had possessed a singular vision and clarity. Several times in the late nineties he had even predicted an imminent and huge terrorist attack upon America, and warned me of its consequences. But now he was gone, and the rest of us had to grapple in reactive confusion with the new challenge as best we could.

I should have been up to the task. After all, as the taxi entered the outskirts of Sulaimaniyah I possessed a wealth of war knowledge stretching back eighteen years, to the point when I had first enlisted in the army. Yet every single assumption I carried with me that day, ranging from my choice of start location, to the trajectory of my life, to the future of Iraq, proved to be totally and utterly wrong.

Kurt played me a tape once, then a few more times at my request. Recorded on a Walkman as he accompanied a peshmerga unit in a full-on assault against an Iraqi strongpoint during the Kurds' uprising in 1991, it remains an unforgettable account of the nature of sustained infantry attack and its aftermath. At first the firing is irregular and haphazard, but it intensifies quickly as the guerrillas advance under increasingly heavy fire, the air ripping with the cracking retorts of incoming bullets, war cries, and the thump of RPGs. Turn up the volume on a good stereo and you are transported right into the middle of it all as Kurt's voice, remarkably controlled considering that men to his left and right were dropping to bullets, narrates the unfolding fight. Then, as the peshmerga storm into the Iraqi perimeter, scores of surrendering soldiers, most of them young conscripts, can be heard pleading for mercy. For a second or two the gunfire seems to subside, then it bursts forth again, rising in crescendo.

'My God,' Kurt speaks again, his voice sharp with shock. 'What's happening here? They're killing the prisoners.'

The Kurds go berserk, machine-gunning every captive, then smashing the heads of the dead with concrete slabs. When they finally cool down and the mutilation stops, the voices of more peshmerga can be heard discussing whether to kill Kurt in order to silence the only witness. The tape ends. Kurt got away. That time.

A political football throughout their history, the Iraqi Kurds' hatred of Saddam's regime had escalated throughout the savage 'Al Anfal' operations of the late eighties, when nearly two hundred thousand of their people were arrested and executed by Ba'athist forces in a bid to crush their separatist aspirations. Chemical weapons were persistently used against rural communities during this campaign, a strategy culminating in the infamous bombardment of the Kurdish city of Halabja, when up to seven thousand Kurds were gassed to death in a single attack.

Crushed by the scale of this persecution and denied a regional ally by the end of the Iran–Iraq war, three years after the Halabja attack Iraq's Kurds had risen again, encouraged by the exhortations of George Bush Senior following the Iraqis' defeat in Kuwait. For a few short weeks the Kurds had controlled almost all of their territory in northern Iraq, routing Iraqi army units and killing Mukhabarat secret police and Amn security service personnel wherever they were found in a time of brutal retribution which Kurt had witnessed at first hand. During this small window they had even seized Kirkuk, a city possessing a Jerusalem-like status in their collective psyche. The discovery of oilfields in the 1920s had made Kirkuk the biggest single economic asset in northern Iraq. (The oozing crude resources were supposedly the location of the flaming biblical pits survived by Shadrach, Meshach and Abednego after their refusal to worship Nebuchadnezzar's golden idol.) Claimed historically as their own, it had long been denied to the Kurds by the successive defeats that had blighted their independence campaigns against the Baghdad authorities. However, their recapture of the city had lasted no more than a few days. By the time I had arrived back in Britain from the Gulf, an anonymous and irritable member of the force that had just returned Kuwait to its autocratic rulers, in the north of the country the Iraqi army had regrouped and was counter-attacking. They effortlessly retook Kirkuk, whose loss marked the start of another catastrophic defeat for the Kurds which sent some two million refugees fleeing in panic to Turkey and Iran.

They had never regained the city, despite some belated Western support which allowed them to return home later that year, their security guaranteed by northern Iraq being made a 'safe-haven' and a 'no-fly zone'. Kirkuk, though, remained in Iraqi control just outside the limits of this territory; and without its oilfields, the Kurdish autonomous zone was technically an economic basket case. Governed in tandem by the two leading Kurdish political parties, who in the past had fought one another in a wasteful civil war, their land was little more than a financial orphan dependent on United Nations subsidies supplemented by local smuggling.

Now, though, as the Kurds saw the coalition building up its military might in readiness to invade, they again made plans to seize Kirkuk from Baghdad's grip. But no one else wanted them back in control of the city. Wary of their own restive Kurdish populations, each neighbouring state was keen to keep the Iraqi Kurds economically neutered, fearing that control of Kirkuk would incite a new pan-Kurd drive for independence. The Turks were especially truculent, having fought their own long and bloody campaign against Kurdish separatists. Indeed, Turkey saw little merit at all in allowing American troops passage through their territory to fight in Iraq. Already wary of Bush's war aims, they presumed that such an operation could benefit only the Kurds. So the game that paralleled the steps to the new war was an intense series of move and counter-move between the Americans, Ankara and the Kurds as each sought to achieve their own ends.

My practical preparations for the coming conflict were more auspicious. I acquired the guns by a garbage-tip rendezvous on a highway at the edge of Sulaimaniyah, standing self-consciously beside the dealer's blue saloon to check the merchandise in his open boot as traffic rolled by and thin vagabond kids poked about in the surrounding waste in search of food and salvage. The supplier resembled a low-grade pimp in a dark corduroy jacket and purple shirt, a mobile phone ringing in one hand. It was a chill day that the shy February sun did little to warm. Adding to the dismal ambience, a handicapped boy, maybe ten or twelve years old, rocked back and forth in the saloon's back seats as we talked cash and calibres. His son? I never asked. The child grimaced and slapped at his face in fear as the dealer loosed off a test clip from a pistol into the surrounding wilderness.

'This is not the time for Plato,' Awat noted sagely. A short penguin of a man, deeply fascinated by philosophy, a born raconteur and a journalist in his own right, he was my interpreter. I had met him in the offices of a Kurdish newspaper in Sulaimaniyah a few days after my arrival and had quickly hired him.

His observation was apt enough: it was not the moment to talk of ethics and philosophy. Although journalists and guns do not mix well, there were so many diverse risks facing us that I figured we might as well set an agenda geared to our own survival. My driver Magdid was a former peshmerga fighter, who in a past era of his life had been trained in close-protection skills by the Americans. Beyond the potential threats of chemical attack, mines, shellfire, air strike and the rest of the conventional war panoply, there were more sinister risks. In a nearby mountain enclave, bordering Iran, lurked Ansar al Islam, an al Qaeda-affiliated amalgam of foreign fighters and fundamentalist locals, men deeply antipathetic to any Westerner and on the verge of killing their first foreign journalist. So it seemed a good idea to arm Magdid and refresh his training.

Some television crews were already employing mini-armies of armed guards. My budget did not stretch that far, but it could run to a couple of guns to be concealed in the car for worst-case scenarios. So I blew seven hundred bucks on a Kalashnikov and a Tariq 9mm pistol, and bought enough ammunition to cope with a significant altercation. Magdid seemed so delighted with the goods that I had to talk him through the rules of engagement five times over, just to ensure that he did not open up at a traffic cop at the first opportunity.

Next I took Awat and Magdid to Sulaimaniyah's bazaar, a winding maze of covered alleys in the centre of the city where you could buy anything from smuggled electronics, televisions and DVDs, engine parts, clothing, food and spices right down to the lowliest wingnut, walnut and flip-flop. Artificial it may have been, but in northern Iraq the Kurds' black market economy was clearly thriving, and life in the urban areas was little different to that in any other Middle Eastern country, and was more affluent than many. Moving into the sector of the bazaar selling military-surplus gear, I kitted out my team in full nuclear, biological and chemical protective clothing, including gas masks, charcoal-lined hoodies, trousers, rubber gloves and boots. Having already been issued with my own kit in London, I knew that I could hardly go into a chemical battlefield with the staff in jeans and cotton shirts. I did not want another interpreter dying on me.

ANTHONY LOYD

We made sure we had enough spare fuel stored in a lock-up to last us all the way to Baghdad should the start of hostilities affect available stocks. We practised changing into our chemical suits in my hotel room, a predictably shambolic rehearsal which proved that we required at least a ten-minute alert of an inbound gas shell, and test-fired the guns in a deserted valley, blowing away a rampaging terrorist hit squad of empty mineral-water bottles.

My final purchases in preparation for the coming apocalypse were some caged birds. I reckoned that a canary would, in case of its sudden death, give us an early warning of gas attack. But the Kurds did not sell single canaries in the bazaar, so I ended up with a job lot of four budgerigars. Naming them after First World War poets in anticipation of chemical Armageddon and death for all, they remained very much alive, getting fatter and triller by the day in their own small, symbolic refutation of the presence of weapons of mass destruction in Iraq. By the end of it all, Sassoon had even laid an egg. Iraq was full of surprises.

Over the following few weeks I waited for the invasion to begin, tracking the local developments, presuming that as soon as the first American troops arrived I could abandon my studies of Kirkuk and regional politics to move south with them to the heart of the matter: the capture of Baghdad. Quickly bored with the luxuries of the hotel in Sulaimaniyah, I drove each day throughout the territory, trying to fend off the growing suspicion that the area felt a little too slack to be on the threshold of receiving an invading army, and that the usual pitch to an atmosphere which precedes open warfare was somehow lacking.

I spoke with the survivors of Halabja and any number of Kurds who had been gassed in other areas during the Al Anfal period. They were among the thousands who had discovered that, having cheated death once, it still stalked them as their health deteriorated with the passing years, early mortality riding on the back of cancers, respiratory failure and birth defects. I met refugees who had fled Kirkuk and lived their days dreaming of revenge. I encountered a hapless and broken Egyptian, badly tortured, who had crossed into northern Iraq after his recent release from a fourteen-year sentence in a little-known prison: Abu

Ghraib. Unwitting victim to a better-known event, the man's offence had been to sell a foreigner a roll of film from his Baghdad photography shop. The foreigner was Farzad Bazoft, the British journalist hanged by Saddam in 1990 as an alleged spy. I met with gun-runners, oil-smugglers, PKK fighters and commanders, peshmerga past and present, businessmen, politicians, trade officials, Islamicists, communists, mystics and dissidents.

And all the while I waited for the US 4th Infantry Division.

But they never showed up.

The entire success of the assignment, so far as I was concerned, depended on the American strike force moving through Turkey and into northern Iraq on their push south. No 4th Infantry equated to no big story, no northern front, no charge to Baghdad. Their absence would leave reporters in northern Iraq sidelined, grinning with stoically masked jealousy as our embedded colleagues in the south waltzed to the capital.

Which is exactly what happened. Negotiations between the Turks and Americans got nowhere. Ignoring the promise of millions of dollars as pay off, Turkey simply refused to allow the American force overland passage.

Depressed? Despite the maturity of years, a deep understanding of the cycles of war, fortune and fate, and all the death and carnage I had already seen, I still felt the burning rage of a jilted lover. The most erosive psychological canker for any war correspondent is usually not the imprint of killings and destruction, the smoking homes, broken bodies and ruined lives they have witnessed. Wartime traumatic stress disorders most commonly affect those upon whom war is imposed, those who are unable to move during protracted exposure to violence, and those who have no voice with which to unburden themselves. By the nature of their voluntary status, comparative freedom of movement, broadcasting capability and the fact that they can spend their evenings getting smashed with comrades dissecting every detail of a bad day, reporters possess a series of defences against extreme trauma. That's not to say that they are immune: most long-term correspondents get more than their share of nightmares and mood swings. No stranger to the scratches, scrabbles and yowls of my own sleeping mind, I viewed my personal dirty-war dreams as I would semi-feral farmyard cats: sometimes there, sometimes not, I was surprised neither by their absence nor by their presence.

However, I suffered from a twisted malaise that was a more familiar scourge of the job: the awful internal corruption whereby personal and professional self-definition merge, glued together by immersion in war and the competitive sense of success in reporting it. Remove that access, marginalise the reporter from the story, and in no time even the most skilled and well-adjusted individual becomes a pathetic and fragmented being, with whatever altruism and belief they once had in their vocation overwhelmed by the infantile squalls of a ravenous and unsatisfied hunger.

So, in northern Iraq, cheated once again by war, I fell into black despair.

'We've been "Turked", there's no other way of puttin' it,' acknowledged Woody, a young American Green Beret, confirming the end result of his country's diplomatic joust with Ankara in inimitable soldier's shorthand. Then he got back to the business of blowing up some more Iraqi soldiers. There was not much else to do, so I lay on my belly in the sand, lifted a pair of binoculars to my eyes and watched him perform. It was a relaxed killing.

March was at an end and the desert around us was enjoying its brief window of spring colour. Dry ravines were gurgling with water, their banks ablaze with scarlet poppies. Spears of grass twisted silver in the breeze, stretching out across the sands, an army of short-lived relief against the siege of heat, throwing the golden glow of foothill rape fields into prominence against the green. The air rippled gently under the sun and hawks floated on the thermals in search of their quarry. They were not alone in the skies for long.

The war had at last begun. Ten days earlier British and American armoured columns had started pushing up from Kuwait, through Iraq, towards Baghdad. Yet the northern front remained all but paralysed, the coalition's concept of a twin front nutcracker squeeze on the Iraqi capital scuppered by Ankara. 'Turked', as Woody so aptly described it.

I had left my Sulaimaniyah base a few days before the start of the invasion and moved south to Chamchamal, an ugly runt of a frontier town populated by Kurds just short of the Iraqi lines. The division between Kurdish and Iraqi territory beyond it was more a security zone than a front line. There had been no actual push across the area by either side since 1991. Instead, the Iraqis had established a long stretch of positions on high ground along the divide, protected by minefields and wire. Several roads remained open through this territory, allowing the Kurds, still technically Iraqi citizens, to cross should they so desire. Few did. Some lacked the right documentation. Others feared intimidation at the Iraqi checkpoints through which they had to pass. Most simply wanted nothing to do with the Iraqis.

Shadowed by a ridgeline held by Iraqi troops, Chamchamal was gateway to the main road to Kirkuk. So, as well as being a suitable forward base from which to follow up on any shift in the lines, it was a prime location to question the few Kurds who did traverse across the zone of separation. Renting a house in the town from a local Kurdish family, my short stay there was stressed and unstable. Paul, a phlegmatic photographer sent to northern Iraq by the paper, was working with me. It was the first time he had been to a war, so I felt responsible for him, an unfamiliar sensation at odds with the freewheeling unilateralism I usually enjoyed. And my plunging mood made me bad company. While Paul remained a model of patience and stoicism throughout the whole assignment, I knew I was growing more irritable and sullen by the day: an awareness which itself made me even more frustrated. Shay had also arrived, having taken a circuitous route in through Turkey, and shared the house with us. But he was working with a mutual friend from a rival paper, which meant that our usual openness was cauterised by a degree of professional tact.

To make matters worse, Awat, my interpreter, had done a midnight bunk. He could not have picked a less convenient moment. We had spent the eve of the invasion on the roof of the house, staring out towards the Iraqi positions. As night fell we retired to the ground floor and huddled around our radios to listen to the BBC, chemical suits and first-aid kits laid out expectantly. I kept the budgerigars with us downstairs. Having fed and watered them every day, it seemed suddenly rather gratuitous and unfair to expose them to gas attack on the roof. Then we drank a lot of whisky and crashed into sleep. Waking at dawn, the view from the roof was unchanged: the Iraqi troops still occupied their usual positions outside the town; Chamchamal stirred from sleep with the same lacklustre crow of cocks and rattle of early vehicles as every morning over the previous twelve years; except for the disciplined excitement of the newsreader's voice on the radio, there was not even the smallest, dullest, most distant boom or bang to suggest war had begun. The only difference to my world of the previous evening lay with Awat's bedroll: it was empty. I was doubly enraged by his betrayal as I had liked his company and had trusted him. Tracking him down to his house in Sulaimaniyah that afternoon, nearly homicidal with rage, I found him embarrassed but unmovable. At heart, similar to many Kurds, he felt he had survived too much to die working for a foreign journalist just at the point when the invasion would trounce Saddam with or without his input. I found a new interpreter. He was old, curmudgeonly and ate his own ear wax. I fired him after a few days and hired another. He was young, rich, spoiled and nervy. I would have fired him, too, given time to find a replacement.

Then, one afternoon, a few days after the invasion had begun, the Iraqis suddenly pulled back from their positions above Chamchamal and on a wide-ranging front to its east and west. Although they had endured some air strikes, their retreat was no rout, more of an orderly withdrawal to a new defensive line nearer to Kirkuk. As embedded reporters moving forward with advance coalition units in the south of the country – the very journalists whom I had assumed would have such limited access to the war – wrote at first hand of heavy fighting, significant battles, desert ambushes and armoured thrusts, I reported on a few old boots and discarded helmets picked up by Kurdish looters scavenging through the abandoned Iraqi positions.

Chancing upon Woody and his fellow-Green Berets, at least I found my disgruntlement shared. I had all but trodden on them as they called down air strikes on an Iraqi position a few hundred yards ahead. On a speculative trawl of the front south-east of Kirkuk, I had spotted a likely vantage point from which to check out the Iraqi lines. As Magdid parked the jeep I walked towards it and, crossing the lip of a berm, literally stumbled upon the Americans crouched in the depression below. Dressed in a mixture of civilian clothes and camouflage uniform, though as surprised as I, they were friendly enough. With a mission in hand, they were too busy to shoo us away, and were content to let us stay with them as they worked, warning us only to keep our heads down and not move too much.

Two attacks by jets – 'fast movers', as the soldiers called them – had already hit the Iraqis, destroying some artillery pieces and vehicles. Through their scopes, the Americans could see that they had also killed between twenty and thirty Iraqi soldiers. However, the group of peshmerga attached to them wanted more, and fidgeted and chattered in anticipation of the late arrival of a B-52 bomber tasked to finish the job.

'You say 52 come ten o'clock,' challenged one of the Kurds as he peered over the berm towards the Iraqis.

'Yeah, well, it's been a kinda slow morning,' drawled Andy, a Californian, as he looked skyward. It was nearly midday.

'52's from United Kingdom?' the peshmerga asked. There was a nod.

Rather than the vanguard of an American division, these men formed one of several small special forces units in northern Iraq, lacking half their usual equipment, tasked to harass and pressurise the Iraqis as best they could in make-do alliance with the peshmerga. The Turks had initially barred their airspace even to these token US troops, so the first few special forces teams had been forced to fly around Turkey, over hostile Iraqi airspace. Their first transport plane to land in the Kurdish zone did so full of holes from Iraqi ground fire.

They had arrived for war without vehicles, heavy machine-guns or mortars. They had to borrow battered Toyotas from the Kurds, something that had already caused near disaster. During an initial night reconnaissance of Iraqi lines, the engine block of one of their vehicles had simply fallen through the chassis. Pursued by the Iraqis, two American teams had made their narrow escape crammed into a single surviving pick-up. It had been an ignominious start.

In this daylight operation, things were going better. The eight-strong team had arrived at the location earlier that morning, pushing forward to the edge of the newly established Iraqi defensive line. Dividing into two groups, one team, 'Moto', moved behind a nearby slope, while Woody and the second group, 'Shifty', secured a position directly facing the enemy in the deserted rectangular pit over which I had so obliviously blundered. On three isolated hills ahead of them the Iraqi troops they were targeting for air strike were easy to identify. Even though they had already endured one bombing run, the soldiers stood up in their trenches in full view, milling around a six-wheeled vehicle with an anti-aircraft gun mounted on the back. In the foreground of one of the hills grazed two tethered donkeys.

We waited. We smoked. We talked. We yawned. We became a little bored. It was hard to imagine that a few hundred yards away some of the men we watched were about to be incinerated. And even the awareness of that disconnection was more interesting and acute than the reality of the Iraqis' imminent fate. The tiny black figurines were reduced in my mind to no more than a transient existential question. Perhaps if they had been a little closer, a little larger, a little more colourful, they would have meant more. At least they would have given me more to write about.

Suddenly the ten or so peshmerga sitting behind the team became excited: '52, 52,' they gabbled, pointing up.

High above us, all the way from an airfield in Britain, a huge silver beast trailed white vapour against the rich blue of the spring sky.

'Shifty to Moto, inbound,' a voice hissed over the radio.

Yet still, even as the roar of the engines grew, the Iraqis loitered above their bunkers. A curious moment followed in the slow-motion extinction of their lives: the contradiction, only a second or two long, as every American in the forward post seemed as one to will the exposed Iraqis to take cover.

'I don't believe it, they're still standing up.'

'Why would they want to walk around now?'

'Go on, get down, you dumb fuckers.'

There was no sound at first. But the saddle-ridge of the largest hill simply disappeared, and with it the standing Iraqi men. A huge series of brown clouds took their place as other elements of the payload flashed white air-bursting flame above them. Then the noise came, more of a sensation of waved banks of pressure than an explosion.

Immediately it was back to business for the American soldiers. As the smoke and dust cleared, Shifty and Moto relayed the results of their work back to the aircrew. Incredibly, there were survivors. The two donkeys grazed on untouched and the Iraqi anti-aircraft vehicle roared out and away from the swirling haze. So the B-52 came in for a second run. It took many minutes to turn, but when it did a second Iraqi position was hit in similar fashion. A hidden fuel store blazed, churning a black shroud of smoke over the casualties.

As the aircraft left – 'empty of casks', we were told – the Iraqis responded, firing a few surface-to-surface rockets at a position that they presumed to be occupied by the Americans. The missiles missed by so far that we never even saw them detonate. The Americans checked over the radio to see if there were more aircraft available for a further strike. There were none. The Green Berets began to pack up their equipment in preparation to move elsewhere. The atmosphere continued to be calm, the men's movements methodical and deliberate, the managerial style of their position completely at odds with what the Iraqis were going through a short distance away.

The Kurds were delighted, though. 'Until 1988 we were all Marxists here,' joked a peshmerga commander who had watched the B-52 strike beside me. 'So we used to see the US and UK as imperialists. Now we see them toppling Saddam for us. So we say, "Viva imperialism!"'

I spent a few more days hanging around in the company of the Green Berets in this small cutting-room-floor clip of a war zone. They had set up an improvised platoon-sized base in an abandoned Iraqi post in the desert, a shabby affair of brown, crumbling-brick barrack rooms most memorable for the three flags – British, American and Israeli – painted long ago on to the flagstones by the guardroom as symbolic doormats for the Iraqi soldiers. Here the Americans gave rudimentary training to a group of peshmerga, between calling down air strikes and moving out at night to snipe at and otherwise harass the Iraqi lines. After a couple of days the Turks even allowed some of their missing equipment to reach them overland: Land-Rovers, machine-guns, grenade launchers and mortars.

'Now we got our machine-guns, we're just gonna go out, fill 'em full of lead and leave their bodies to bloat in the sun: see if that gives 'em the message,' said Andy, squinting and spitting a stream of tobacco juice on to the sand as he prepared to go on a raid against yet another remote and inconsequential Iraqi position at the head of a column of peshmerga.

They received televisions, too, so they could watch Fox News at night between missions in their little corner of the desert, and be reminded that the war was just, the world was behind them and everything was going to plan: hush-a-bye lullabies for American dreams. Yet, whatever differing opinions we may have had concerning the war, I liked them. Far from being a bunch of dumb grunts interested only in upping their kill count, behind their gung-ho vernacular they were well-travelled soldiers who could debate the issues. Besides, Americans had always seemed like natural allies to me.

Their new kit arrived on the same day as word filtered through of the fall of Baghdad. The news only added to my sense of complete futility. I may as well have been on Mars for all the relevance my situation had to the bigger picture. Saddam's regime collapsed along with the last of my morale. My depression was further cranked by the number of reporters getting killed and injured in the northern territory as they tried to cover this footnote event. Ansar al Islam, routed from their mountain base above Halabja by a combined peshmerga and special forces assault, had slain an Australian cameraman in a suicide-bomb attack. In the little town of Kifri a cameraman was killed and a producer badly wounded by mines. In Sulaimaniyah a correspondent friend died in a fall from the hotel roof. And near the city of Mosul Big Sim and his boys found themselves on the end of a mistargeted American air strike which to one degree or another wounded the entire crew and killed their interpreter along with a dozen or so peshmerga.

If the fall of Saddam's statue in the capital sent shockwaves around the world, it did not immediately seem to affect the Iraqi troops protecting Kirkuk, who for another day held their lines, bastion to a block of territory between my location and Baghdad that seemed to ensure I would never reach the Iraqi capital. Even when Kirkuk fell, it did so with the shy squeak of a spinster's fart. To call it a damp squib would have been a bellicose exaggeration. On the front line an hour beforehand, there seemed barely a plan for lunch, let alone a battle. Though the area still rumbled with a vacuous mix of sporadic shellfire and air strike, in the meadows north of the city the peshmerga guerrillas lounged around playing dominoes, listening on tiny transistor radios to the news of Baghdad's liberation, or taking siestas in the spring sunshine. Their senior officers were absent, receiving orders elsewhere, and a few Green Berets loitering near by had little more on their mind than listening in to the Kurds' talk. Or maybe it was just meant to look like that. Wary of Turkish threats, the Americans could not openly hand Kirkuk to the Kurds. But they also had to satisfy their peshmerga allies with some sort of token gesture.

Equipped for little more than a heavy skirmish, the idling Kurdish fighters each carried a Kalashnikov and a few magazines of ammunition. Most were youths eager to prove themselves in action, but they were accompanied by a few hardened veterans of previous wars. There was even one old goat of seventy-six. Haji Baez was a sniper, and had been a peshmerga for forty years. He claimed his eyesight was still up to the job, and that he had turned up at the front of his own accord for a piece of the action. If the Americans and Kurdish authorities had concocted a public relations deception plan concerning Kirkuk, then no one had told him about it. 'I'm on fire,' he cackled, patting his Draganov rifle. 'I'll be the first in Kirkuk.'

Some Iraqis in the city had already raised a white flag the previous afternoon. It had fluttered on a road junction just north of Kirkuk for about twenty minutes before an internal gun battle broke out between government troops wishing to fight on and those wanting to surrender. The flag had been lowered before the Kurds had any opportunity to respond.

Eventually a peshmerga produced some bread and rice, and we were just sitting down to eat when there was a flurry of activity from the road, sudden news, and a ripple of energy passed through the lethargic fighters. I heard the word 'intifada' – uprising.

A peshmerga walked up to us and remarked: 'I think the Iraqis are fleeing. It's time now.'

Five minutes later we were in the middle of a chaotic jamboree of peshmerga vehicles storming down the road to seize Kirkuk. There was a little smoke in the sky, a few sporadic rattles of gunfire, and at the roadside a couple of short columns of dazed Iraqi soldiers tramping back in captivity.

The gunfire picked up as we entered the city, but it was more in celebration than combat. The bulk of the Iraqi forces had pulled back towards Tikrit, leaving the lines held by a light screen of conscripts who surrendered immediately and, perhaps because of the presence of the Americans, appeared to be well treated by their captors. Indeed, the first hours of liberation seemed characterised by looting rather than vengeance. Shop windows imploded as mobs charged inside to seize the spoils, joined by most of the peshmerga vanguard. A department store was ransacked along with government offices, the mêlée working itself into an almost orgiastic fury, smashing windows and destroying furniture as an outlet for their feelings.

Ignored by the looters, a body lay prone by the central Tabak Chaly Bridge over Kirkuk's River Khasa. A balding man in grey slacks and city shoes, he had been snatched from his Nissan by a group of armed men and shot on the pavement. His attackers stole his car and drove away. He seemed a particularly forlorn sacrifice at that late moment in the war, murdered for his vehicle and left to lie alone on the tarmac.

There was unadulterated joy there too, though, and the Kurdish civilians who had remained in Kirkuk despite the Ba'athist purges of the last decade ran from their homes to greet their liberators with rapturous applause, the air reverberating with the victory-cry ululations of the women, some of whom bowed down to kiss the feet of the city's new masters. By mid-afternoon, although shooting, smoke and breaking glass still shared space in a few places across the city, the celebrations in the centre had reached a point of some conformity. In Kirkuk's main square a crowd ringed a statue of Saddam while the more gymnastic scrambled over his head, beating it with shoes and horse whips. Someone sprayed 'USA' at his feet, just in time to honour the arrival of the Green Berets. An hour later and the statue was toppled, already a clichéd event.

Then the looting stopped as Kurdish police units, specially tasked and waiting to move in behind the peshmerga, entered to secure the city, taking control of hospitals, communication and business centres. Of any liberated city in Iraq, Kirkuk's transformation was perhaps the smoothest. By nightfall, American regular troops had appeared on the scene and the peshmerga had begun to withdraw, calming Turkish fears of a takeover. Within twenty-four hours there were even traffic police controlling the roads.

So much was to change in so little time in Iraq that even the Kurds would probably no longer remember that day as being particularly significant. The question of Kirkuk's ultimate status inside Iraq remains as unanswered as the bigger Kurdish question. With hindsight, the city's capture may be judged less a conclusive point than an addendum in the prelude to a new conflict. On the day itself, however, some Kurds at least revelled in the moment, untroubled by the deeper complexities of the war's ultimate rights, wrongs and future. As my memories of the heat and smoke, the crash of glass and the rattle of Kalashnikovs dim, I still vividly recall a lone middle-aged Kurdish woman. On the downslope from frenzy, she stood alone on the auditorium stage in the Ba'ath headquarters on the east bank of the Khasa. Swaying with the weight of an iron bar in her hands, she clubbed and slashed at a huge portrait of Saddam Hussein in repeated slow-motion strokes. Her husband and son had both died in 1988. Deserters from the Iraqi army, they had sought shelter in Halabja and were gassed in the attack.

'I've been waiting for this day,' she gasped, exhausted by her efforts, almost in a trance as Saddam's ripped face looked down upon her. 'I always knew it would come. Oh, how I've waited for this day.'

*

I left Iraq less than a week later, travelling overland into Iran to catch a plane home, my mood identical to that with which I had returned to England from the Gulf in 1991. Instead of wisdom or enlightenment in my mind that day, each and every experience of the previous twelve years seemed to have bequeathed me no more inheritance than a block of psychic salt: the more I bit it, the more thirsty I became; no ice cold in Alex for me. If I was happy during the long drive out, it was only because I was saying goodbye to Iraq and leaving behind the ill-fortune that always seemed to dog me there. As I crossed the border, I wished the country quick peace and great prosperity, if only so that I would never have any reason to return.

EPILOGUE

Baghdad, Spring 2004

Staring out from the narrow balcony of my hotel room as the day drew to a close, I watched the heavy orange sun drop slowly into the city's smog-hazed horizon. Between us stretched a jumbled flat expanse of brown masonry, most of it modern, the details fading into a smudge by middle distance until it was cut suddenly by a frontier of green bulrushes and the oily drift of the Tigris, empty of even the most resolute fisherman's coracle. On the western bank the city began again with a wall, wire and watchtowers, part of the huge security zone separating the coalition's headquarters from the rest of the Iraqi population.

So this then was Baghdad, land of the *Arabian Nights*, I mused to myself, thoroughly unconvinced, and listened to the capital's medley of beeping car horns, rotorblades, the occasional crackle of gunfire and, just once or twice, the faraway thump of a bomb. Here I am, after all these years. It seemed rather fitting that I had arrived at the very moment when I cared least to see it, just as the city was falling to its knees in a new phase of war that would swiftly consign the memories of the coalition's speedy invasion and military victory to virtual irrelevance.

I did not even have any baggage to unpack. It had all been lost in transit, rerouted somehow to the Sudan, so I had landed at the airport that morning possessing no more than the clothes in which I stood, Kurt's ashes still around my neck, and a small rucksack containing my laptop, sat-phone, passport and cash. Perhaps this, too, was a suitable condition for the stripped isolation of that lonely moment.

For I had just witnessed my first close quarter peacetime death. It was my mother. My mother was dead. There had been little forewarning.

I thought back to an afternoon the previous year, when the war was only a few days old and American units were still fighting their way up through southern Iraq. I had been standing on the roof of our rented house in Chamchamal, talking to her on the sat-phone. So zestful and quick-witted, so old a friend, talking with her was always an uplifting experience, and our conversation carried none of the awkward weight of obligation and division that so often characterises communication between those on different sides of the war-peace divide. In the far, far distance came the tremulous reverberation of an air strike. No stranger to the sound of background violence during calls, she was unconcerned, her voice clear and calm across thousands of miles. We were talking about the war and her life in Somerset, a combination which somehow spliced flawlessly in our easy relatedness, when the word 'pain' made its debut intrusion. As an almost shy admission, she briefly described a fleeting but severe succession of painful sensations – sometimes stabbing, sometimes burning – that had occurred on the right side of her face over the previous few days. I felt instantly uneasy. Her pain threshold had always been phenomenal. She was the strongest and most enduring member of our family and pain was a stranger to her. I could not recall her ever having used the word before.

'Uh, well, you've got to go and see the doctor, Mum,' I said finally. 'Promise me you'll go, right?' I knew that the entreaty was useless: she indulged doctors no more willingly than discomfort. Then I brushed the moment away.

The memory of it re-emerged, though, to chafe against my thoughts from time to time during the rest of that assignment. Her death had been the one which I had hoped I would somehow never have to face. Enough grief. No more goodbyes. Not my mother. But I read our conversation that day as no more than the scratching of a twig on a window in an autumn breeze, not the bony-knuckled knock on the door at a minute to midnight. Little could I have I imagined how desperate a fugitive time would become.

There had been nothing to suggest death on my return home from northern Iraq. Far from it. A local doctor lazily suggested neuralgia, assuaging our fears but not my mother's pain, for which he prescribed ineffectual non-prescription tablets. She saw him a number of times but the diagnosis never alluded to anything more ominous. By late autumn the attacks had become more severe, more frequent and longer in duration. She never cried but the pain made her tremble as she fought it. I saw her shake like a leaf. With a naive faith in the medical profession, we did what we could. It was just neuralgia after all; and, though excruciatingly painful, neuralgia would not kill her. Then in November the sight in her right eye suddenly blurred and faded in the space of a few days. She adorned a black patch similar to that worn by her decorated grandfather. Some neuralgia. We bypassed the GP and arranged for specialist tests. In the meantime, to ease her discomfort, I brought her St John's wort tablets and bath oils. They were still in the medicine cabinet in Somerset as I stared out across Baghdad, I realised, and wondered whether when I returned home I should throw them away or stuff them down the doctor's throat.

Unaware of exactly what we were dealing with, my sister and I had stayed at her house over Christmas. A couple of weeks later the test results came in. I sat with my mother in a hospital room to receive them.

'It is cancer,' a man in a grey suit told us in the same way one says, 'Rain today.' Jesus, could he not even have managed to say, 'Sorry, it's cancer'? In an instant the words threw my world into crisis. I expected NASA to call in its space missions, factory sirens to wail across the planet, the World Health Organisation to announce an emergency summit, yet the grey suit simply walked out of the room carrying its man and left us there with nothing but silence. The tests had revealed a small tumour at the edge of her brain.

'Let's go to Marks and Spencer and get a sandwich,' she said, still calm, as we walked out of the hospital together. 'Are you OK, Ant?'

'Yeah, I'm OK, Mum,' I replied, tears stinging my eyes, trying not to be sick as we tapped down Poole's grey January pavements.

All those wars, all that danger, all that familiarity with death counted for nothing now. I thought I was fairly tough, inured even, but at that moment I felt little different from the four-year-old who had wept upon first realising that his mother would die before him. 'Do something,' my brain screamed. 'Save her.'

'We're going to fight on, all right?' she added, stalwart as ever. 'We'll fight it and beat it.'

A course of chemotherapy was scheduled to start in February. Why February? I wondered. Why not now, immediately, this second? My mother accepted the fact that she might lose her hair without complaint, even cropped it in anticipation, and posed laughing in newly bought hats. With her eye patch, shorn hair and the challenging blue stare of her undamaged eye, she resembled a resistance fighter, as intrepid as our family's bravest hero. We laughed a lot during this period, and walked for hours and hours with her terrier and lurcher through Somerset's winter landscapes. Defeat was not an option as we geared ourselves for the coming treatment, but my heart was afflicted by naked dread masked by desperate resolve: my mission was to save my mother's life and I would do anything, strike any deal with God, to ensure its success. I should have known better by then. I should have remembered the useless impossibility of saving Kurt, recalled the futility of my desperate clinch with Allieu. There is no acceptable plea bargain. God cuts no deals.

As a change from the more familiar assignments I had done back in Afghanistan after leaving northern Iraq, the boss asked me to cover the close of the prosecution case against Slobodan Milošević in The Hague, where he was on trial for war crimes, a week before my mother's chemotherapy was due to start. It was a three-day assignment and I had been reluctant to accept it, but did so in an effort to back her courage. She did not want to see other people limiting their lives on her account. On the penultimate morning of my work there, though, I knew something was badly wrong.

'I feel very calm, Ant,' she told me over the phone, without elaborating. Though she had soundly beaten me at Scrabble when I had visited her only a few days before, now she sounded distracted and unfocused. I put it down to the effects of steroids, prescribed after the tests.

She collapsed two hours later, dragging herself across the floor of her

Somerset home to the telephone, calling my sister Natasha in London. 'Don't tell Ant,' she cautioned before the ambulance arrived. 'I don't want him to worry and come home from the job early.' Minutes later Natasha called me with the news, and I seized a cab and headed to the nearest airport.

There was never the time for any treatment and all our best-laid plans to fight the illness stood as nought before the rushing tide. 'Bye-bye time,' she said to Natasha and me as we stood stricken by her hospital bed. 'Say goodbye to my friends in the village.' She raised her hand and gave us a little wave. I promised that I would get her out of there, realising that the only battle left was to persuade the doctors to let us take her home to die. The ward doctor, a saintly young man whose compassion and understanding tempered my homicidal feelings towards the GP, explained that while she remained in hospital the inevitable might be delayed, but if she went home with us death would come quickly. He repeated the choice directly to my mother. She said that she wanted to go home.

'Then I will authorise your release,' he said, standing. 'It was good to meet you.'

From her bed, she stretched out a thin arm and shook his hand. 'It was good to meet you, too, Doctor.'

So there, then, in that handshake and steady gaze of appraisal, was courage revealed. Not the bravery of a glorious battlefield gamble, but the wilful might of humility and composure, the absolute courage of calm at the end of a life that she loved and did not want to lose. It was to be the final gift from a woman who to me would always be too young to die; one who coolly faced the moment and never tried to escape. There, too, came death, not sought but seeking, not part of the ravage of war but no less certain for the size of its claim in peace in Somerset.

Time ran away before we could get her out, thwarting even my last promise. She slipped into a coma before she could be moved from the hospital. A doctor warned us that she could stay in that condition for many days, even weeks. Very carefully, and using few words, he also let us know that should we suspect she still suffered any pain then he would administer morphine. Yet if that were the case, he said gently, death would be fast. A very short time later, just long enough to seem credible, we found the doctor and told him that we were sure she felt pain. Then we left the hospital and walked to a nearby church. We stayed there for about half an hour. On our return, our mother's laboured breathing had eased. She died then and there as Natasha and I held her scarred, callused hands. It was only four days since she had fallen.

I learned heartbreak well. It cracked the February sky and broke the lines of my palms. We took her body home to rest for a single night so that her dogs and house had time for their farewells. The winter was kind on her funeral day: the sky a blazing blue, a light dusting of snow over the first blossom of the year. It seemed almost all the village was at the church, so I said goodbye to them as she had asked me to do.

I spent March sorting out her things in Somerset, then drove to my flat in London. I flew to Iraq a couple of days later. In Fallujah a marine force had become bogged down fighting insurgents after a failed raid to apprehend those responsible for the murders of four American contractors, whose burned bodies had been hung from a bridge in the city. The holy cities of Najaf and Karbala had been seized by fighters loyal to the militant cleric Moqtadr al Sadr who clashed with American troops around the clock. In Baghdad the new peak in bomb attacks, shootings and murders was overshadowed by events in Sadr City, the Shia ghetto in the capital, where Moqtadr's men also indulged in running gun battles with coalition patrols. Every significant road through Iraq was interdicted by insurgent activity, either Sunni or Shia, and fighting had spread to most of the major population centres. The slow fuse to mayhem, lit when the invasion began, had burned to its end.

I arrived feeling expendable and slightly crazed, grasping an invigorated sense of mortality with a carelessness that seemed like an ironic, sure-fire guarantee of survival. If raw grief gave me a certain empathy in sharing the vista of loss with those around me, I did not presume that in sorrow I shared the tragedy of the Iraqis, who had neither any choice in their predicament nor any opportunity to say their farewells: wham-blam and there was just a smear of blood and gristle on concrete.

But there was no sense of defeat, standing on that balcony, gazing across Baghdad, wondering at the thirteen years of war that had brought me there. Quite the reverse. Death seemed diminished, friendship undimmed. A feeling of profound fortune emerged to cloak me; an awareness of great prize and intense gratitude. The realisation was gentle, but no less absolute for the power of its touch. Though not what I thought I had been looking for when it all began so long ago with that first war, and not what I expected to discover in that city of all cities, on that day of all days, as an inheritance it was inestimable. No venture has richer reward. As unquantifiable in its essence as love, I had been bequeathed with life's great defiance, the unwinnable struggle's only possible victory: hope. I lived in hope.

Staring out again at the Tigris, I watched the last of my youth meander away with the river's current, and felt life burn hard. And I thought that I should write of the places and the people that had given me so much; whose lessons could perhaps never have been learned one without the other; who had gone but would never leave me. I could have known none better.